A
SLOW TOUR THROUGH FRANCE

FROM AVIGNON TO SAINT-MALO BY BICYCLE (MOSTLY)

Marie Madigan

Wood Sorrel Books

www.mariemadigan.co.uk

Book Layout ©2013 BookDesignTemplates.com

A Slow Tour Through France/ Marie Madigan. -- 1st ed.
ISBN 978-1-5395897-2-3

For Margaret and Peter,
helping me still

PART ONE

Of Trains And Wind

CHAPTER ONE

To Avignon

I think they'll be all right.'

Adi regarded the two polythene-wrapped bicycles that he'd just shoved one on top of the other into a luggage shelf on the Eurostar from St Pancras. It clearly hadn't occurred to the woman Adi had phoned to check the current restrictions, as it hadn't to us until this moment, that the on-board luggage size restrictions might have something to do with the actual dimensions of the shelves on the train. 'Don't worry, no one's going to be there with a measuring tape,' she'd assured him.

Our bicycles looked as if they'd been beheaded: front wheels and forks removed, handlebars turned, sundry delicate bits taped up, the whole wrapped in industrial strength polythene. They earned suspicious glances from the customs staff at St Pancras, who nevertheless let them through. The regulations on the website had stated a maximum length of 120 cm; our bikes were 125 cm and 130 cm. We'd considered removing the rear wheels, then thought, 'Nah', especially after the reassuring conversation with the woman from Eurostar. Too much hassle, we decided.

Hassle I blearily wished we'd suffered. During the early morning journey from Bangor to Euston and across to King's Cross St Pancras I'd already grown to hate my lovely bike. How could it weigh so much more than in its natural state? How could it have grown so many shin-whacking extra bits?

Tense moments in customs had ensued. Adi's corkscrew in the bottom of a pannier had triggered a total luggage search in customs, and we'd had to decant our fuel into an empty cordial bottle because - duh! - you can't take petrol through customs. But at least we'd got through, despite the suspicious glances at our polythene- wrapped bikes.

Adi gave them a last push, then we shoved our two huge hockey bags, each filled to bursting with four panniers and assorted extras, into the lower luggage racks. We looked at our baggage for a moment. Our slightly too-long bikes were wedged diagonally into the letter-box shaped shelves, the frames forming a shallow angle with the shelf base. I worried for a moment about bending the forks, then decided I didn't care and moved to let other passengers get to the shelves. We'd caught the train. We were going overseas! Well, underseas.

'We're going backwards again,' Adi said when we'd found our seats. He looked around to see if there were any seats we could move into. I ignored him – this is a train travelling ritual – and settled into my seat.

As we were welcomed in French, German and English, and the train pulled away from John Betjeman's statue, I began to relax. This was the second of three trains that would take us from Anglesey to Avignon, for a two-month cycle tour south to north through France.

We'd fallen in love with cycle touring three years previously. It was Adi's idea. We'd tried it for the first time after the death of our elderly, opinionated fell terrier, Sharron. (Being carried in a basket, or on a bike trailer, would have been something that she would have had Views on.) The first trip, the summer after she died, was a coast to coast ride from Whitehaven to Robin Hood's Bay, immaculately planned by Adi, in horrible weather. Those four days getting to Robin Hood's Bay with nothing but the power of my wheels and my legs turned me into an instant convert. Cycling of any kind, but especially cycle touring, I realised, was capable of both inflicting great pain and bestowing immense self-satisfaction, not to mention being an excuse for sampling the best scones and cakes that northern England had to offer. Doggedly pulling a heavily laden bike up the hills of Yorkshire's Esk Valley in driving rain was definitely not fun at the time, but the smugness of achievement more than compensated for the pain and the weather. Many was the happy dance at the top of a hill, once I'd managed to get up off the ground where I'd collapsed.

That same autumn we toured around southwest Scotland, leaving our campervan on Arran and hopping on ferries to the long finger of Knapdale and Kintyre and over and back across Loch Fyne. On that trip we tried wild camping for the first time. The evening by our tent on a sandy beach looking west as the sun set behind Iona sealed it for me. This was how I wanted to spend my holidays, every holiday.

And for the next three years, we did. Our work in nature conservation has a highly seasonal element, with a dip in the hardcore physical work of chain-sawing and vegetation management from April through to July, corresponding to the bird and mammal breeding season. For a couple of years we took three and a half weeks off between mid-May and mid-June and toured around the Scottish islands and highlands. It never disappointed. We normally managed to fit in at least another week later in the summer or early autumn, as well as a few weekends of touring in England and Wales.

When I say it never disappointed, I mean it. Yet a hankering had arisen in my Adi's heart.

'Scotland's lovely,' he said. 'But someday I wouldn't mind touring somewhere you don't get rained on every day.'

We might not have been widely travelled but we were certainly wetly travelled. On one trip it was so wet that the campsite manager in Lochgilphead gave us the use of a caravan for the night at no extra charge. We weren't there for the weather, of course – it was Scotland in September and we're not dense. We were there for the scenery, the colours and the lack of midges. Likewise, you don't go to Wales, Ireland, Yorkshire and Northumbria for cloudless skies and toasty temperatures. You go prepared and you see stunning landscapes, to see what you'll never see anywhere else, any other way. But we had occasionally thought, shaking out the tent after a storm that had rolled in just when we were dismantling it, how nice it would be not to get wet and cold all the time. We felt this especially strongly as we work outside. Working stoically throughout autumn, winter and what had passed for spring that year of 2012, we had begun to feel that we had credit in the bank when it came to cheerfully enduring bad weather.

Still, left to myself I probably would never have thought of coming to France. I hadn't been overseas, apart from home to Ireland, for nearly ten years. Not because I don't have any desire to travel – I certainly do – but because the list of places to explore in these gorgeous islands just keeps on growing. There are all those lanes in yellow on the Ordnance Survey maps that I haven't cycled along yet. Scottish islands we have yet to visit. Hills and lanes and footpaths that I haven't yet cycled along or walked up. It's my ambition to cycle around the coasts of Britain and Ireland, and to visit every county in these countries on my bike. But Adi had been thinking for a while and had come up with convincing arguments and practical ideas about where we could go. Somewhere that would satisfy the triple needs of budget (not bottomless), accessibility by train and more than average chance of sunshine. He laid the evidence out for me.

'You can get to Avignon from Bangor in a day, for less than £100 each,' he said, 'and there are millions of campsites, millions, the French are well into camping. I've had a look, and with a budget of £17 a day on average the Nice Things Money should pay for all our accommodation, with wiggle room for tea shops and wine tasting, for guess how long?'

Nice Things Money is the account that is never, ever used for dull necessities.

'A month?'

'Two! A two-month cycle tour! Wouldn't that be a challenge?'

A two-month cycle tour... It would almost certainly be less expensive than cycling around England and Wales for the same length of time. Wild camping in Scotland brings the costs down, but after three days of pulling a heavily laden bike up those hills I need a shower before coming within hailing distance of another human being. And there was the food to think about. We are both vegetarians, but we always cook our own meals so that wouldn't be an issue even in meat-loving France. Adi had already bought the Rough Guide to France, and the authors were fulsome in their praise of the fresh produce at French markets. I was definitely interested.

And, of course, the weather would be better.

'It will be warm in the south when we start and as we cycle north it will be getting warmer, keeping pace with us,' Adi had gone on to clinch it for me. 'All the way across France!'

I was sold.

No quest of self-discovery. We weren't looking to find ourselves on the road. We just wanted not to get drenched all the time, and to immerse ourselves in a different country. With two months, on a bicycle instead of anchored in one spot or cocooned in a campervan, we'd get to know the contours of the land and experience some of the everyday life of the country, so close but still essentially foreign.

To distract myself from the thought of the English Channel over my head, I pulled out my book while Adi looked up the weather in Avignon. (He was still beside me. He hadn't found any forward facing seats.)

I still had some butterflies and qualms. Two months isn't a long time, but it can seem long when you know that you can't see the friends and family you love. We'd planned this for nine months. We wouldn't be coming home early except in case of a disaster. We couldn't afford to. We had bought our tickets out and back. We were leaving.

I was startled awake by Adi shaking me out of a doze. We were approaching Lille. I looked at the time.

'That two and a half hours flew!'

'It was only an hour and a half,' Adi said. 'We're in a different time zone now.'

As gently as possible, we extracted our bikes from the shelves in which we'd wedged them and struggled with them and the pony-sized hockey bags to the train doors ahead of time so as not to be trapped on the train to Cologne. We staggered out with our burdens and dropped them on the platform. Crowds of disembarking and embarking passengers swarmed around our awkward mass. I ran to find a shop to get change for trolleys and arrived back five minutes later to a spookily abandoned platform, just Adi and a mountain of baggage in a vast empty space.

When we finally found the information screens it transpired that our third train was delayed and the platforms changed. The bit of my brain that was listening to the tannoy announcements and hauling out my rusty French ached like a pulled muscle. Everything felt surreal; I felt sweaty and panicky. I blamed the glass of wine I'd had the day before while ironing and listening to Absolute 80s. Do not ask me why I was ironing clothes that would be living in a pannier for nine weeks. I have no sensible answer.

The TGV from Lille to Avignon made up for everything. We waited with our hockey bags and increasingly tatty-looking polythene-wrapped bikes in the correct part of the platform for our carriage. We knew we were in the correct place because of a helpful little map on the platform illustrating where each carriage would slide to a halt.

'Last leg,' Adi said, as our carriage pulled up, exactly where the sign had indicated it would. 'If it all goes wrong now, it doesn't matter. If the train breaks down in the middle of nowhere we can put the bikes together and ride off into the countryside.'

'Or end up in Marseille by accident.'

'How bad.'

We were thrilled by the TGV. The space! The luggage racks! The not being looked at as if you had ruined the other passengers' lives by bringing bikes on board! The upper landing on our duplex had seats for mobile phone users, racks upon racks for luggage, and even more racks inside, at each end of the carriage and in the middle I sat down in the landing contentedly to label all our luggage, and tried not to get too excited by the fact that the man sitting next to me was texting in French (foreign country! Proof!)

When I finished I found Adi in our carriage, lounging with a grin at a table seat.

'This is not our seat,' he said, 'but I'm not moving.'

'Backward-facing?'

'Again!' He waved an arm around. 'There's loads of room. Anyway, all these people will be getting off at EuroDisney.'

Adi is given to optimism, a perfect counter to my natural caution. I sat down but, caution winning out, moved to our designated seats whenever we approached a station. He had to join me when a million children got on at EuroDisney. 'Don't say a word,' he said.

During the four-hour journey the sun disappeared and the weather turned distressingly Welsh. Hills, then mountains, rumpled the landscape to the east. During a delay in Lyons the sun came out and we sat with noses pressed to the glass, watching people on the street below going around being French, on bicycles and on foot. Way after eight in the evening we endured the final sweaty struggle off the train into Avignon TGV. We wiggled the trolleys down the long ramp to the doors and out into a bright windy warmth. The taxi driver shrugged gallicly at us as we stood nervously with our oversized luggage, wondering if he'd give us the look that British taxi drivers excel at: the one that says, 'Look, I'll drive there and back for you but I'd prefer if you didn't actually get into my nice clean cab.'

Unfounded worries. He wedged them in, in much the same way as we'd wedged them onto the Eurostar shelves.

Fifteen minutes later I was sitting on a low wall in the dusk at Camping Bagatelle, guarding our bikes while a couple of cats eyed each other and Adi searched for reception. One last struggle through the darkening campsite to our pitch. Oh, the joy of throwing down the unwieldy baggage for the last time! We erected the tent by torchlight, had a quick drink on the terrace outside the campsite's bar and fell into our sleeping bags. Wind roared in the trees above us all night, but I smiled into the dark. We were there.

CHAPTER TWO

Avignon

I knew only two things about Avignon. One was that there was a bridge; 'Sur le pont d'Avignon' inevitably became the first of many earworms. My shoddy attention in primary school history meant I was shocked to find out it was only half a bridge. The other was that it had briefly been the residence of the popes. An improbably story in ' A Child's Lives Of The Saints', a book I read many times as an eight-year-old, related how one of the Saint Theresas had walked to Avignon at the age of three and admonished the Pope to go back to his proper place in Rome. I still remember the illustration, a chubby, earnest child hectoring a stricken-looking Holy Father.

We looked at the map over breakfast in the campsite's cafeteria (croissants, yoghurt, and tea served with the tea bag outside a pot of hot - not boiling - water). Adi had done most of the planning, such as it was. For our first tour across England he had booked campsites ahead each night, but our subsequent tours had been more loosely planned, due to the geography and general dearth of roads in Scotland. (Sometime it was just 'Will we go south or north along the Western Isles?') Adi loves nothing more than getting his head in a map. I'd been really busy with work recently, so I had let him get on with the planning.

Today would be a rest day, a chance to put the bikes together and to get used to cycling on the right before we launched ourselves eastward into the valley north of the Luberon Mountains. We intended to follow the signed Luberon cycle route. It would be a gentle introduction to Provence and to cycling in France in general. We would return to the Rhône at Saint-Rémy-ce-Provence, cycle south to the Mediterranean, along the coast west to meet the Canal du Midi, and along the Canal, which would launch us east and north. We'd then go straight north at speed until we hit the Loire at some unspecified spot. West along the Loire to Nantes and around the coast of Brittany to finish in Saint-Malo. I thought it was a good plan, if a bit on the wiggly side.

'It's a long way,' I said. I'm the one who points out the problems.

'But we've got loads of time.' Adi's the one who points out the positives. 'It'll be great.'

But I did have worries. Was I fit enough for this? Would my schoolgirl French get us through? And what if we wanted different things?

This was what really concerned me. I love exploring and I love Adi. We both love cycle touring. It is a way of seeing the world and feeling the landscape unfurl itself around and beneath you. It is a way of travelling that can change in a moment into a mooch through an old town or a peep over a hedge at a colossal standing stone in the middle of a field, or a moment to pause to inhale a view you simply wouldn't see any other way. But I also loved the physicality of it. In the past, I had usually been the one who wanted to cycle a bit further and who was ready to move on earlier after stops. This had sometimes led to heated discussion. They never persisted long, but the point was that we did have different views.

This had troubled me on the train and during the night. Here, we wouldn't have our normal outlets. We wouldn't even be able to moan good-naturedly to a shopkeeper about the other's shortcomings. No way to let off steam except by cycling. Adi would be the only person in the entire country that I knew.

But the biggest worry assailed me over breakfast as I looked at the tea pot. If it did all go belly up, how would I get through it without a proper cup of tea?

Avignon didn't disappoint. It glowed. It sits just at the point where the main channel of the Rhône makes a 90° bend, and the old town is still surrounded by its medieval towers and ramparts. Our campsite was across the main channel on an island, formed by the Rhône splitting a couple of miles north of us, so we walked up the slip road onto the busy bridge towards the city. My worries about cycling in traffic were put to rest (almost) by the green-painted cycle paths lining the road and by the number of cyclists of all kinds. They were clearly treated as equal members of the vehicular traffic. We entered one of the larger gateways in the old town walls and went exploring.

Avignon was capital of the Catholic Church during the early middle ages, from 1309 to 1378, and was the seat of Benedict XIII, now deemed an antipope, from the late 1300s until 1409. It was he who had the city walls built, to protect himself and the town from forces loyal to Rome. After the schism ended and the papacy settled in Rome for good, Avignon remained a centre of culture and art. There's a huge arts festival each August. There was a palpable buzz about the town; it managed somehow to be both relaxed and exciting at the same time.

We avoided surprisingly aggressive charity donation seekers in the Place du Palais by visiting the Cathédrale Notre Dame des Doms. A huge edifice itself, it was dwarfed by the Palais des Papes that formed one entire face of the enormous square. An organist was practising cheerful early-Classical music as I inserted a euro in one- and two-cent coins into a coin slot, to light a candle for my mother. If my mother were abroad in a cathedral like this, she'd light a candle for me. Lighting candles for her has become a ritual for me and my sisters, a connection to her across the land and sea. But my mother probably wouldn't have started a league table of candle-value based on the size of candle to the euro.

For the record, the Avignon candles were moderately good value, if a bit slender. As the last of my coins dropped, a crowd of tourists entered, all mutterings and camera shutters. Adi and I escaped out into the sunlight and the wind, up to a little park high up on a rocky bluff, the Rocher des Doms, behind the cathedral.

'Is this the Mistral?' Adi wondered, looking at the shrubs bending while I took photos of our first French ducks in a pond in the park

'Hope not.' We knew of the Mistral's reputation, the wind that comes hurtling down the Rhône valley, warm and cold by turns and always strong. The sun was shining today, high clouds striped a white-blue sky, but when we came down off the bluff via narrow wriggling streets, the warm wind was rattling cups on the café tables, snapping the canopies and lifting the hair and skirts of elegant women.

In Avignon's enormous indoor market hall patient vendors smiled at us as they handed over yummy breads and peppers and tomatoes, dripping freshness. We went back to the campsite to lunch and to assemble the bikes.

I woke guiltily, after lying down in the tent for a short siesta, to find two complete and eager bicycles. I'd slept for an hour and a half, while Adi had got on with it.

'You looked as if you needed it,' he said.

Payment in pints was promised.

Refreshed, we cycled into the town and pootled around, getting used to riding on the right, getting used to the sensation of being a respected member of the vehicular community. Narrow cobbled one-way-streets were marked with the sign 'Sauf Vélo' and we rode joyfully down them, following relaxed and confident-looking French cyclists. To our delight, drivers seemed entirely patient, content to idle along behind bikes on the narrow streets until they could overtake safely. Best of all, we were in the company of other cyclists. All sorts and ages and sizes and shapes of people, a proper cross-section of society; not just students, or racers, or die-hard commuters - just people. In Britain you only get that in a few cities - London, I guess, York, Bristol, Cambridge. You definitely didn't get it in north Wales. To be cycling among other ordinary-looking people, with not a high-viz jacket or a helmet in sight, was intensely liberating.

Errands completed, we cycled back over the bridge and rode around the island. Instant countryside; the only houses were large farmhouses surrounded by fields. To my surprise, it was quite easy to get used to cycling on the right. Junctions were difficult at first, but after just a couple of hours, reminding myself to aim for the distant side of the road when turning left, I felt quite confident. It's funny what takes longer: it was about three weeks before my brain, watching cars overtake each other on the road ahead of me, stopped screaming, 'They're on the wrong side of the road there's gonna be a crash oh god – oh. It's ok. We're in France.'

That evening set the template for the evenings to come: me chopping and Adi cooking, a delicious concoction with spices and vegetables from the market, mopped up with a new discovery: fougasse bread. We'd bought it from a tiny boulangerie run by a narrow, slightly unhinged-looking woman waging war with a broom on the pigeons outside her shop.

Into the town for the third time, in a wind grown disturbingly chilly, to get fleeced in a bar on the Place d'Horloge. As we told ourselves when we looked at the bill, we ought to have known it would be a costly mistake. €2.70 for a glass of red wine - ok - but a whopping €7 for Adi's beer! The bar dog, a plump and solemn black Scottie, stared at us as we resolved to avoid bars on pretty, touristy main squares, then returned to his contemplation of the world, clearly having heard it all before, while we huddled out of the wind and vowed that come what may, we were going to wear our sandals.

PART TWO

The Beautiful South:

From Avignon to Apt

CHAPTER THREE

To Maubec

Most cycle-touring books I've read are, firstly, written by solo cyclists, and secondly, about much longer journeys than ours, achieved in much shorter times. Thirdly, almost all of them feature a scene within the first ten pages where the writer is sitting with head in hands, with sore backside, usually in tears, wondering what they are doing. I'll tell them what they are doing. They are cycling eighty bloody miles on their first day and they have to ride a hundred miles on their second day and already they can't face it. Of course they can't face it! How did they think they would not be crying?

No such problems would assail us.

'We don't want to overdo it and be miserable,' Adi said, looking at the map over breakfast. I agreed, quelling the little voice inside me that said, yes, yes, I

25

do want to overdo it! I suspect it was my legs talking. I would have liked to test them. But it's true that I didn't want to be miserable, and based on our previous tours, eighty miles a day was not an option if we wanted to stay together. Besides, another voice in my head said to the first voice, we're in kilometres here. Eighty kilometres was entirely respectable. Sixty would do to start. Sixty kilometres was what we expected to do that day, a leisurely, circuitous route to Apt.

The Luberon cycle route started in Cavaillon, about 25 km south-east of Avignon, and wriggled east to Forcalquier, 65 km away by the main roads, before winding around the back of the Luberon range and back to the start along the south-facing slopes of the mountains. 'We'll pick up the route between Cavaillon and Apt, and follow the signs from there on in. We'll easily make it to Apt,' said Adi, waving a casual finger over the map as we ate our late breakfast.

'For God's sake. I'm sure we should be halfway there by now.'

'Don't start that already.'

'How far have we come?'

For answer, Adi rattled the map and frowned at it.

We're never going to make it to Apt, I thought. I stamped on my impatience and tried to eat a banana.

We were sitting in the shade in - I checked the map over Adi's shoulder - Caumont-sur-Durance.

It had been nearly midday by the time we finally cycled through the walls of the old town and out into the suburbs, delayed by several chores we should have done yesterday. This was the source of mild tension fizzling in the heat between us.

'I can actually hear you trying to be patient,' Adi said. 'You actually make a noise.'

I grinned and made myself relax. At least we were on our way.

Despite the behind-already feeling, the best bit of the morning so far had been pedalling up the small slope from the campsite entrance to the bridge over the Rhône, fully laden for the first time. I'd had no time to practise at home, so wobbling up and down the campsite's alleys for ten minutes was all the preparation I'd had. But up that little hill I could hear my legs and the bike sighing happily. 'This,' they said, 'is what we were born to do.' After a pause, my legs added, 'You could have paid more attention to packing. We thought you'd learned.'

As we'd cycled south-east out of Avignon's centre the sun had come out properly, the wind had fallen to a brisk breeze and the sky was a blue-white dome. We fell into a map gap in the suburbs, that no-man's-land where touristy town centre maps end and the Michelin regional road maps don't show quite enough detail. We blundered for a while. At least, I blundered. Adi has an excellent sense of direction, and without a map I had no choice but to trust him. After some terrifying moments - a terror borne more of our uncertainty than any aggression or scary driving by the traffic around us - we negotiated a series of dual carriageways and found ourselves cycling in the safety of the broad hard shoulder of the D900, the equivalent of a British A-road, in approximately the right direction.

'Exactly where I was aiming for,' Adi said with satisfaction. Anxiety over whether we were permitted on this category of road was put to rest when we met other cyclists coming the opposite direction, friendly hands raised in greeting. Sun bounced brightly off the road surface; infrequent cars passed us at respectful distances. A low ridge of hills appeared in front and to our right.

And so we came to our disputed siesta a whole hour after starting off.

'It's hot. We have to stop for a bit,' said Adi.

It was hot, true. But still. Only an hour… I tried hard not to bounce with impatience and took in our surroundings instead, which was a bit of a mistake. Caumont-sur-Durance looked like the set of a spaghetti western, and boasted a disgusting public toilet, a small, sweet fountain and an aged woman on the other side of the square doing verbal battle with a small crowd of be-scootered teenagers.

'Can we go yet?' I asked after ten minutes.

'It's still too hot!'

'But I thought we wanted to get to Apt.'

'We will, but we have to wait a bit. It's still too hot.'

Adi's positive nature can lead to an optimistically casual dismissal of terrain, heat and distance. I, on the other hand, am a worrier. I also had the uneasy feeling that we were being judged. A great P.E. teacher in the sky was marking our performance, and we were being marked down. We were not Proper Cycle Tourers.

Fortunately, Adi gets bored easily. When he suggested that maybe we'd find it easier to cope with the heat while cycling and making our own breeze, I leapt onto my bike.

There was gorgeousness already. Cycling into the bright sun, I rolled up my sleeves and the hem of my shorts and revelled in sensation of warmth on bare skin, the like of which I hadn't felt except for brief not-freezing spells in March, fleeting half-hours of promise-of-spring that had never delivered.

Soon we passed a roadside vegetable stall, where we bought a huge ridged tomato and a bag of sugar snap peas from a pretty girl. A pair of ducklings with clipped wings quacked apprehensively inside a crate.

What happened if you bought one: did you take it home yourself, to let it live or die, or would the pretty girl wring its neck for you on the spot? I wanted to ask, but the mechanics of translating my questions eluded me. The risk of being taken for a genuine customer loomed and the spectre of two vegetarians pedalling with a freshly slaughtered duck - or a live one - that we'd been too polite to refuse kept my mouth shut.

High clouds slid over the sky but didn't damp the sun or our spirits. A friend texted Adi to let him know that May 14th, the day we'd left, had been the coldest May day in Britain on record. We did a little dance.

We picked up the Luberon cycle trail in Robion, a village of two halves, the lower a ribbon development along the main road, the older half set flush up against a greenery-draped cliff. Robion had what we would come to know as all the trappings of a Provençal village: towering town hall, war memorial and fountain surrounded by plane trees, and buildings and roofs of warm sandstone in shades of honey. The steep, rocky walls of the Luberon rose behind, clad in pines and trees unfamiliar to me. We sat for a few minutes, refilled our water bottles at the fountain and watched a shifty-looking little brown terrier slinking around the flower beds with half an eye on the old men talking on a bench in the shade. The reason for his shiftiness became clear when he cocked a leg and peed on the flower beds before scuttling away at speed.

The signed route headed east, with small and friendly blue signs pointing out the way at junctions. The roadside verges sang with colour, poppies, irises, barley, harebells and cranesbills. Sometimes there was a little ditch - bone dry with fractured plates of crusted mud - between the road surface and the fields; sometimes the flower-filled verges melted seamlessly into the fields and meadows with sudden blazing patches of poppies. Vines and olive trees stood in ranks, with no fences or walls between fields. Just a change in crops, from wood to meadow to vineyard to olive to cherry. Some of the lanes were lined with clawdd-type walls, a dislocating taste of north Wales in this totally foreign landscape, and so narrow my plump rear panniers almost scraped the walls.

We climbed up our first hill - 14%! - to Oppède Le Vieux, a picturesque hill-top village. Arcaded paths and warm stone cottages climbed up to the ruined chateau and twelfth-century church at the top. We paused in the square, admired the view upwards and the view of the valley below us. It was a gorgeous setting for our second minor row. It went like this.

Me: You said you wanted to get to Apt.

Him: You never want to stop and look at anything.

Me: What do you mean, never? It's the first day!

This was over his wish to explore the village for half an hour. Yes, I'd love to, I thought, but did we have time to stop in every single village? But it was gorgeous, so we left the bikes in the square (unlocked - after three wobbly hours on mine I was already thinking, 'You want to nick this? Good luck to you') and headed up through tiny passageways to the old village and the ruins of the chateau. It reminded me of Robin Hood's Bay, with its narrow stepped and cobbled streets, differing in that it wasn't on the sea, was warm, and that in Robin Hood's Bay you don't turn corners and come face to bumper with a Smart car squeezing along an alley that would challenge a well-fed donkey.

The views north across the valley to the Vaucluse plateau and bald-topped Mont Ventoux in the far distance restored our slightly chafing tempers. We could still make it to Apt, we thought, until ten minutes after getting back on the bikes. Someone had removed my leg muscles and replaced them with goo. We weren't going to make it to Apt. The P.E. teacher in the sky put a big cross next to our names but I didn't care.

We got lost, found the route again, cycled on a little, but realised that the next campsite was 16 km away and that we were far more tired than we'd expected to be. I blamed the wind in Avignon. Adi reckoned we hadn't eaten enough. We searched for a campsite in Oppède but failed, rode around a little aimlessly and ended up retracing our route in part to the lovely little village of Maubec, the nearest place where we were sure of finding a campsite.

We fell into our old familiar routine. Tent up. Into the showers. Adi cooked while I sorted out the bedding and made our pitch our home. Rain spat, but not until after the tent was up and everything was inside, and there was no venom in it. After a fabulous dinner of couscous with onions, garlic, tomato and petit pois with the remains of the fougasse bread, we wandered up to the tiny hill on which Maubec sits to a friendly pizzeria, for pudding and wine. It was almost dark as we walked back to the tent. In the indigo sky above was a plane flying east, and bats, and Venus. I fell asleep reading David Copperfield on my Kindle, after writing my diary. Only two disagreements. Win!

CHAPTER FOUR

To Apt

In the whirl of work leading up to our departure I'd lost sight of the fact that Avignon was only about a thousand miles south of Anglesey. Provence is hardly equatorial, but I was still looking forward to a climate utterly unlike the one we'd left behind. And we had all that bad-weather-cheerfully-endured credit. The weather bankers would be smiling on us.

The weather bankers had other ideas.

'I hope this is only a blip.' Adi was in the awning, peering out at the drizzle through which we'd just scuttled to the showers and back. I was in the inner tent, lying on my stomach and scribbling notes on birds I could hear.

'What does it look like doing?' Jay squawking, great tits, robin singing.

'Nothing much.' He scowled out. 'Oh, a buzzard just flew over.'

The drizzle had started after breakfast, which was porridge. Over the years we'd learnt, often the hard way, about the best foods to eat when cycle touring. On our early tours we'd usually countered the afternoon dip with an energy drink or an emergency glucose sweet, especially if we could see a hill coming up. This would give the desired kick to the muscles but, we realised after a couple of tours, there would be a steep and tearful crash on the other side of that kick. We'd been getting better at using real foods to keep us going and avoid the dreaded bonk, that horrible, all-over-nauseous sensation that your legs have turned to jelly and that you are going to murder someone in order to obtain sugar. I still clearly remember my first bonk, on the first afternoon of our first ever coast to coast ride. A brambly hedgerow had never looked so inviting.

Our favourite breakfast comprised potato cakes. Wild camping experiences in Scotland, miles from shops, had given us a great fondness for them. They are wonderful foods, with an early energy boost combined with a steady release that keeps you going through the hardest morning. If we couldn't buy them we usually contrived to have a couple of emergency spuds and small stash of flour to make our own.

Chunky oatcakes, with flour and porridge oats, were another favourite. To make sure we wouldn't get caught out miles from shops in France we'd brought - rather misguidedly - half a kilo each of flour and porridge oats with us. Yes. A kilo of flour and porridge. Try to control your mirth.

Through the gap in the awning I could see campers trotting to their campervans with baguettes protruding from under their jackets. I looked down at my bowl of porridge. Hmm.

An Englishman called John overheard us speaking in English and came over to chat. He was from Wiltshire, and he and his wife (hiding in their campervan from the drizzle) had been coming to this campsite for twenty-four years to go walking. The Grand Randonnée 9 passed through the campsite on its way from Saint-Amour in the Jura Mountains to Grimaud on the Mediterranean. Over the coming weeks we'd get used to seeing the discreet signs that marked the GR paths, double-coloured marks on trees, posts and walls. But at the moment we were more interested in the weather forecast John had just heard on the radio.

'Showers?' repeated Adi in alarm.

'Showers,' confirmed John, and went off to prepare for a day's hiking.

We put off starting, hoping John was wrong and that it would improve. I stood on the sheltered verandah of the shower block holding my Kindle up in the air to access the campsite's shaky wifi and bought 'French for Dummies' from Amazon. I'd already become frustrated with my limited vocabulary; the forms of French had come back to me fairly easily, but the actual words for stuff had slipped away and refused to come out when urgently required. I had great hopes for the book but gave up when 20 minutes of impersonating a Kindle-holding Statue of Liberty had resulted in only a 35% download. Back at the tent Adi was hunched over the map and his bike computer.

'This doesn't make sense.'

We'd reckoned it was about 38 miles to Apt from Avignon, allowing for our indirect route. The computer said we'd cycled 39 miles yesterday afternoon. You'd think we'd have learned from three previous summers' cycle touring, but it seems to be like a variation of Murphy's Law - let's call it Madigan's Law - which goes: 'No matter what the map and the road signs say, it will be half as far again as you think, even when taking Madigan's Law into account.'

Bored with the drizzle, we eventually packed the tent up, slightly damp.

'At least it's not cold,' Adi said as we rolled off into the morning.

The spitting rain couldn't dim the beauty of the landscape. The trusty little Luberon à Vélo signs led us along little roads, between meadows and vineyards and sloping fields of lavender not yet in flower, the plants like big green hedgehogs squatting in rows. We stopped in Ménerbes, a beautiful village perché upon an elbow-like sub-spur that curled out from the main mountain ridge and enclosed sheltered vineyards in its crook. The sun peeped out and hid again. An elderly gentleman from eastern France talked to us, well, to me, about his car trip, ignoring Adi completely and drooling slightly, as we stood by a wall dropping down to the rooftops below.

This is what I remember from that day: roofs! Earthy colours, every hue from honey through to toffee, like sunshine trapped in warm sandy earth, baked into tiles and laid on roofs to warm the houses beneath and the spirits of all who looked on them. Even in the dull light they made me feel cosy. The sun emerged briefly again as we walked the narrow streets to the park at the top of the village, giving us hope.

'That rain was just a blip,' Adi said confidently as we unlocked the bikes.

Ten minutes later we were cycling into a nasty headwind. I called it names; it tried to knock me off on the bends. The skies darkened and the wind abruptly stopped. This was apparently the cue for the rain to take its turn. By the time I'd found my waterproof jacket I was wet through. We pedalled on through it - at least it was warm - and ten minutes later shook out our jackets by a field of glorious poppies. A bit prematurely. Soon the jackets were on again as we pedalled through hailstones. Hailstones! Shaking our waterproofs out for the second time by another field of glorious poppies, Adi said, 'I've worked it out. It misses us.'

'What misses us?'

'The Scottish weather. It's come to find us.'

My mood, I must admit, was vicious. We rode on, criss-crossing the main east-west road from Avignon to Apt, and my mood lightened, as moods unfailingly do on the back of a bike. My stomach - still full of the morning's porridge - was already rumbling as we chugged slowly up and around a little hill and freewheeled down a gentle slope, looking across the valley to delightful Bonnieux perched on its ridge. I was so intent on gawping at Bonnieux and pausing to photograph it that I was completely taken aback when we rounded the next bend and rode straight into Lacoste, clinging to the hillside. Unmentioned in any of our guides, as pretty as anywhere and utterly unexpected, we were entranced by this tiny gem of a village. As if in response to our wide-eyed enchantment, the sun came out.

This was worth a pause. We bought a pain au chocolat each and a can of Orangina and sat eating on a sunwarmed stone bollard overlooking the valley to Bonnieux. A pleasant American-sounding couple paused to ask us if we were doing a whole trip on bikes. Turned out they were Brazilian-Canadian. When they heard we'd come from Wales they were delighted: their daughter lived in South Carolina, with a Welsh neighbour who flew the Welsh flag in her garden every day.

'Sod the weather,' Adi said as we rode off, full of sugar and fats. 'Less than twenty-four hours on the road and already four villages like that!'

Four villages of of jaw-dropping, smile-making loveliness. We'd cope with the weather, I thought, rolling up my zip-offs to expose another inch of white thigh.

The climb to Bonnieux was steady and gentle, the pause in the little square restful, the bread from the artisan boulangerie divine. We munched it with apples and oranges sitting by the town fountain, underneath a picture taken in 1980 of the last laundresses to use the public lavage, the laundry, beneath the fountain.

From Bonnieux the breeze still blew into our faces but it was warm. The friendly signs led us on a largely level route along tiny roads, keeping us up on the hillside with glorious views, both down the main valley to the east and around corners into teeny side valleys. The slopes were terraced with vines and with meadows blazing red and purple and green, unfenced and unwalled. Rows of cherry, olive trees and vines stepped cross the fields. Some vines looked ancient, thickly muscled as a rugby player's thigh; some young and supple, with tramline supports stretched along the rows above them. Fresh green tendrils strained upwards, seeking support.

For someone who works in the countryside it's a bit embarrassing that it took me well over twenty-four hours to work out why there weren't any fences.

'No sheep!' I said to Adi in triumph, riding along the lovely lane in the sunshine, looking down on Apt, our destination. In sheepy north Wales, a bike ride in early May from Anglesey into the Snowdonia will take you past all the stages in The Life Of The Lamb, from the barely week-old Welsh mountain sheep born at last in the shadow of Snowdon to haunchy four- and five-month-olds, born in sheds around Christmas. The landscape is green and grassy and crisscrossed with stone walls and fences to keep these far from stupid creatures from escaping to find the next juicy mouthful of grass. Here, there wasn't a herbivore to be seen: no cattle, no goats, and not a trace of a sheep. No bleating or mooing.

'At least we know we're not going to meet a herd of Highland cattle,' Adi pointed out.

This is one of the hazards of cycling in Scotland. Gentle, timorous beasts those shaggy brown cattle might be, but those horns are intimidating. I've waited, jelly-kneed, for up to half an hour before deciding to brave a track through a scattered herd of dozing cows, trying to neither startle nor threaten. It's terrifying.

Apt spread out below us, a friendly-looking sprawl. We freewheeled down a lovely lane for the last three miles. Swifts screamed over us as we entered the cheerful, scruffy town and pulled up beside the tourist office. Shortly afterwards, we rolled up to the cheapest campsite, Camping les Cèdres, down in the middle of the town.

In the queue for reception we met other cycle tourers for the first time, and my chronic comparisonitis went into over-drive. The Dutch couple had proper touring bikes; each wheel - each wheel! - had a little stand, designed to cope with the extra weight of panniers. Our bikes had no stands at all. They sported identical yellow-and-black Ortlieb panniers front and back. (Checking later with Adi we found that we had simultaneously and silently christened them The Bumblebees.) The woman was friendly but frighteningly efficient. They'd come from Avignon this morning by a new, cycle-specific route, much more direct than the Luberon route, she said, looking doubtfully at my skinny legs and laden bike. John from Wiltshire had mentioned this road during our chat that morning, a paved road high up on the mountain ridge that was only accessible to cyclists, horses and Luberon Natural Park vehicles.

'Some of the inclines on the Luberon à Vélo are 14%,' said the female Bumblebee.

My stock answer to this is, 'I just go slowly,' instead of pointing out that I've been up 25% hills in Yorkshire fully laden - gravity-defyingly slowly, with frequent pauses to replace my popping eyeballs, but pedalling every inch.

'It will be very hard,' she insisted.

There's only one thing to do when someone persists in pointing out difficulties, and it's to agree fulsomely with a great big smile. Yes! Yes, it is going to be hard! It'll be great! Just what I want! I like hills!

Adi is of a cautious disposition, and while we had already agreed that we would stay in Apt for two nights, allowing us to enjoy the Saturday market the next day, he said he'd just pay for the one night for now. 'Just in case.' This sort of caution on his part is entirely normal, as is the fact that I nodded and agreed, not really listening. I had already decided that we were staying for two nights because I had visited the toilets while he queued and had found, to my joy, toilet seats, toilet roll and a hair dryer

Toilet roll! Not in the cubicles, in a holder in the bathroom, but at least it was there. The campsite and public toilets we'd found so far had mystified me. Did everyone carry tissues and handwash around with them all the time? Mind you, I do that at home.

Apt was barely a twenty-mile ride from Maubec but we'd read great things about the Saturday market in our Rough Guide. Another reason we stayed, and that I didn't protest, was that there was a paucity of campsites between Apt and Forcalquier; if we went any further it would only be another eight miles before we could be sure of somewhere to stop, which hardly seemed worth it. Even with my sneaking desire to be one of those epic-miles-on-the-first-day sorts, I didn't really want a 70-mile day so early in the trip.

My diary that night was full of colours. Poppies, vetches, knapweeds and little purple bellflowers I didn't recognize on the road verges and in between the rows of vines. A hobby above Ménerbes. A cuckoo calling just outside Lacoste. Jays upon jays. Crickets singing us along all the afternoon. The smell of warm earth; the road throwing the heat back up at us. We drank wine from a vineyard just outside the town and toasted our bikes. It was the 18th of May and we had two calendar months to go.

CHAPTER FIVE

Apt

The day off in Apt was a blur of colour and smells. We woke and rather dutifully ate our porridge. The efficient female Bumblebee, we noticed, had approached a neighbour in a campervan and obtained the location of a bakery. The scent of the croissants did not endear the porridge to me. (Just to warn you, I'm going to refer to bakeries as boulangeries from here on in. It's such a lovely word.)

The sky was striped in thick bands of blue and white and a strong, warm breeze blew. After rinsing out the cycling shorts and t-shirts - normally the first thing we did on arrival at a campsite but neglected last night in view of the early rest day, headed into the town.

Apt's centre is compact, almost entirely pedestrianised. From the packed market square, stalls snaked out down the narrow streets, squeezed wherever there was space. Under the town clock, the mairie, beside the small cathedral, you could buy earrings, rugs, cheeses, spices, preserved meats, nougat - at least three stalls selling nougat - or chickens. I left Adi deep in discussion with the man at the spices and herbs stall; in a mixture of sign language and basic French and English they were managing to have an in-depth discussion about the best spices to go with various vegetables.

Passing quickly by the relatively few just-for-tourist shops - easily identifiable by the deafening rasp of toy cicadas - I had a quick look in the Maison du Parc du Luberon. It was a cheerful museum, with playful exhibitions on the natural history and culture of the park, with a particular emphasis on the geology. The palaeontology section, in the thirteenth-century vaulted cellar of the building, was certainly the most atmospheric setting for a museum display I'd ever been in. I came away with a bundle of leaflets on the natural history and on other cycle routes in the area.

I loved the French attitude to eating in cafés and bars. I found a seat on the terrace of a bar at the square and felt as if I was in a film. The sun was shining, a guitarist was playing authentic-sounding French music (although what would I know). I watched in wonderment as a couple came up with a big takeaway pizza box and sat down at one of the outside tables. No irate proprietor coming up to say 'Oy! Can't you read?' and pointing at a sign with the usual 'Only food bought here to be consumed on these premises.' As long as the bar isn't actually serving food itself at the time, or only snacks, no-one seemed to be bothered as long as you'd bought a drink. What a civilised way to be.

Adi met me and we went back to the tent to do a little re-organising of our panniers. It had become clear that I had failed the packing test.

On our first coast to coast tour we left our campervan at a campsite in Robin Hood's Bay, cycled to Whitby and took four trains across the country to Whitehaven. This meant that when we arrived on our bikes in Robin Hood's Bay four days later we had a campervan full of clean, dry, deliciously unsweaty clothes waiting for us. Instead of rushing straight to the shower, I made a cup of tea, sat down with a notebook and pen, and slowly went through all my panniers, removing items one at a time. I listed every item and noted whether or not I had used it, and if so, how often. If I'd used it out of pure stubbornness instead of need, I noted that as well. I was scrupulous. I was honest. I was immensely proud of myself for thinking of this plan and for actually carrying it out before the shower and the self-congratulatory pints. For our next few cycle tours the list served as a template for my packing.

I don't know why I abandoned it as I packed for France. Perhaps I felt that because we wouldn't be bringing woolly hats and gloves (never, never, never go to Scotland in any season without your woolly hat and gloves) there was room for oodles more stuff. What was I thinking?

To France, I brought: two pairs of cycling shorts, three pairs of socks, four pairs of knickers, three bras, two light merino wool t-shirts, two cotton t-shirts, two long-sleeved merino wool tops, one fleece, two pairs of zip-off walking trousers, one pair of cotton trousers, one merino wool vest-top, two light cotton hippy-ish tops, two wrap-around skirts, one windproof jacket, one waterproof jacket, one pair of sandals, one pair of trainers, one pair of cycling shoes with the cleats taken out (don't ask), bike lock, wash bag, travel towel, sunscreen, tub of body moisturiser, Kindle, the Collins Bird Guide to Britain and Europe, two novels, two notebooks, two pens, camera, despised Blackberry (buried), charging cables, tiny First Aid kit, the Rough Guide to France, the Rough Guide to Provence, the Rough Guide to Brittany, sunglasses and a tub of lip balm. All this was squeezed in my four panniers around the sleeping bags, mats and liners that it was my job to carry. Also squashed in were the bags of flour and porridge oats that we'd brought. I also carried the hockey bags that we'd put the panniers in whilst on the trains, now rolled to the size of large tins of beans and wrapped up with gaffer tape. Adi said they were expensive, so I carried them on my rear rack for two months.

Oh, and a hula hoop.

Adi carried the tent, the emergency tool kit, the stove and cooking equipment, as well as the staple foodstuffs. Except for the wretched flour and oats.

Our bikes were sturdy types. My Dawes Tanami was - is - technically a hybrid designed for commuting, and had already served me well for ten years of pot-hole and gutter riding at home, and many months' worth of cycle touring. I'd treated it to a steel Tubus rack on the front after my first season of touring, and a low-geared chainset, but otherwise it was as I had bought it. I occasionally gazed at the shop windows of specialised touring bike companies, but I loved my dependable, dogged bike. Which didn't have a name, other than Bike. (I have not much imagination when it comes to names. Most of my cats have been called Puss.)

Adi felt the same way about his bike. He'd been riding his Marin Sausalito for six years by then. A hybrid with front suspension, which he normally cycled with the suspension locked off, it had carried him comfortably up wicked Yorkshire hills. Unlike me, he hadn't invested in a granny chainset, but then he has bigger thigh muscles than I do. A couple of years before, he had fitted it with butterfly handlebars, often seen on Dutch touring bikes, and he loved them; he liked changing his hand position, giving his arm muscles a bit of a break.

After pushing things around in the panniers for a bit, we went out for a short ride along quiet lanes, and found the cycle track the other tourers had come by. The Luberon route, we agreed, was much prettier. Over dinner - salad and a Mediterranean spiced vegetable stew made from the toothsomely fresh ingredients and spices from the market - we discussed our onward plans. I was itching to go. The forecast looked dire, but we decided not to believe it. I fell asleep to the sound of crickets

PART.THREE

Heart of the Luberon:
from Apt to Cucuron

CHAPTER SIX

To Forcalquier

I was scribbling in my diary outside a bakery on a Sunday morning somewhere in the backstreets of Apt. There was a bright, warm breeze and we had 12 miles of easy cycle track ahead before we hit any hills. Reasons for good cheer, yet my scribbles were irritable, because the reason I was scribbling in my diary on the deserted Sunday street was because I'd been abandoned by Adi. He was scouring the streets for coffee. The supply of grounds he'd brought from home had run out and he didn't have enough for another hit - a dreadful situation. Time was creeping on and I was starting to fidget, with that feeling we were failing some sort of test.

We'd been up since seven but it had taken ages to get going. It was the bloody potato cakes. I don't know what we were thinking. The porridge oats, flour and emergency potatoes strategy was perfect for Scotland but that morning in Apt, watching everyone around us eat their fresh bread and make their coffee and dismantle their tents while we boiled the spuds, mashed them, mixed them with flour into potato cakes, then fried them, I felt like an idiot. I was rigid with tea-withdrawal by the time they were ready, by which time everyone else had driven or cycled off. It had seemed like such an excellent idea. It is an excellent idea, just not when you're in a country that has excellent and numerous bakeries in every village stuffed with energy-giving breads of all description. The Bumblebees smiled at us as they rolled away at half-eight. I smiled back weakly and vowed to eat double portions of porridge. We had to get rid of the bloody stuff.

Adi finally arrived with a takeaway coffee and glowered up at the sky. It was darkening. He colourfully pointed this out. I agreed that it was darkening, said, 'Shall we go?' brightly, and pedalled off.

The problem with being a couple - I mean two people, not necessarily having promised to love and cherish - is that there is only one other person to listen when you need to vent. Adi didn't expect me to do anything about the weather. He didn't want me to cheer him up. He just wanted to let off steam, and maybe strangle a weather god or two. I was just a sounding board, but it can be depressing being a sounding board. Though I know he didn't mean to bring me down, it is never a cheering experience listening to someone calling the clouds rude names. I cycled on, ahead of him for once, into the darkening wedge of sky between the valley walls.

The great thing about cycling is that there are always other things to think about: the wonderfulness of cycle lanes, for instance. We ignored the tortuous route of the Luberon à Vélo out of Apt, which wriggled through no doubt stunning villages, and kept instead to a traffic-free cycle lane that stayed close to the river Calavon, which flows through Apt and eventually joins the Durance. I kept hopping off my bike to take photos of the track and its signs, junctions and general furniture. Two lanes! Little bicycles painted on the road! Junctions where cyclists had priority! We met a lone male cycle tourist at a junction and shared a shrug of fellowship in the headwind.

We picked up the Luberon route again near Le Boisset and followed lanes through hamlets and farmland on the south side of the river to Céreste, getting a sudden, swift soaking on the way.

'The wind stops when the rain comes,' Adi said, shaking out his waterproof beside another glorious meadow strewn with poppies. 'I wonder why that is?'

'Variety?'

We paused to nibble some bread in Céreste, a pretty village with a sloping main street, and ticked off the essentials: big town hall, fountain, three boulangeries, shifty-looking little brown dog. Onwards to the north side of the valley, where the hills were beginning to tighten on the valley floor. The rain began again, a heavy drizzle that felt as if it had some staying power. We didn't comment on it, just kept pedalling, a little mechanically.

At the ruined Prieuré de Carluc we stopped and explored. The pentagonal choir of the chapel, grey and smooth and forbidding in the rain, was the only part in good repair, but was closed. The priory was founded in the 11th century, and was partially troglodytic: the builders had taken advantage of caves and overhangs and used them to connect the priory buildings to each other. We stood in a trough that ran through a tunnel - we later found out it had been a tomb - and sheltered out of the rain for a little, munching a fougasse.

From there the road, tiny and winding, started to rise, undulating over the spurs and ripples of the hills on our left, the southernmost fingers of the Vaucluse plateau. The view opened out; ridges of green, scrub-covered hills marched into the distance. Gently but inexorably the road climbed, our first long hill and our introduction to the evils of French road engineers. I clicked down the gears and pedalled stoically. My legs were getting into a rhythm and I heard them speaking to me. 'Keep clicking down. It's not a race.' Their voices - they sounded like identical twins - competed with the 'Pont d'Avignon' song still playing manically in my head.

We rode up into the heavy drizzle, between the still-brilliant colours of the road verges. The clouds sank to meet us and we rose into a land of scrubby oaks and holm oaks and other trees. Just before Reillanne the road took a heartbreaking dip before climbing steeply up towards the village square. The rain was sluicing down by now and as I rounded a corner twenty yards behind Adi a woman under an umbrella caught and held my eye. It wasn't difficult for her, I was crawling. 'Vous êtes courageuse, Madame,' she said.

This cheered me greatly. Not wet and mental, but courageous!

Adi and I shook out our waterproofs under the awning of a café before dripping inside. All the young and middle-aged men sitting over their tiny coffees and glasses of pastis greeted us with courteous nods. Everyone, men included, kissed their friends three times when they met, which I found charming. My Earl Grey tea was lovely and Adi's coffee visibly improved his mood. He even said he was looking forward to the next bit of the climb. I decided to keep him in coffee no matter the cost.

The road kept rising but the rain kept easing. The Legs – I'd begun to think of them in capital letters – pedalled away stoically, and I caught myself giving them little pats every so often. Up into the edge of the Vaucluse plateau, twisting and climbing, gentle and endless, with the headwind making things interesting on the bends. Just south of a village called Vachères, where the road reached close to 800 metres, we took a minor road to the right. And then our reward: descending, down and down.

At least it should have been a reward. I'd never been comfortable descending, especially with panniers playing with my centre of gravity. I don't actually know what difference panniers make. I only know that I take bends at an even more upright angle than I do without them (usually 89°). I could only admire Adi's graceful confidence for about fifteen seconds before he disappeared joyfully down the hill. When we met at the bottom he had thoroughly cheered up, grinning though soggy. Aha! Coffee and big long descents, I thought, grinning back happily.

The road rose gently again through the dripping, deserted forest of Scots pine, oak and beech. When we joined another road and turned down the hill we could see the white domes of the astronomical observatory of

Haute Provence among the wet green woods on the plateau.

'You know they built it here because on average 170 days and nights a year are completely cloudless?' Adi asked me. He looked up at the sky and shouted, 'Did you hear that?'

We were now on the D5 and freewheeled down and down, out of the woods and into the meadows below. The reliable little blue signs led us across the valley bottom, through Dauphin and finally north towards Forcalquier, perched on a hill above the river Laye.

It was drizzling again when we arrived and we lost the Luberon route signs for the first time. When we finally found the campsite we pitched up quickly and went straight into the bar for tea and wine (those great rehydration drinks). The lone male cycle tourist we'd seen not far from Apt was in there and I overcame my shyness to introduce myself to him.

'Vous faites un tour à vélo?'

He turned out to be English. He always toured by himself.

'I'm happy on my own most of the time, but it must be nice being together,' John said (for that was his name). 'My wife won't come with me. At least -' he waved at the windows where the rain drummed '- you've got someone to moan with when it's like this.'

Adi and I exchanged glances.

'If you don't moan too much,' we said together.

John told us about the solo ride he was planning next summer, across Canada, Atlantic to Pacific. He was going on to the Gorges of Verdon tomorrow. Envy afflicted me. We had been tempted by the Gorges but decided that we weren't yet fit enough and didn't have quite enough time.

We parted to shower and make dinner. The shower was excellent, huge cubicles (though still with push button taps) and perfect, steamy water - but the rain poured so relentlessly that we didn't even try to cook. Adi and I shared a squashed emergency flapjack and a slab of chocolate and went to eke out a glass of wine in the bar.

No actual rows, just one long mood that lifted. Win!

www.LivingWatersEU.com

JN37L1Z551

1M

John Wesley 1703–1791

100,000

United Kingdom

ONE MILLION

Pounds

1,000,000

What's most valuable to you? Money, health, eyesight, your soul? How about this million-pound question: If Heaven exists, are you good enough to go there? Have you ever lied, stolen, or used God's name in vain? Jesus said, "Whoever looks at a woman to lust for her has already committed adultery with her in his heart." If you have, you will be guilty on Judgement Day and end up in God's prison, Hell. But the Bible says God is rich in mercy and offered us a way out of Hell and into Heaven. Sinners broke God's Law and Jesus paid their fine by suffering and dying on the cross. Then Jesus rose from the dead, defeating death. Today, repent and trust Jesus, and God will give you eternal life as a free gift. Then show your gratitude by obeying His command to be baptized. Make sure to also join a church, and read the Bible daily.

www.WhyDidIGetThis.org **JN37L1Z551**

CHAPTER SEVEN

To Beaumont-de-Pertuis

It is perfectly acceptable,' said The Rough Guide To France, 'to sit for hours over just one cup of coffee.'

I wanted more than an hour. I wanted a day sitting around a pot of tea, indoors, in the dry. We were sitting outside a small, slightly seedy-looking bartabac in Manosque, underneath the awning, watching traffic slosh through the solid, functional streets. It was still drizzling, we were still wet, but we were warm. I was munching a baguette stuffed with pungent cheese and red onions, and I had a large cup (no teapots yet) of blissfully hot Earl Grey tea on the table in front of me. A man who looked like an extra from The Sopranos sat at the next table along, reading a newspaper over a tiny cup of coffee. A young man with a satchel stood in the doorway of the bar, smoking and talking over his shoulder to the old men and the bartender inside.

I was ready to fall in love with this barman. The morning had been hard. It started pleasantly enough, with tea and croissants actually indoors in the campsite bar, followed by a mooch in the market in Apt, where we bought cheese and fruit from a bright-eyed young woman. We'd found the signs for the Luberon route and cycled southeast through fields. The road headed into a small hilly area, the last gasp of the Luberon range butting up against the Durance river. We ignored a small section of the route in favour of the D4096 and quickly regretted it when we found ourselves stuck in a lunchtime traffic jam outside Volx. A church with a tall, white steeple looked down on us as we inched through the large village and found the Luberon signs again. Easy, if soggy, cycling ensued along a path by the unromantically named Canal Électricité de France, parallel to the Durance.

Squatting beside the canal, Manosque had presented a sturdy, industrial face to us as we rode in. Need I mention it was raining? We were wet again, slowly becoming resigned to the fact that one of us must be some sort of weather deity. Adi was all for sharing the blame but I thought it was just me. When the sun came out in Avignon I had smiled too loudly at it, or written about it too noisily in my diary or something.

We searched for somewhere to stop and eat our baguettes. Manosque was clearly not a touristy place, but Adi spotted this bar-tabac. We leant the bikes against a wall, squelched over and chose a table. And then I announced our arrival by sweeping an ashtray off the table with my bar bag.

The splinter of glass went on forever, leaving an awful silence. Sopranos Extra and Satchel Youth stared at me. Conversation in the bar stopped. The barman appeared. Puce-faced, I stumblingly apologised.

'C'est pas grave,' he said gently, 'pas grave,' and made me sit down while Satchel Youth swept up the glass. Still flustered five minutes later I went in and ordered at the bar, when I should have known he would come out to us when he was ready - after all, I'd made sure he knew we were there - and then fumbled in my purse and tried to pay him there and then. At which point this lovely man spread his hands, palms down, and made soft downwards gestures. 'Tranquille,' he said. 'Tranquille.'

And suddenly I was. He must have been some sort of hypnotist; tranquillity flooded me. He led me out and sat me down beside Adi at our table. He cleaned it, laid napkins on our laps and in a few moments delivered the best tea I'd had since leaving home. As I sighed in bliss after the first sip Satchel Youth and Sopranos Extra both smiled at me. Things didn't seem so bad.

This courtesy was everywhere. Being addressed as 'Madame' - I was getting very fond of that - and the way everyone says bonjour to everyone else when they walk into a bar: it just makes you feel like a person. I often feel like a person in at home in Wales, I admit, but sometimes just walking along a public footpath by the coast near my home I meet people who I almost have to poke in the ribs before they'll make eye contact, or respond to a polite hello.

The combination of the tea and the baguette, stuffed with strong smelling 'Dent du Chat', was warming and cheering. So we were weather gods. So what? We looked at the map. The next campsite marked on the Luberon route was in a tiny place called Beaumont-de-Pertuis.

Adi studied the map for far longer than, in my opinion, he needed to. They're his thing, maps. In any photos of groups of family and friends out on walks, he's the one holding the map while everyone stands around looking over his shoulder or holding the corners for him so he can point with authority. As I mentioned earlier, he's got a great sense of direction, and an ability to absorb the two-dimensional information from the map, the three-dimensional information from his surroundings and make a completely useful internal map that he walks through, or cycles through. This is a part of the brain that is not switched on in me. I love to ponder maps at leisure, but it's no fun over someone else's shoulder. As for directions, if I have to follow a route I memorise a sequence of turnings – left, left, straight, right, left – into a chant that I can remember, and refer to the map again when I've run out of directions in my head. On the other hand, Adi likes to refer to the map frequently so he can check it against the physical world and the map in his head. 'So that village over on the other side of the valley should be Ballysummat, let's just have a quick map check – Hah! It is!' That kind of thing.

When I went in to pay an old man at the bar said, 'Anglaise?'

'Non. Je suis irlandaise.'

His face lit up. 'Aaahhhh!' He put both arms by one hip and brought them back and forth repeatedly in a shovelling motion. 'Hhhhhheuuugby!'

Seeing my confusion the barman joined in, but as he explained in exactly the same way, shoving the word at me with his hands, it took a moment for the penny to drop.

'Rugby!'

'Oui! Irlande! Hhhhhheuuugby!'

When I explained that I now lived in Wales, there were backward whistles and looks of respect (entirely undeserved as at the time what I knew about rugby you could paint on a rugby ball with a five-inch brush). When we departed everyone, Soprano Extra, Satchel Youth, lovely barman and everyone in the bar, raised a hand and wished us 'au revoir'.

'I love French people,' Adi said as we plodded away.

'Me too.'

'We didn't really think we were going to get away with it, did we?' Adi said, cheerfully, a little later. We'd left the canal and the broad plain and were rolling along little lanes on the southern slopes of the Luberon mountains. If not for the rain it would have looked - well, sunny and southern. The Rough Guide said that the northern slopes of the Luberon mountains were damper than the 'Mediterranean-scented southern slopes', so I'd been clinging to the hope that the dire forecast we'd accessed last night wouldn't count here. It was not to be. At least the chantable phrase 'Mediterranean-scented southern slopes' took over from the Pont d'Avignon tune as my earworm.

And those slopes were beautiful. Even in the drizzle hundreds of swifts wheeled and soared. We rode up through little woods of oak and hawthorn.

Tiny purple flowers of thyme pinned the soil between the trunks. Poppies and orchids glowed. The slopes were gentler here, down to the Durance plain with a range of smaller hills beyond to the south. Where fields met the road edge the mud was riven with huge cracks, baked by the three rainless months that had preceded our arrival.

I never know how to feel when we arrive somewhere to find people clutching hats and coats, looking at the sky and exclaiming, 'It's never like this at this time of the year. Never!' On the one hand, it's a sort of upside-down and inside-out validation of our planning. Discovering that this was genuinely unusual weather for the time of year meant I hadn't missed a glaringly obvious fact that everyone on the planet knows. ('But everyone knows about the tornadoes in Swaledale in March! What were you thinking?') This is a very tiny silver lining, because to look at it another way, we have once again arrived during freak weather. Or brought it with us.

By the time we reached Beaumont-de-Pertuis I felt knackered. We'd only cycled 34 miles but I'd had hardly any sleep with the rain doing an all-night drum-roll on the tent. Everything – panniers, bar bag, Bike, me – felt heavy and sluggish. The campsite wasn't signed, but a chain of helpful people in the village asked each other until a one woman who knew where it was appeared and directed us. It wasn't actually open for the season yet, but a wiry man with a big smile who was strimming the grassy pitches under the cherry trees made us welcome.

It was the first real test of my French comprehension. Everyone else we'd met spoke quite slowly, either out of kindness to us or because the Provençal accent is quite slow and deliberate anyway. I loved it: heavy and deliberate, with a good weight on the final, silent 'e'.

Not this man. He rattled away like a runaway horse. I managed to interrupt and convey that I only understood a little French. 'Ah, mais vous comprenez assez!' he smiled, and rattled on.

To my surprise, he was right. I did understand enough. A part of my brain lunged at the words as they came sleeting past and glanced at them for a nano-second until the next recognisable word came past, and the next, and the next. I swear I could feel a part of my cortex buzzing as synapses snapped and fused. The bathroom, the showers and the tokens for hot water. ('Why was he asking if we wanted hot water or not?' I wondered aloud to Adi later.

'Because most people want cold showers because it's usually THAT HOT HERE!' That last directed upwards through the roof of the tent at the drizzling sky.)

The man - I never got his name - showed us where the ladder to climb the cherry trees was kept. 'Vous voulez, vous montez!' he said, with a beaming smile.

Pitching was a soggy affair. We'd packed the outer and inner separately that morning. The inner was still damp, the outer sodden. We erected the outer first, and I spent twenty minutes on my knees with a huge wodge of all the tissues and toilet paper I'd robbed from assorted toilets during the day, swabbing at the footprint and the inside of the outer skin as best I could. The inner was damp but sufferable, and we got all the bedding and panniers in without contaminating what was dry with our wet clothing. (There is nothing, nothing, that makes me as incandescent with rage as a soggy waterproof jacket brushing against warm, dry clothes or skin.)

Adi managed heroically to cook in the drizzle, which was gradually lightening. By the time dinner was ready, we could sit in the awning with our legs out to eat it. We talked to the cat who'd come to stare at us. We were in the shade of rows of cherry trees, on the edge of a gentle hill that fell to a stream. The village sat slightly higher than us on the other side of the stream, about a mile away. Not a bad view for dinner, we agreed.

After washing up we cycled into the village and walked around. No tourists. A bass clarinet and a

French horn were practising above the library, repeating a phrase over and over. We found little streets leading up to a church, and walked right round the little mound on which the village was built. It wasn't the most dramatic of perched eminences but it was lovely. I wrote up my diary sitting outside the bar, munching free peanuts, listening to the chink of dice from the old men playing inside the bar and a man and woman in a house down the street singing loudly and cheerfully. We turned in for the night with rain on the tent again. 'I don't care,' I thought up at it defiantly. 'You're not going to get us down.'

CHAPTER EIGHT

To Cucuron

Even with earplugs in it sounded as if John Bonham had been practising in the tent all night. Adi was trying to time a sprint to the shower block to put his coffee on the stove - because there must be coffee - when the proprietor appeared in a full-length rain-cover, looking like a hobbit on stilts.

'Venez, m'sieur-dame! Venez à la maison!'

Lovely, lovely man. He waved us after him, up steps on the outside of the farmhouse wall to enter a large kitchen on the first floor. His mother greeted us, waving a coffee pot.

'Café?'

Adi nearly knelt in front of her.

They made me tea by boiling a tea bag in a saucepan of water. The old woman was portly, with a bright turquoise tracksuit, bad legs, a stick and a lovely smile. 'Triste, triste,' she said, waving a regal arm at the pouring rain outside. Three months without rain, and now... She shook her head. 'Triste.'

We talked - well, mostly the man talked - but we managed to discuss the Olympics, English people who come to Provence to walk, the price of accommodation in London, their grandchildren, whether Wales will ever be independent, and the quality of fruit and vegetables in our respective homelands.

For I had made a discovery: I loved cherries! Cherries off the tree, by the handful. I had never tasted anything like these. When we left, full of tea and home-made biscuits, he pressed two large bags of wine-red, freshly-picked cherries into my hands.

It rained, and rained, and then something funny happened as we made our way up the side of the mountain towards La Bastide-des-Jourdans. It stopped! We looked at each other but didn't say anything in case whatever mischievous weather sprite that had been plaguing us overheard. (I'd decided to blame someone other than myself for the weather.) We carried on, through the woodland scrub, still climbing up and up until Adi looked at the map and said, 'This is wrong.' We were heading up a tiny mountain road that would have brought us right over the range and back to Céreste.

We paused to admire the view, shadowed by thick stripes of white cloud with narrow bands of blue in between.

And then, as we freewheeled back down the mountainside, the sun came out! We stopped on the edge of Vitrolle-en-Luberon. There was an electricity pumping station just outside the village, surrounded by a small fence. Within moments it was festooned with the inner tent and our sleeping bags. The sleeping mats and the outer we spread out on the ground in front. We ate our cherries and studied the map, trying not to even think about the sun that really was shining and the steam that was starting to rise from our belongings.

Over dinner the night before we'd made up our minds that we would stop in Cucuron, about 20 miles away. (Oh, you long distance cycle tourers, try to control your disdain.)

'I'm sure we could get to Cavaillon if we wanted to,' I said, but my heart wasn't really in it. The countryside was hilly and I didn't want to rush. (Excellent, excellent, murmured The Legs.)

'I'm sick of cycling in the rain,' Adi said. 'We could stay in Cucuron until the rain stops properly. Just have a break from cycling in it. The countryside around sounds lovely.'

I agreed, but still had a niggling feeling. It was only our fourth day of moving onward and we'd left home a week ago. Stop-start-stop-start-stop. Much later I realised that the feeling I couldn't articulate was due to a lack of momentum in our trip so far. Certainly, I didn't want to cycle in rain all the time, but I felt instinctively that the best thing to do was just to keep moving forward and take everything as it came. I felt - but again, didn't fully realise until later - that I needed to get into a rhythm, and that cycling even a short distance of thirty-five miles a day consistently would have been more enjoyable and settling than stopping and starting.

But I didn't work that out until much later. At the time, sitting on the ground beside the pumping station, enjoying the lovely sensation of rain droplets vaporising from the skin of my calves, all I could feel was that niggling, inarticulate fidgetiness, fighting with the fact that I didn't want to disagree with Adi. It was his holiday too, after all.

'So far, it's rained on all our cycling days and been lovely on the days off in Avignon and Apt,' I said in the end. 'So maybe we'll get a sunny day off in Cucuron tomorrow.'

'Maybe we should stay everywhere for two nights.' Adi rolled his eyes when he saw my face. 'JOKING!'

'I know! I'm sick of cycling in the rain too.'

'We can go for a day ride without panniers,' he coaxed. 'See what the southern slopes of the Luberon have to show us.'

I grinned at him. 'Sold.'

The rest of the ride to Cucuron was charming, even though the rain did find us again (twice). The road descended from the pumping station and then stayed more or less level, low down on the sloping shoulder of the hills, wending through vineyards, olive groves and meadows below the wooded upper slopes. We passed through scattered hamlets, past isolated churches. In the fields an occasional worker walked the rows of olive trees, or hoed at the grasses around the vines.

The tourist office efficiently gave us campsite information and we chose the closest.

Camping Lou Baderou lay about a mile outside Cucuron, a farm of olives and vines, honeyed-stone outbuildings and a large old swimming pool full of frogs. It instantly jumped to the top spot in our nascent campsite league table; it was by far the prettiest yet, with extra marks for having its own wine for sale at reception.

We pitched up quickly and went back into the village to find the boulangerie. We ended up wandering for an hour. Cucuron was utterly fetching, and we mooched contentedly along the narrow streets, finding parts of ancient ramparts and gates butted up against houses. In the oldest part of the town stepped streets led up to a green, shrubby park surrounding the donjon, or keep, of the original citadel. A view of lovely, curved-tiled roofs over to the church of Notre-Dame-de-Beaulieu, the delicate campanile of the village's bell tower protruding from the roofs, with the rumpled tree-covered hillsides stretching away.

We found the boulangerie, and slender tawny cats, and settled down in the place de l'Etang beside a long pool (I found out later it was the old town reservoir) for a dangerously cheap and delicious glass of wine (me) and an expletive-inducingly expensive glass of beer (Adi). After venting briefly and colourfully, he said, 'I don't care. This makes up for it.'

He waved a hand at our surroundings. The pool bordered by plane trees. Houses and hotels plastered in yellows and ochres. Wooden shutters painted blue and green. Potted ivy plants draped from tiny balustrades in front of upper story windows.

I raised my glass and we chinked, smiling at each other. My fidgets were quelled. I could enjoy this.

CHAPTER NINE

Cucuron

I don't think they bear us any ill will,' said Adi, watching a battalion of ants making off with a thumb-sized flake of croissant. 'They are the Borg.' We added searching potential pitches for ant nests to our list of rituals.

I was lying on a rug outside the tent in the sun. Sun! We'd been right: stopping in Cucuron for two nights had tricked it into coming out. There was genuine warmth in its rays, though the campsite owners and the crew of seasonal vineyard workers camping across from us were still in long sleeves.

The fact that we must be the slowest couple to cycle the Luberon cycle route ever no longer bothered me (much). I had been sun-mellowed. For the first time since we'd set off everything was dry: I kept touching the tent and various items in wonder. Not a hint of dampness, I reported to Adi. Having such creature comforts as a bone-dry sleeping bag filled me with giddy delight.

'This is what we ordered,' said Adi in satisfaction.

'Lovely,' I agreed happily.

'Not too fidgety yet?'

'Not yet. I'm enjoying this.' I raised my tea mug to him. Not moving onwards meant there was time for a second mug of tea, or as many as I wanted - an unexpected bonus! It had actually been three days - the morning in Apt - since I had started the day with one of my own Earl Greys.

As we lay on warm grass in the morning sun, surrounded by guide books and maps, the pretty campsite proprietress was driving a ride-on lawnmower, slowly mowing around the few tents and the olive and plane trees. She wore slim-fit jeans, a flowery tunic top and shades, and was smoking as she steered the machine one-handed. She looked utterly French, thoroughly cool.

'I don't want to start smoking again,' I said to Adi, 'but I wouldn't mind looking like her.'

Everyone seemed to smoke! Under the plane trees in Cucuron's town square last night, it was clear that smoking was not just for middle-to-old aged die-hards. Here, young people smoked. And yet they looked so healthy. All those treats in the patisseries and boulangeries that should by right turn them into great lardy lumps, all that smoking, and still they looked incredibly attractive.

Adi, meanwhile, was performing sums. He'd been noting our daily mileages in his diary and had just totalled the first week. 'Christ!'

'What?'

'We've only averaged 26 miles a day!'

The obvious retort was 'Why are you surprised?' which I swallowed, because there are things it is not helpful to say. Anyway, I knew the answer to my unvoiced question: he'd been busy enjoying himself doing what he was doing and not comparing himself to other cycle tourists, as I had been. There's a lesson in there somewhere. Death to comparisonitis!

We spent the morning washing clothes, reading and moving the tent (above-mentioned ants). When the sun got too hot and watching the ants had lost its novelty I found a tiny shaded balcony for guests, overlooking a small courtyard formed by the cluster of outbuildings. I browsed the bookshelf - five languages - and watched a black redstart flying back and forth to her nest in the stone wall of the courtyard below. When the fidgets struck in the early afternoon we cycled out to Sannes and Ansouis, making a triangular ride.

Released from the panniers, the bikes practically skipped underneath us, skittish as colts. It's the loveliest feeling. They raced along with hardly a twitch of the pedals, covering the few miles to Ansouis in a blink.

In Ansouis, a village even prettier than Cucuron, we separated and I wandered up steep streets, greeting the inevitable chic cats and smiling at the sun. Ansouis was tucked into a nook on the northern side of a lumpy hill, its church and alleys looking over the drop below and across to the southern slopes of the Luberon mountains, now green and warm in the sun. Adi found me again - it wasn't a large village - and we climbed up to the church of the chateau at the top, a formidable structure, blinding light stone outside, cool as a tomb inside and stuffed with statues of the saints. I lit a candle for my mother under Sainte Thérèse, (tall candles, as thick as my finger: good value at €1 each). Everything was white, glinting and warm; I couldn't get over the warmth.

The bikes sped to tiny Sannes and back to Cucuron with barely any effort from us. Sunshine lent our wheels wings. We locked the bikes and went for a second wander; it really was the most appealing village. This time we found the sixteenth-century mill I'd read about, in a hollow in a rock face on, naturally, the rue Moulin à l'Huile. Still being used to press olives!

The sandstone houses were shuttered against the sun. Narrow cobbled streets were softened by flower beds and small, palm-like trees, with slender, bare trunks and frond-like leaves throwing parasols of shade over doorways. We took photos from the church end of the village this time, over the roofs and towers to the old keep.

We had a drink at the second bar in the square and soaked up the sun, congratulating ourselves on working out why the squares in all the villages were edged with trees, invariably soaring plane trees with their patchwork bark. It was for the same reason that the nice man in Beaumont-de-Pertuis had offered us a cold shower.

'Because usually it's HOT!' Adi said, and burst out laughing.

A metallic crash shattered the peace, breaking through the chatter of the young men outside the bar. On the corner of the square, a young woman emerged from the driver's door of her car. She'd been turning right from the square onto the main street, and stood now regarding the damage to the right wing. It was now apparently surgically attached to the boot of a car parked on the corner. The young men got up as a bunch to have a look. The car seemed to belong to one of them. There was a moment of much hand waving and excitable shouting.

'Oh, it's all kicking off,' said Adi.

Then they all, the offending young woman included, pulled out cigarettes, lit up and settled back into hand-on-hip poses, contemplating the meshed cars without apparent rancour.

'Imagine that at home.' Adi grinned at them. 'I love France.'

Back to the tent for dinner, a tasty affair by Adi again. Tonight's dish was a chunky, spicy tomato-based vegetable sauce served with what we christened 'spicy oatcake splats' - an innovative use of the wretched oatcakes and flour. After dinner we drank wine from the farm, from grapes grown on the vines we could see in the next field, pressed here in their cellar, sent a mile up the road to be bottled and brought back to the farm to be sold to us.

'Where do you want to go tomorrow?'

Adi rattled the map open and laid it on the grass in front of me and looked at me expectantly.

'Well, we were just going to follow the route, I thought. Back to the beginning at Cavaillon, then on to Saint-Rémy.'

He was looking thoughtful.

'We could...'

'But?' I was smiling.

'But look here.' He held out some of the leaflets we'd picked up in Apt, showing some additional loops of the Luberon cycle route. 'The guide book isn't really bothered about the villages it'll lead us through down here, but it says that Roussillon and Gordes on the north side are amazing. Look.' He pointed at the map. 'There's a way through the mountains on this road here, through the Combe de Lourmarin to Bonnieux. We could stay in Roussillon, and take it from there.'

'Ok,' I said, carefully. 'Sounds lovely. It'll put us another day behind, though.'

'Behind what? We're making it up.'

'I know, but we do want to head north at some stage. We're not out here forever. But I'm happy to go to Rousillon. It sounds lovely.'

He lay back on the ground. 'We've got *loads* of time.'

I looked at the maps. France is *big* north to south, and we hadn't reached the Mediterranean yet.

Adi opened an eye. '*Loads.*'

'Loads,' I agreed.

Nothing to worry about. And, I thought, hugging the thought to myself cheerfully, if we slow down a bit now, we might start actually doing long day rides to make up for it later. Yay!

I guess that old comparisonitis hadn't vanished completely after all. I fell asleep to the sound of the frogs sawing away under a sliver of a moon and dreamed of David Copperfield cycling up a hill in the rain, a soggy map flapping about over his handlebars.

Of Cats and Sheep: Cucuron to St-Rémy-de-Provence

CHAPTER TEN

To Roussillon

I reckon we're near the top,' Adi said, nodding up along the road through the Combe de Lourmarin. 'The gradient's eased off. We've done the steepest bit.' He grinned at me. 'Well done!'

Apart from the tiny road we'd almost taken by accident a few days ago, the Combe is the only road north-south through the Luberon range, and the only option for anything bigger than a car. A few campervans had overtaken us as we'd pedalled steadily through the chasm with the Aigue Brun river tumbling on our left, but it was peaceful enough.

'And look at this,' Adi went on, gesturing at the sun. 'It's still out!'

The weather demons must have fallen asleep on the job, because for the first time since the day we left Avignon, we had been cycling, fully laden, in sunshine for a whole hour. The sunny breakfast at Cucuron (croissants, not wretched potato cakes or oatcakes) had sent us, replete and content, scooting along the Luberon route towards Vaugines. Cicadas, which we'd only heard making timorous, muted calls until yesterday, now sang us on our way with a full-throated chorus, the poppies thrumming with them. In Vaugines, a football came bouncing over a playground wall followed by a forest of little waving hands and a chorus of calls. 'M'sieur, le ballon s'il vous plait!' Adi's blonde hair clearly gave him away; when he threw it back to them they all shouted, 'Thank you, Mister!'

The small lane held to the south-facing slopes, through woods, yellow fields of corn, meadows of wild flowers in vivid reds and purples. A gentle descent brought us into Lourmarin on a broad river plain. The chateau glinted across the river at the village; in the river meadow between, a huddle of donkeys stood in the sun, resting chins on each other's backs.

We paused to buy bread there, leaving our bikes leaning against a wall in the Aires de Camping-Cars as we walked to the boulangerie. We'd noticed quite a few of these Aires, service areas dedicated to campervans and motorhomes. For a few euros, you could pull up for the night. For a couple of euros more you could empty waste water and toilets and fill up on fresh water. It seemed entirely sensible: by turning a few car park spaces in the village car park into overnight spots for campervans and charging a modest fee for a couple of services, the village invited passing travellers, who might not want to pay a full campsite fee if they were on route to somewhere else, into the village centre rather than parking up in a layby up the road. The campervanners woke up in the middle of the village, a couple of minutes from a bakery, a grocer's, a butcher's. Winners all around. (As soon as we came home I started suggesting it to our local council. No joy yet.)

We left Lourmarin and the Luberon cycle route and we rode into the Combe, a north-south cleft in the hills. The temperature had increased to the point where I welcomed the cool and shade of the gorge. The road climbed very gently beside the tumbling, blue-grey river, and I was just thinking how easy it was when the zigzags ahead hove into view. The Legs, who had been quiet since the day we rode to Forcalquier, piped up again.

'Slow and steady,' they cautioned, so I clicked down the gears and didn't even bother trying to keep up with Adi. Despite our leisurely pace and low mileage so far, The Legs clearly had been getting stronger. I found the zigzags relatively easy, just testing the thighs a little. A good dollop of stubbornness helped, as it always does.

'Ready for the last bit?' Adi said.

Oh, you evil road engineers. Much later, someone told us that steep gradients are common in the lower sections of climbs. Higher up, where snow is guaranteed, the gradients must be gentler to allow the snow ploughs to get through. This is especially so in the Pyrenees and the Alps, where there's an economic incentive to keep roads open to the ski resorts, but it applies to an extent in hills all over the country.

Bastards, I thought, pedalling slowly up the attritional slope. Bastards. And they'd stretched it out evilly, sending us along the edge of a ridge that seemed to go on forever. But there were trees and groves where I was sure deer and goats were watching us, just out of sight, and wrens and cicadas were singing.

'Gently, gently,' counselled The Legs. I heeded them, plodding in low gear up through the pine forest, until suddenly I was over the almost imperceptible crest, clicking up the gears and catching up with Adi. The descent into Bonnieux was lovely, with the golden statue on the church steeple at the very top of the town glinting through the trees as the road twisted down to the village.

We drank a tea and coffee at the terrace of a bar with a stunning view across the valley, until we were moved to the second class seating on the pavements when the waitress realised we weren't going to order food. For the first time, the bar staff were inattentive; we totally failed to catch their eyes. Eventually, in irritation, we guessed the price of our tea and coffee, put the change down and left to sit on the wall, just beyond the café's terrace.

'I hate feeling I'm wearing an invisibility cloak,' Adi complained.

'It's an old problem,' I said. 'Waiters have been ignoring people for decades. Wasn't there that moment in a P. G. Wodehouse story, in a restaurant in Paris – something startled him and he yelped so loudly he almost attracted the attention of a waiter.'

An awful lot of lycra-clad cyclists were pedalling up the road beneath our perch. Lurid club colours, challenge-ride jerseys and American and English accents abounded. Most of the cyclists were wearing very expensive-looking kit. 'Mont Ventoux Finisher' featured across many a chest.

We left before we could start to feel inadequate, and walked around finding shade and churches and new vistas and tiny streets, and of course cats. We ended up having a chat with a nice couple from New Zealand, who were sitting outside a tiny ice-cream parlour. I noticed the English voices as soon as we sat down but had been reluctant to engage them in conversation right away because they were clearly in the middle of a minor domestic disagreement ('All I'm trying to suggest, Vera, is...') But Adi arrived with our ice-creams, noticed, said 'Hello!' and that was it. They were really nice, on the last week of a six-week trip that had taken in Scotland, London and the Peak District as well as Paris and Provence. They couldn't wait to tell us where to go in St-Rémy-de-Provence.

'The Carrières de Lumières. All about van Gogh and Gauguin, an audio-visual show in the middle of the old bauxite quarries in Les Baux, in the hills south of St-Rémy - you have to go.'

'You have to.' Their smiles were infectious, domestic disagreement forgotten.

'And the asylum.'

'And the trail following his paintings.'

Three o'clock came and we thought we'd better get a move on. The air was becoming heavy and charged; over Forcalquier in the east we could see thunderclouds. They thickened as we descended the easy few miles from Bonnieux and traversed the valley bottom. We crossed the river Calavon by the tiny Pont Julien, a Roman bridge of three stone arches built in 3 B.C. It's been used continuously for over 2000 years. The supporting columns have holes in them to allow floodwater to pass through. Looking at them over the shallow trickle that was the Calavon, it was hard to imagine the raging flood levels that would make those necessary.

A black kite floated low over us as we continued towards Roussillon. The air turned heavy, warm and moist, and lightning flickered as we approached the outskirts. Pedalling madly through the oppressive air, frantic to reach shelter before rain that never came, I'm sure I've never looked more like an Irishwoman abroad, purple of face and white of leg.

We pitched up and went straight out for a wander; the clouds were so threatening we thought we might not get a chance later. Roussillon was undoubtedly stunning, but there was something about it neither of us quite warmed to. The rock - barely hard enough to qualify as rock - has been quarried for years for ochre. Seventeen tints of ochre, to be exact, reflected in the plasters of all the buildings in the village. You can see why it's been popular with artists and film-makers for decades: all those warm hues on picturesque houses and churches perched on that plug of vivid red rock. It was a beautiful tourist trap on top of a soft red cheese. We didn't feel right there, but there is always a compensating moment. This time it was a ginger cat whose fur blended into the colours of the town; he permitted me to touch a finger to his gently questing nose before hopping gracefully onto a wall to contemplate the square.

Our campsite was large, 70 or so pitches on gently sloping land that had been terraced under pines and young oaks. After dinner we perched on an old railway sleeper. Through the trees we could see the reflection of a dramatic sunset, thrown back onto clouds and turning them the colours of the houses we'd just seen in Roussillon.

These were the sounds of our evenings: frogs and collared doves. Do-DOOOO-do, do-DOOOO-do, do-DOOOO-do. I heard a Radio 4 programme on collared doves a couple of years ago, charting their expansion from the continent across southern Britain. One presenter said that he thought their call sounded like football supporters doggedly chanting 'U-NIII-ted, U-NIII-ted.' I couldn't get that out of my head. The south of France full of doleful avian football fans chanting morning and evening.

That night there was another strand to the chorus: dogs, dotted around the campsite and the nearby farms, all set off by one grumpy terrier while we sat on the sleeper and it darkened.

CHAPTER ELEVEN

To Robion

I woke cheerful and happy, the happiest wakening yet. Even the sight of another pair of cycle tourers departing while we were still boiling our potatoes didn't awaken my comparisonitis.

Lovely start to the day, swooping down into a broad vale. I disturbed a hare, sent it leaping through a lush, green field of wheat. The last seven kilometres to Murs took us up a long, gentle, relentless climb. We had stunning views back towards Roussillon to distract us from the pain as we pedalled up the slow rise to the edge of the Vaucluse plateau. By now The Legs were getting used to this. For some reason I coped with the climb a little better than Adi; an aura of discontent and hard consonants floated back to me all the way up. (He was still in front. My Legs were clearly made of stronger stuff than his, but they were still smaller.)

'Your legs can't have a better mental attitude than mine,' he said. 'Legs don't have attitude.' But he stopped complaining.

We stopped at the quiet village of Murs and sat by the old laverie, still full of cool water, to eat oranges. We were in a notch on the edge of the Vaucluse plateau, with views down wooded and meadow-covered slopes and across to the Luberon hills, shimmering khaki. Heat bounced off the stones. A road cyclist sped past with a friendly smile.

The road to Gordes was delightful, descending gently for miles on a narrow, winding road. We saw nothing but lizards and birds and one small beat-up Citroën. Arriving in Gordes gave us complete culture shock. Coaches and car parks, pale buildings gleaming in sunshine and hordes of tourists.

'There aren't hordes,' Adi said when I remarked that it was heaving. 'It's just that we've hardly seen any at all yet.' And when I look at the photos now, it's true. It was just the contrast. It felt like a great press of noise after the soft whirr of bicycle wheels and the chirp of cicadas. I discovered recently that one of the characteristics of an introvert is a heightened sensitivity to stimuli, which explains why sometimes just being in the proximity of other people makes me want to run into a quiet, dark place.

For the first time we saw whole shops given over to tourists. Toy cicadas rasped away. Plump tourists wandered through the streets fanning out down the hillside. We followed a narrow ginnel down to a pathway protected by a wall from a sheer drop. Below and around us other paths, balconies and houses clung to the bright wall of rock. Gardens of lemon trees and flowers squeezed anywhere the slope deviated from the vertical.

We treated ourselves to lunch and accidentally ordered a litre of wine. It wasn't until it arrived that we realised that the waitress and I meant different things by 'a carafe'. The salad was huge and delicious, and we took our time in the siesta-time heat, sipping at the wine and a huge jug of water.

We spent most of our four-hour break talking to people. An American couple sat at the next table in the café. The man had business Lyons and Geneva, so he and his wife were making a week of it. A New York city couple; she was slender, dark-haired, fidgety in a quiet, anorexic sort of way, but a sweet smile. They talked about how cycling in New York City had changed over the last ten years.

'It's great having a mayor who knows he's not going to run for office next term,' said the man. 'He just happens to be into cycling and it's changed things incredibly. I love riding in the city - it's exciting, but it's not like you're courting death.'

'Not always,' said the woman.

'Not always.' He shrugged. 'You must get scared sometimes, even in quiet places like where you live.'

We said goodbye and sat on the steps in the shade outside the chateau, which houses the tourist office, among other things. A tanned, attractive Canadian in his mid-thirties threw himself down next to us with a grin and a 'Hi!' He was the cyclist who'd smiled at us in Murs this morning. He lived in Gordes during May and June, in Toronto from July to December, then in Mexico from January to April, following his wife's job. Their little boy went to school in three continents and two languages. His wife joined us and chatted briefly. Her eyes lit up when she heard that we were cycle touring.

'Camping all the way? That's amazing! I'm fifty next year and I want to do new things, fifty at a time. Fifty nights in a tent - that'll go on the list.'

They left us with smiles, making plans. I felt warm, as if I'd inspired someone just by being on a bike. I also felt a bit like a fraud - after all, it wasn't as if we were doing ninety miles a day, or cycling across a continent. Then I chided myself. How many times have I been inspired, on days when the rain and the dark has defeated me and I've driven to Bangor rather than cycled, by the sight of some dedicated cyclist, lit up with lamps, pedalling steadily in the rain? They always look so free, even though they're probably just doing their normal commute. It doesn't have to be an epic to inspire someone. It's still real.

I popped into a shop, tempted to buy a sweet white cotton t-shirt with red poppies on the front. It was not a short transaction. The chatty shopkeeper gave me his honest opinion on a selection of tops and sizes, then, sale completed, he whipped out a map of Gordes which he annotated with everything a tourist could need: the best viewpoints, the Cercle Republicain ('Just go through the bar, the Cercle is for the people, a balcony, you can see everything, it is beautiful'), the toilets ('Fill your bidons, the water is fine, I do it all the time'), the best shop to buy fruit from.

The Canadian lad had said the view back to Gordes from the road downhill towards Cavaillon was one of the best in the world. He wasn't joking. A hundreds yards down the road we pulled up and looked back over the wall protecting us from the sheer drop. The town was in full view, in all its impossible clinging glory on the side of the hill, buildings in and under the rock, tumbling above each other. The only possible reaction was to say 'Wow! Wow!' continuously, so to save effort I just let my jaw hang while I used up my camera's battery life.

We had intended to visit the nearby Village des Bories, an uninhabited hamlet of dry-stone huts and beehive-shaped buildings, similar in shape to but infinitely less dreary than Irish oratories, having the advantage of being in Provence rather than Kerry. We paused at the head of the track to the Village, reading the information sign.

'You have to pay to go in,' said Adi.

'And it's a kilometre down the lane. Down,' I said.

The silence spoke of our unanimous opposition to the idea of going down. What goes down must come up, with baggage and a slight afternoon hangover. So down the main road to Cavaillon, we went: a horrible busy road which, after several easy but loud and dusty miles, bisected Robion's new village.

The campsite lay a couple of kilometres outside the village, a very pleasant spot with lots of leafy, shady pitches and paths through the cherry orchard. It boasted the most characterful shower block, housed in a venerable, stone-built barn. Plentiful wash basins lined the corridors. The shower cubicles and separate washrooms were enormous, with hot, hot water and deep sinks like Belfast sinks, and chunky yet elegant chrome taps and fittings. A mysterious object projected from the wall beside each sink, a slender curve of chrome piercing a long yellow object that looked like a cross between a banana and a lemon.

When I worked out what it was I shouted to Adi excitedly.

'Come and look at the soap!'

Odd looks from other campers.

After a long session under a showerhead the size of a dinner plate I'd recovered from the slight post-Gordes dip in mood. Also cheering was the picnic table, just round the hedge from our pitch. It wasn't in our section but we carried the cooking things and foodstuffs around the corner. Dinner AT A TABLE!

'No! Not fair!' shouted Adi, slapping his hands down on almost-airborne bits of cooking and food. It wasn't the first breeze that had tried to wreck our dinner, but it had no chance against our appetites. We weighted down the lighter things and ate our fill.

Over a post-prandial cup of tea we looked at the map. On the advice of the young Canadian man, we decided to go through Cavaillon and on to St-Rémy-de-Provence.

I knew that I was well on the way to kicking the comparisonitis when, after dinner, a lone cycle tourer who'd arrived late approached us and opened the conversation with 'Combien de kilomètres par jour?' and a mad-eyed stare. He didn't really know what to do with my response of 'Ça depends.'

'I'm not going to turn into one of them, I promise' I said to Adi.

CHAPTER TWELVE

To Saint-Rémy-de-Provence

In the morning the cherry farmer came to take orders for the bakery. We breakfasted on pains-au-chocolat.

'We're becoming too fond of these,' I said.

'It's okay to indulge as long as we're working it off.'

'At our current daily mileage?'

We looked at our half-eaten pastries.

'We'll reassess it after we've started riding longer days,' Adi said.

We got going early and then spent what seemed like forever in Robion because we needed 'a few bits'. We seemed to cycle up and down the long and charmless main street a dozen times, looking for a shop that met Adi's standards for the needed bits. He finally disappeared into an epicerie and I caught up on my diary.

I had plenty of time to. After recording everything from the last few days and a summary of wildlife heard and spotted so far, I was scribbling something about the injustice of menfolk throughout history complaining about the amount of time womenfolk can spend in a shop when he came out, arms full of yummy stuff: oranges, a melon, artisan pasta, chocolate, nuts, seeds and snacks.

'I could have come out with twice this amount,' he said, throwing the oranges to me.

It was the one downside of cycle touring that we had found. Too often already we'd cycled past little wooden signs bearing the words, 'Cave. Vin. Fromage' and pointing up farm tracks. We promised ourselves that some day, when we were old and The Legs had retired, we'd come back with a campervan and visit every single one of them.

The last gasp of the Luberon cycle route. Adi was seized with a desire to get on and suggested we take one of the major roads, but I argued for seeing the end of the signed route, and won. It hadn't let us down yet and still didn't. Utterly peaceful, only cicadas, cuckoos and collared doves. Lanes wound past lavender fields and vineyards, through hamlets twisted into the last spurs of the steep green hills on our left.

I was beginning to feel like a France fan girl. The countryside was just so foreign. Riding along, I recalled all the people I'd heard over the years saying that they were bored with France, or that there was no point going because it's so close, or that they were sick of the French (yes, really), and I wondered if they'd been going around with ears and eyes shut.

Mind you, I feel like that when I hear people saying they've 'done' Snowdon or 'done' Arran. What the hell does that mean? 'What did you think of Y Lliwedd?' I'll demand. 'Or the south ridge? Which was your favourite stream?'

We paused in Cavaillon's main square in the shade of the plane trees, and ate oranges and watched the old men playing boules.

It wasn't long before I got twitchy.

'Shall we go?'

Adi looked at the temperature displayed on a pharmacy's green cross sign. 'It's too hot still.'

'We'll make our own breeze. It worked before.'

It was definitely better than sitting and waiting it out. We took the direct route along the D99, a straight road west lined with trees whose shade didn't quite reach us. The most interesting thing on it was a man who stuck out an ironic hitching thumb.

Until we came within shouting distance of St-Rémy-de-Provence. We paused by a huge fragment of a mausoleum and an enormous triumphal arch, the entrance to Roman Provence. Known as Les Antiques, the ruins are inscribed all over with pictures, images, carvings of important men (always men) leading much less important men with chains and collars around their necks. Under the arch, protected from the weather, the intricately carved rosettes and figures were as sharply defined as if the stone mason had laid down his chisel last week.

We stayed two nights. We couldn't not. St-Rémy cast a spell over us both the moment we entered. Broad boulevards encircled a tangle of enchanting lanes and narrow alleys that made up the old town, and called to us as we rode through to find the tourist office. Plus, we had arrived just before one of the town's great spectacles: the festival of transhumance, when sheep from all around are gathered from the lowland fields where they winter into a flock two thousand strong, to be herded around the town centre before going up to the Alpilles for their summer grazing. If we stayed two nights we could hang around on the final morning, see the sheep go through at noon and then push on south to Arles, our next stop.

We pitched up speedily at the busy campsite a mile or so out of the town centre. It seemed to be a holiday weekend, with lots of families as well as the retired campervanners and caravanners who'd been our companions until now. We'd encountered almost a monoculture of French, German and Dutch retired couples - almost no English - so it was cheerful and noisy, and for the first time we spotted that obligatory summer-campsite feature: a small girl turning cartwheels.

Quick showers, then back into town. We locked the bikes and wandered the old town's charming streets, entirely pedestrianised. Tiny madonnas high up in niches on street corners. A white cat outside a window on a minute balcony, looking down on the square and being photographed by a small group of tourists.

I bought a pastry made with aniseed.

'C'est á l'anise,' said the pretty shop assistant, concerned that I understood. My brain had trouble parsing the syllables.

'Á l'anise,' she repeated, and expertly mimed an old man knocking back a shot and going cross-eyed. It clicked. Absinthe! Aniseed! Fortunately, I like this.

I wandered around eating it on the street and noticed something: nobody else was eating on the go. I wondered if eating while walking is one of those things the French just don't do. No businessman stuffing a sandwich into his mouth as he sped from one meeting to another. No podgy people eating burgers.

Even the few fast-food places that we'd seen had little tables outside for people to sit down and eat in a civilised manner. It's a different country.

Adi and I had frowned over our budget and decided that we were actually going to pay to visit some of Saint-Rémy's tourist attractions. On the advice of the New Zealanders we'd met in Bonnieux, we decided to visit the asylum of Saint-Paul de Mausole, where Vincent van Gogh voluntarily lived for fourteen months in 1889 and 1890. Also on their advice we'd chosen to go to the sound and light installation based on the relationship between Van Gogh and Gauguin, situated in a disused quarry a good bike ride away up into the Alpilles. St-Rémy nestled in the northern feet of the hills and we could see them, a small range of jagged hills stretching east-west, rising up behind the town protectively. We'd also visit Les Baux-de-Provence, an almost-uninhabited hill-top village, close to the quarry where the installation was set. Les Baux gave its name to the aluminium-rich bauxite ore that was discovered and mined on the hills.

'That's a good hill,' Adi said, looking at the map while dinner simmered in the pot over the stove. It was dusk; we'd spent a long early evening wandering in the old town. One of our neighbours, a cheerful German woman, made lip-smacking faces as she walked past. 'I'm looking forward to that.'

'Me too,' I said with relish. There were swifts and good food, and not enough cycling miles (of course) but there was wine and happiness.

CHAPTER THIRTEEN

St-Rémy-de-Provence

The sun was still shining next morning. I stuffed myself with French phrases over breakfast. While Adi had been collecting the necessary maps and information from the tourist office the day before, I'd used its free wifi to download the rest of 'French For Dummies', entertained all the while by the expensive cars trying to find parking spots that weren't rumpled and cracked with tree roots. My bedtime reading had been vocabulary lists, tables of useful verbs, readings of conversations. I couldn't wait for someone to ask me about my hobbies.

Saint-Paul de Mausole lay on the edge of the town, and was still a clinic for the treatment of mental illness. We entered the gates, paid our fee at a little booth and followed the ticket-seller's directions. Reproductions of Van Gogh paintings hung on a stone wall above raised beds of flowers and herbs. In odd corners hung other reproductions, some in the spot where he had painted them, where you could see what the artist would have seen. Sometimes the prospect had changed completely, a modern wall in place of a corner of a field; sometimes it was virtually unchanged. Both were heart-twisting.

Signs, neither overbearing nor apologetic, kept us to the permitted areas and away from the working hospital. In a serene courtyard low box hedges quartered flowerbeds of crimson begonias in full bloom. Outside, a small field of poppies where van Gogh walked every day. Rows of green spiky lavender, like giant sea urchins. Inside, the tour led to a small room, a replica of the artist's. A hard chair, a tiny bed. The red shout of poppies outside, seen through bars.

Visiting Les Baux-de-Provence after that was surreal. The bike ride was lovely, the bikes tossing their metaphorical manes and rolling happily up the steady climb through beautiful woods clothing the north face of the Alpilles. The Legs were also loud in their praise of this no-panniers thing. We dropped from the lovely wooded ridge down the southern slopes past gently sloping fields of vines and olives, before another gentle climb towards the fantastical fortified village gleaming in the sun.

Every building in Les Baux seemed to have grown out of the rock; churches, chapels and houses, mostly 16th and 17th century, straddled the ridge beneath the chateau. Half of the buildings seemed to have at least one cliff for a wall. Many of them were in ruins; I read afterwards that only 22 people actually live in the old village now.

We bought ice-creams and wandered with other tourists though steep twisting alleys. Up on a high, quiet rock outcrop, the highest you can reach without paying to go into the chateau, we looked south and fancied we could see a shimmer that might be the Mediterranean. Green plains fading into blue. *Glas* means blue in Welsh but green in Irish, so I am forever getting confused, not least because many meadows in Welsh, lovely naturally grazed *marians*, are called *glas*, after the blue-green hue of their grasses in sunlight. From our perch above Les Baux the colour we could see in the blur where land met sky was *glas*, in either language.

A little further along the ridge on which Les Baux was perched we found the Carrière de Lumières. The limestone is so workable that it can be sliced like a cake, but it hardens over time; hence the fresh-looking carvings on the sheltered parts of Les Antiques. The stone was quarried by removing great regular blocks; what remains is a sort of mirror illusion, a great cavern that looks as if it has been constructed, supported by pillars of rock scored with the marks left when the blocks were removed.

No-one within a hundred miles should miss this installation. A dark space the size of a football pitch, the height of a three-storey house, held up by two great pillars of rock. Cameras and speakers hidden in the heights projected enormous images all over the almost-smooth cavern walls. The images were skilfully broken into their elements and animated, telling the story of Gauguin's and Van Gogh's close but fraught friendship. The scale of the images moving over the walls and floor almost overloaded my senses; the figures of watching visitors appeared tiny and black at their feet. Elements from paintings appeared in rhythm with music. A dance sticks in my memory: first flowers appeared; then the girls' faces; watching mothers around the room; the wooden floor; the young male dance partners. Sometimes the paintings rippled; sometimes there was music, sometimes readings of letters. Towards the end there was a dialogue: Gauguin's letters, van Gogh's replies, illuminated by self-portraits turning increasingly lined and weathered. The final image, of van Gogh's almond tree, the blossom blowing away in a rushing wind, was unbearably sad.

'That,' said Adi afterwards, when we emerged from the cool quarry into 30 degree sunshine, 'was worth €20. €7.50 was cheap.'

High praise.

A little subdued - it's the sort of experience that clings to you, unmissable but poignant - we cycled up to an even higher viewpoint, actually looking down on Les Baux, then took a zigzag spin down a minor road. We met absolutely no-one; they were all in Les Baux and, we soon discovered, in all the cafés in St-Rémy. It was while we were searching for one with spare seats in the old town centre - we hadn't yet realised that all the bars and cafés were on the surrounding boulevards - that Adi stopped suddenly.

'Halen Môn!'

'What? No way.'

But it was; in the window of a spice shop full of jars of pinkish, whitish and greenish salts from around the world, was a huge jar of chunky crystals of Anglesey Sea Salt.

'Non! Vraiment?' The proprietress whipped out a notebook and scribbled something in it. 'I love to meet people from where the spices come from,' she said in English. 'Last week there were people who lived on the shore of the Black Sea - I have also salt from there! You are on my list now!'

She and Adi fell into a deep discussion about spices. She cautioned us to be very careful when pronouncing the words 'vegetarien' or 'vegetarienne' in French. 'Because the people who do not eat eggs and milk, what do you call them?'

'Vegans?'

'The vegans - in French they are vegeta-li-en. And no-one knows what to do with them.'

Back for a late siesta before dinner. On the pitch opposite us was a Dutch campervan with an immaculate awning and its own decking, swept twice a day by a thin man supervised by a neat Jack Russell terrier. The campervan's wheels were covered with little caps that matched the colours of the awning. The man always greeted us nicely, and almost managed to hide the sideways looks at our shorts and underwear drying on the guy ropes between our picnic table (a decisive factor in the pitch-selection process) and a tree. After dinner we took a bar of chocolate and a bottle of wine and went to call on the New Zealanders.

We'd met them the previous night, on our ramble around the campsite to check out tents and campervans and awnings. It's a ritual. We never get tired of it, looking at funny-looking tents, varieties of awnings, original modifications to campervans, the weird things people bring with them. And of course, searching for the Dutch campers. (There are always Dutch campers.

There's a regulation or something.) Adi had spotted the UK number plate and said hello; they replied with smiles and antipodean accents. Aaron, Robyn and thirteen-year-old Jessie had been on the road for 22 months, around the world. They'd spent extra time in some countries, teaching English to fund their exploration, particularly in Thailand and in China. They'd sold their house to fund the trip. Their experiences would fill a book: lovely people, full of life, enjoyment, optimism and open-heartedness. On this leg they were on a three-month trip around Europe. They were going on to Japan before going home at the end of September.

Breakfast next day was a leisurely affair. We made some oatcakes with the flour and the oats. We were nearly through the wretched stuff. The oatcakes were great though, thick and tasty. Unbelievably, the sun was still shining. Quick wind check: none. Rain: none. Sun: one, visible. Tent: dry as a bone.

We rolled past Aaron to say goodbye; he admired our neatly-panniered steeds. ('Awesome set-up, mate.')

In town there was already a festival air. The boulevards encircling the centre were thronged with locals and visitors. In the square at the northeastern corner a band had set up on a stage, and market stalls filled the broad pavements. Smells of fresh pastries and cheeses called to me, rising on the warm air with the voices of the crowd, the sound of a contented throng with a hint of expectation.

We found ourselves a spot on the inner pavement of the boulevard.

'We live in Wales,' said Adi. 'How can we be so excited about seeing a load of sheep?'

'French sheep.'

'Ah, that'll be it.'

The sense of anticipation was rising; the musicians in the square had stopped playing and heads were turning back down the boulevard. A wave of excitement rippled up the street towards us and the unmistakable arthritic rumble of a farmer's four-wheel-drive grew louder. A tinny tannoyed voice came closer and a Landrover with loudspeakers strapped on top rattled into view. A leather-faced smiling man in a black peaked hat, evidently a venerable shepherd, Master of Ceremonies and owner of the voice, sat in the passenger seat, waving out the window. A vocal exclamation mark Mexican-waved its way up the boulevard, followed by the sound of hoofbeats and something else, loud and clanging. A donkey and cart followed, laden with buckets and sacks of hay, led by a man in traditional shepherd's dress of dark waistcoat and small black peaked hat. Behind him, three donkeys carrying wooden pannier-frames filled with enormous brown bags. Behind them, a single small boy in a brown cloak and flat cap strode down the centre of the road, a stick in his hand and a small sheepdog at his heels, leading a line of solemn shepherds the breadth of the street, staffs in hand. And behind them, the sheep.

A baaing, creamy, woolly-smelling river of creatures with thick, tightly-curled fleeces filled the road. Every ten yards, on either side of the river of sheep, a shepherd with a staff and a sheepdog strode, keeping them moving.

And the noise! Some of the larger rams wore bells, but most of the clanging came from the huge bells on the goats, strapped on with leathern harnesses. I feared for the hearing of the wearers; they really should have been provided with ear-muffs. They formed little islands of brown with great spreading horns in the creamy stream of fleeces. For ten solid minutes it went on, the noise of bleating, the clanging of the bells, the chatter of the crowd and the occasional bark of an excited dog. At last the stream thinned. A few suddenly panicked sheep raced to catch up with the herd. The creamy seething mass curled around the corner of the boulevard, followed by another line of shepherds and the final donkey and cart.

There's only one thing to do after a French festival, and that's to go and sit at a café with everyone else.

With our newly bought cheeses and pastries from one of the nearby stalls, that's what we did, and sat with my last Saint-Rémy tea (Earl Grey, no pot), watching little street-cleaning lorries hosing down the trampled remains of sheep and goat dung. Within half an hour there wasn't a trace of the animals, we'd finished our tea and coffee, the sun was out and screaming, and we were starting our ride south in the hottest part of the day.

We grinned at each other. Released the brake levers. Onward.

The Road to the Sea: St-Rémy to Saintes-Maries

CHAPTER FOURTEEN

To Arles

At midday the next day we sat having a cup of tea (no pot) and a beer at a little bar in Arles, charming and down to earth, with one of those lovely, solemnly polite barmen that Provence breeds.

I could hear: a very light breezy wind; the clattering of scaffolders at work on the amphitheatre; a pair of men talking over tall glasses of Leffe; Essex accents behind us. A huge party of schoolchildren chattered down the street while another streamed out of Les Arènes, the 2,000-year-old amphitheatre that had once been the largest Roman building in Gaul, in what was once the capital of Roman Gaul, Spain and Britain. We'd just walked around it, counting the sixty arches on each of the two tiers on the outside, feeling suitably small and impressed.

The ride to Arles the day before had been hot and uneventful. We'd cycled easily up the Alpilles, with only gentle protestations from The Legs, and admired Les Baux-de-Provence shimmering on its ridge as we descended. For a while we followed the line of a Roman aqueduct, one of a network that used to supply Arles. We took a break to clamber on its stones, enormous blocks quarried from God knows where. 'Imagine humping that lot down from Les Baux,' Adi said.

A plaque to an archaeologist who'd worked on the Roman monuments for decades, erected by his friends and colleagues and mounted on the side of the aqueduct, shone in the harsh sun. We rode on.

Arles' suburbs didn't inspire. We'd found the campsite easily enough, two miles from the town centre, scruffy but just passable. Showers and toilets were clean, the staff indifferent. We met a lovely couple of Canadians in their sixties, also cycle touring, pitched just across from us. They were from a little town in British Colombia.

'Most Canadians call it "Up North". Anywhere more than 50 kilometres from the US border is "Up North",' Jan explained. Gerry used to work in the Forestry Service, Jan as a school counsellor. They began cycle touring a couple of years ago and this was the last night of their second six-week tour this year;

they were flying early the next morning from Marseille back to Canada. They'd spent six weeks in Cuba in February and March. On this trip they'd been around the Luberon, the Gorges of Verdon and up Mont Ventoux, which put them on the level of gods for me. We had dinner with them at a little bar-tabac, sitting on street tables next to a little shaded park. Jan, you could tell, was a wonderful counsellor; she had a way of listening attentively and asking pertinent questions that made you feel as if you'd been speaking intelligently, even if you'd been waffling inarticulately.

My comparisonitis wriggled. They were in their sixties and they'd been up Mont Ventoux! On touring bikes! But I managed to crush the worm of discontent. There would be other tours. For now, I was on this one with Adi, and it was great. I smiled at him. He didn't know why I was smiling. Or maybe he did, I realised. I was smiling because I was happy.

But by morning my niggles were back.

'Why are we staying two nights here?' I asked again.

'For a rest.'

'From all those massive mileages we're doing? Now you're just winding me up.'

'To get some culture, then.'

My wanderlust was back, fuelled by Jan and Gerry's tales, helped along by the fact that I couldn't work up much enthusiasm for Arles. It probably wasn't Arles's fault. It was that cyclus-interruptus feeling again.

'Are we having a good time or not?' Adi asked me.

'Yes, but...'

'Then it doesn't matter how far we ride in a day.'

And he was right. But against that is the fact that I love the physicality. I really enjoy testing myself. I am neither strong nor fast, but one thing I have in abundance is stamina, which is almost matched by my stubbornness. Keep feeding me little bits of food and someone telling me that I won't ever do it and I'll plod on, perfectly content.

'Oh, for God's sake, let's go to the museums - there's dozens of them.' Adi waved the Rough Guide at me. 'You can buy a day ticket that will get you into loads, it says.'

I managed to curb my impatience. The slow pace of the day irritated me, but it had to be slow because of the heat. It affected Adi particularly, and though I didn't want to admit it, I was also finding the humidity difficult to bear. How were we going to manage if we couldn't cope with the heat we'd sought all along? Would the weather gods ever smile on us?

But there were moments of loveliness during the dragging day. First of all there was the simple pleasure of being amongst other cyclists, just going about their business, using the bicycle to get around or, in the case of one teenage boy leaping over benches in the place du Forum to show off. I cherish the hope that small towns in Wales will one day have as many cyclists of all ages.

We visited an exquisite collection of Picasso drawings in the Musée Réattu. Named for its founder, a seventeenth century artist who entered art competitions again and again with not much success, the museum was housed in a lovely building, constructed around a central courtyard, gargoyles snarling over the space. I especially liked Réattu's a self-portrait, and his depiction of the Dream of Jacob in two versions: a daubed sketch in miniature less than a foot square, and the final 8 by 5 foot framed painting of the beautiful young man asleep, the angels at the foot of the ladder from heaven behind him. Anatomically perfect: the toes, the muscled legs, the tiny wrinkles of the torso at rest, the lashes and eyebrows all beautiful.

We'd decided not to include Les Arènes on our ticket, advised by the Rough Guide that it was only worth going in if there was a concert or a bullfight on. Instead we went on to the Cryptoportiques, dark, dank and atmospheric underground galleries. Nothing we read seemed entirely sure of their purpose, other than that they propped up the Roman forum above. They were quite the place to be on a scorching day. Fragments of colossal pillars and capitals lay on the floor of the arched subterranean galleries. We entered through the Hôtel de Ville, a building with doors either side of its ground-floor foyer, creating a lovely breeze through. The ceiling was extraordinary, long narrow white tiles laid in a maze-like intricate pattern that pulled my eyes. For some reason I can't remember a thing about the cathedral, although I do remember its huge impressive doors. Perhaps the candles were particularly bad value, and the shock has wiped the experience from my memory.

The Cryptoportiques won for atmosphere, but the loveliest place was the Alyscamp, which gorgeous name became my new chanting earworm as we pedalled from the Hôtel de Ville. 'Fields of the dead of heaven' is a lovelier phrase even than Elysian Fields, or Champs Elysées. A long, lovely avenue lined with empty sarcophagi and plane trees, the sarcophagi increasing in size the further along we went. At the end stood a medieval church, high and lovely, bare now but for massive sarcophagi where the main and side altars would have stood. Some of the original plasterwork survives high up where walls meet the curved ceiling; figures in hazy colours, softened by centuries. A curtain of light chain hanging in the doorway failed to dissuade the pigeons; they would land, carefully nose their way through and fly to their perches.

An expedition to the Intermarché for an expensive shop - the prices of insect repellent and suntan lotion! - then back to the campsite through rush-hour traffic (still as generous to cyclists as ever). Dinner was a variation on what was becoming Adi's standard: a mixture of fresh tomatoes, onions, aubergines, garlic and Italian spices with spaghetti, a hard goat's cheese crumbled over the lot and a cheap, delicious Ventoux wine.

Some years ago, Adi started listening to Five Live, the BBC sports radio channel, while preparing dinner. It was the feather that tipped the balance of him-cooking/me-cooking/us-cooking-together, which had steadily been leaning towards him cooking almost exclusively. I was more than happy to wash up instead. Still, for a few months I kept offering to help, to chop or something.

'No, I'm fine,' he'd say, and happily I'd let him be, listening to the football as he chopped and seasoned and sizzled. I'd never really enjoyed cooking anyway. Before long it had become accepted practice that Adi cooked and I washed up, a task I much prefer. You wash dishes and cutlery, pots and pans, and then you dry them and put them away. You can break things, but you never get the wound-up tension of cooking, wondering if it's going to turn out alright. Or maybe this is just me?

Our early cycle tours evolved a similar pattern. I chopped; Adi cooked; we washed up together. He's good at it, good at taking ordinary ingredients and a little bit of spice and herbs and making a tasty, colourful, satisfying meal.

We'd gradually learned more about nutrition, how bodies behave when cycling long distances with panniers up hills, and how different foods are processed, and how to avoid the dreaded bonk, that horrible, all-over-nauseous sensation that your legs have turned to jelly and that you are going to murder someone in order to obtain sugar, just as soon as you can get those legs to obey you and move. I still clearly remember my first bonk, on the first afternoon of our first ever coast to coast ride across northern England. A brambly hedgerow had never looked so inviting. Since then we'd tried to make sure we always had a stash of something to eat that would quickly release energy.

Much of it we learnt the hard way. On early journeys we tended to fill the afternoon dip in energy with an energy drink or an emergency glucose sweet if we could see a hill coming up. This gave the desired kick to the muscles to get up the hill but, we realised eventually, there would be a correspondingly steep crash on the other side of that kick. We'd been getting better at using real foods to keep us going.

To France we brought a gem of a book, *Moveable Feasts* by Amy-Jane Beer and Roy Halpin, marked with recipes we wanted to use. (I don't know why we didn't photocopy them, or just take photos of the pages we needed. It was a hefty tome. We'd probably reasoned that the extra weight meant we could eat more guilt-free treats. Heavy book = more croissants.) Some of our favourites were potato cakes and chunky oatcakes to fire us up hills. Hence the over-enthusiastic bringing of the flour and porridge oats with us.

Rating croissants and baguettes became one of our rituals. We had a boulangerie league table, as well as specific tables ranking croissants and baguettes. A boulangerie might rate very highly over all, yet might not have produced a croissant in the top five. It was a nuanced scoring system, one that we enjoyed discussing very much as we munched.

Bread became the most important part of our diet - at least it was of mine. 'More bread!' was the normal answer to the question,' What would you like to eat tonight?' We went through up to three substantial loaves, usually baguettes of some kind, every day. Breakfast, in-saddle munchies, lunch, after-dinner mopping up: bread was ever present in our meals. And the smells of the boulangeries! I am constantly at war with my sweet tooth, and it was almost past my powers to ignore the smells and the pastries and tartlets laid out in front of me.

We discussed this over our evening in Arles, with protracted sipping of wine and water and nibbling of chocolate as the sky turned indigo and swifts and bats wheeled over the campsite. The mystery to us was, why weren't there more tubby French people? Boulangeries were full of the most fattening, toothsome confections imaginable. The shelves were invariably empty by the end of the day. Yet most of the people we met were far from overweight. Where did it all go?

'Everyone cycles to the boulangerie,' said Adi.

CHAPTER FIFTEEN

To Saintes-Maries-de-la-Mer

I practically leapt out of bed in the morning.

'It wasn't that bad, was it?' Adi asked over breakfast, watching me stuff sleeping bags, roll up sleeping mats and dismantle the tent with joyous abandon.

'No, not that bad. But I'm looking forward to moving on.'

There was a short silence.

'I wouldn't mind going to the market this morning. It's a clothes market,' said Adi.

'I'll go to the museum,' I said, quickly.

'Sure you can wait for me before you go speeding off?'

'YES!' There was a pause where we both heard me very   loudly   not   saying 'Pleasepleasepleasedontbetoolong' and Adi not saying 'Pleasepleasepleasedontrushme'.

Even though I took the map of the city, leaving Adi with memorised directions on how to get to the Musée Départementale Arles Antiques, I managed to get lost on the way, something I decided not to tell Adi. The museum sits beside the faintly visible remains of a second-century Roman chariot racetrack. It was excellent, worth making the time to visit: open-plan, airy, full of excellent exhibits, artefacts and scale models of Arles through the ages.

'Come on then.' Adi's voice over my shoulder shook me from my contemplation of a model of medieval Arles. 'I've been waiting for you all morning while you've been dawdling around in here.'

We had only cycled five miles during the day off, so The Legs were in fine fettle and Bike was clearly raring to go. First treat was crossing the Rhône on an enthusiastically graffiti'd cycle track underneath the road carriageway. It was like riding through a box, with a slit high up on the upriver side so we could see the river rolling towards us. There should be a name for it. A véloduct?

South into flat lands, first on roads and then on a long, dusty track beside a waterway. This was the beginning of the Camargue, the lands of the Rhône delta. Just south of Arles the Rhône splits into two main branches, the Grand and Petit Rhône, which in turn split off into myriad creeks and distributaries in the broad triangle between the Mediterranean and Arles. We were roughly following the Petit Rhône south along its western edge. Everything was sand, low-lying grasses and reeds and...

'Is that rice?' Adi was waiting for me in the tiny patch of shade of a rare tree. He pointed over the reedy hedge.

It was. We were cycling through giant paddy fields. Flat, flat, flat. In the heat we started to seek out anything taller than ourselves for its shade-giving qualities. For the first time, I wore my sun hat. We cycled slowly enough not to bake but quickly enough to make some progress, and stood on the wheels, peering over the reeds and grasses and rice to catch glimpses of pools and sand banks. Somewhere out there was one of the reasons we'd come to the Mediterranean.

'There!' Adi braked hard and pointed. 'Got your bins?'

I pulled out my binoculars. Result! Out on the mudflats was a small flock of pink flamingos.

Pink flamingos! This was why I wanted to come this far south. I had never been bothered about reaching the Mediterranean - images of sun-baked bodies and high-rise apartments rose like nightmares in my imagination - but the guide books promised birds we'd never seen before. And there they were, slightly miraged in the distance, long necks curled over to feed.

'They don't looked *that* pink,' Adi said. 'More of a rosy blush.'

We carried on. A purple heron took flight in front of me, a second one ten minutes later. The next time I caught up with Adi he was grinning hugely; a beaver had just waddled across the track fifty yards ahead of him. Heavy-shouldered, curve-horned black cattle glistened silkily as they stood in the shallows of the creeks and pools. The faintest of gossamer clouds hung high and far away to the east.

The vegetation was strange, a low herb layer that looked heatherish but clearly wasn't. Willows lined the ditches beyond the fence. Phragmites reeds spiked up from damp slacks and hollows. Suddenly the eastern view opened out and we were cycling beside a widening ribbon of river, bordered by a broad strand of sand, dotted with livid green hummocks of vegetation. Ahead, the river widened into a shimmering blue-gold mouth, the colour of shining water over barely-submerged sandbanks. Even further south I could just make out what looked like green-fringed islets.

Pausing in the shade of another rare tree, we checked our location on the map. We were looking across one of the lagoons, deliciously called *étangs* in French, to the great long spit that projects east from Saintes-Maries-de-la-Mer before curling away to the south many miles from here, enclosing the Parc Naturel Régional de Camargue to the north and the Golfe de Beauduc to the south.

The track became a road and we passed dusty fields with herds of black cattle and beautiful, strong white horses. It looked the way I imagine Argentina. The Camarguais horses are reckoned to be one of the oldest horse breeds in the world and they've lived in these marshes and wetlands, feral and semi-feral, for possibly thousands of years. They've become a romantic symbol of the region.

Saintes-Maries-de-la-Mer sits at the end of the long, solid spit between the Grand Camargue and huge lagoons to the east and the Petit Camargue to the west. The road led us straight into the centre, where we noted the second, less romantic symbol of the region: the instantly rocketing number of rude drivers in big, shiny cars. We visited the tourist office to get the necessary bumph (Adi had started calling it 'intel'), then dipped our toes into the Mediterranean and did a quick circuit of the town. It was like Skegness, we decided. We had found Skeg-on-the-Med.

The annual music festival celebrating the feast day of Romany patron saint Sarah had just ended. According to legend, Sarah was the Egyptian servant of the two Maries of the village's name. Driven out of Palestine, these Marys, one an aunt of Jesus and one the mother of two of the apostles, washed up here after being driven out of Palestine and landed safely after crossing the Mediterranean in a boat with no oars or sails. Or so it is said.

It was still early in the afternoon when we'd pitched up at the campsite so we cycled back in, split up and explored separately. I bought a pen and met my first jaded shopkeeper. She had the tired look of someone who'd been through the first bank holiday weekend of the year, had remembered why she'd promised herself she was going to get out and find another job that would take her away from people before the next season started but here she was again for another season and there was no way out, all uphill from here, more people, more people, more people... But she was still courteous. Everyone was courteous.

I spent a couple of euro to climb the stairs up onto the open, gently sloping roof of the church of the two Saint Marys. Views to sea, views inland to the shimmering Camargue, sun bouncing back from white buildings with wooden shutters and sand-coloured tiled roofs. I could easily look down on the tops of the few small trees in the village square. A parapet around the church roof protected giddy tourists from themselves. A thick wall continued up from the gable at one end of the church, with five arch-shaped holes cut into it, a bell hanging in each.

I was dying to head for the Canal du Midi. We'd seen the pink flamingos; now for the long cycle south to north. The last few days had felt like a hiatus after the Luberon; this would be the start of another section.

'We'll be heading north now.'

'Sort of,' Adi said cautiously. 'Along the coast, along the Canal and then north.' Then caution left him and he waved a finger dismissively over the entire middle of France. 'When we get off the canal we'll get through this in no time.'

'How much time have we got left?' I'd lost track of the days.

'Exactly seven weeks.'

A huge swathe of time. We could cross France twice if we wanted to in that. I smiled. We were moving onwards now. A new beginning.

PART SIX

Along the Med: Saintes-Maries to Le Grau d'Agde

CHAPTER SIXTEEN

To Grande Motte

Y'know, we could stay here another night.' Adi passed me a plate with the camp-stove breakfast oatcakes. The last of the porridge oats!

'Why?' I managed not to scream. I blamed the sun. It had made him almost terminally mellow. 'I think we've exhausted Saintes-Maries' possibilities,' I went on. 'Unless we go for a walk out along the spit.'

'Hmm.' He looked up at the sun. 'Might get a bit hot.'

'Or pay for a boat trip into the Camargue.'

'Sounds lovely. But… Budget?'

'Budget,' I said.

'We'll leave it till next time so.'

I cheered silently. Boat trips and long walks did have their temptations, but neither was as tempting at that moment as just getting into the saddle and cycling west. I was definitely itchy now.

One of the most contemptible habits of English-speakers abroad is that of tittering at English

145

translations of official signage. I hate the habit myself, but had to scuttle away, doubled over to hide helpless giggles, after reading the following notice while Adi settled our bill at reception:

'The animals must be tattoo and cowpoxes to stay on the camping site.'

It sent us off with a grin anyway.

We took the quieter one of the two roads out of Saintes-Maries, sweeping west and then north with the small Étang des Launes on our right. More Wild-West landscapes: huge dusty fields with a sort of succulent patchy heath-style vegetation, and little ranch-style houses. Herds of those graceful and muscular white horses and the black cattle too; poignant, as I thought how many of them were destined for the bullfights of Arles and Nîmes.

We passed a small sign marked with a bicycle and an arrow, informing us that we were on a circuit, Autour des Saintes Maries. Since we'd left the Luberon we'd been on the lookout for similar signed routes wherever possible. We kept tripping over signs for them, but had so far failed to find any information on them at the tourist offices.

We crossed the Petit Rhône on a small river ferry.

'And that's bye-bye to Provence,' said Adi.

'Really?' I thought we'd left Provence behind at Arles, but the river is technically the western boundary.

The landscape changed once we crossed the river. Ranches and paddy fields declined, vineyards crept in. We stopped at a road-side stall, one of the large, permanent ones with shelves of local goods: bottles and jars of sauces and pickles, sausages, rice and spices. The stall-keeper gave us each a tiny plastic cup of a divine, vaguely apple-y alcoholic drink - delicious but lethal! I'm still not sure what it was. He also offered us a slice of a sausage. He took our decline with understanding - I'm always afraid of offending against such hospitality - but clearly he'd encountered vegetarian types before. We did buy a punnet of drool-inducingly fresh strawberries to make up for not being meat eaters.

We joined a busier road - busier by French standards, that is, which means not too busy at all - and followed it to Aigues-Mortes. Carried away with fidgety legs and the easy, open road, heading north around the massive waterway criss-crossed by what on the maps look like tiny flimsy causeways, I cycled far too quickly and ended up with a big purple face.

'Drink loads of water,' Adi said when he caught up with me, 'and let's stop for a while.'

Aigues-Mortes was full of American teenagers. It's a strange place, fortified walls surrounding the old town centre. Built by Louis IX as the departure point for the Seventh Crusade in the thirteenth century, it became a centre for the production of salt. Great salt pans lined the dry Étang de la Ville, surreal beside the massive, almost perfectly preserved stone ramparts. Unusually, within the ramparts there were no trees to soften the glaring sun reflecting off the walls and paving stones. We bought sensible items first - bread and fruit for lunch - and then a frivolous purchase: a dress made from the most gorgeous Provençal cotton, entirely unsuitable for cycling. Sometimes you just need clothes that make you feel like a human.

We escaped the oven of the old town and sat down under a tree beside the canal to eat our picnic lunch. There's a wide bend in the canal here and clans of swifts were calling to each other and swooping down to drink, impossibly graceful and balletic. They dive straight for the water, wings pumping, then bend their wings right up and back near the bottom of the curve; a tiny dip of the head and up into the air again. I could watch them forever.

All was lovely until we start cycling along the Canal du Rhône à Séte. We (I hope you understand by now that when I say 'we' with regards to any sort of preparation, what I really mean is 'Adi') intended to use it as a pleasant off-road route to the next bit of the Mediterranean.

It seemed innocuous enough at first. A narrow rutted path on the bank soon opened out into a wide gravelled bank - but what gravel! Huge, angular, pointed stones, horrific to cycle along. Fishermen watched us with interest as we bumped along, trying to protect our tyres. Poor Bike kept trying to fall over. My arms ached from gripping. Sweat trickled down my face. I was turning that attractive hue of purple again.

When we looked at the map later we realised it had only been a few miles. It felt like ten. The dismal, sweaty experience was partially alleviated by all the glorious bee-eaters we saw perching on fenceposts, blue of chest and yellow of throat. They were probably noting, along with the fishermen, how unusual it was to see idiots on those wheeled contraptions here.

After an age we escaped along a track. We had no idea where it went, but it was leading away from the horrible stony bank, so we sped gratefully along it, and found ourselves on a motorway slip road, just at the point where it peeled away from the motorway.

'For Christ's sake,' shouted Adi over the roar of cars whooshing past. 'At least it's the slip road off. Okay, don't panic, nice and calm. We'll just wait for a gap in the traffic. Wait. Wait. Now, now - GO!'

He exploded out onto the slip road. I pedalled frantically behind him trying to grab his slipstream, purple in the face for the third time that day. I experienced real terror for the first time; the motorists approaching from behind would be slowing down but would still be doing seventy-plus and they wouldn't be expecting any idiot cyclists...

Around the curve and up the slight incline, thighs pumping furiously, to a traffic-signalled junction, and suddenly we were in a different world. It was like sliding into a cool woodland pool. From the heat and discomfort of the canal, the roaring of the cars on the motorway, we were now cycling through wide, regular streets softened by huge lawns and flowerbeds. Tall trees dappled the light. The traffic was calm, the sounds muted. We reached a cycle path and followed it, not knowing where we were going. We slipped further into the relaxed, fairytale calmness, sounds becoming even softer. We passed a huge boulodrome divided into smaller playing areas, and it was full: old men playing each other, couples teaching their children, a young woman in shorts and bikini top practising by herself.

The path brought us to another track above the east-west road through Grande Motte. In front of us expensive-looking yachts filled a marina that stretched away in either direction. Blue sea shimmered to the horizon. To either side rows of crazy hotels stretched away. In a funny way, it was all cheerful and likeable. There was an immense feeling of space; nothing was crowded. I hadn't particularly been looking forward to the rest of the Mediterranean - now that I'd seen pink flamingos it held no more specific attractions for me - but the good thing about low expectations is the capacity for pleasurable surprises.

We cycled towards the marina, then westward along the promenade underneath the huge white hotels. They were all very geometric and Sixties-looking, but somehow managed to charm: big white pyramidal structures, with round holes opening onto the balconies. They looked a bit like a game of Connect4.

We found the tourist office, where it was Adi's turn to collect the necessary bumph. He came out with a grin.

'The state of that towpath? It's deliberate. A thick cyclist fell in a few years ago.'

In a strikingly un-French attitude to personal liability, the canal authority had forbidden any more cycling on it.

'And they threw down that horrible stuff so that nobody would.'

'No wonder the fishermen were looking at us oddly. What happened to the Gallic shrug and "But did you not see all the water and the big big drop, m'sieur?'"?'

'The police can give you a ticket for cycling on it. They won't, the girl said, but they can.'

'Change of plan so.'

He saddled up. 'We'll think about it after dinner. Let's find our campsite.'

'I love my card,' said the campsite manager. While he took our details a huge, placid chow sniffed my sweaty knees. 'This card is for the shower. It's wonderful, you wave it and the shower it works!'

We were tired and hot and happy to have found this lovely place, an oasis in the middle of the ageing sun resort. He continued, 'And for one night, am I right?'

'You're right,' we confirmed. He noted it on his form, smiling. 'The cycling people, always they stay one night and they are up early and gone!'

'Well, you're right about the one night.'

On the Mediterranean coast, in a leafy, lush, beautifully laid-out campsite with quality facilities, we had just paid the princely sum of €13.50 for our pitch. This was decidedly better than the €31 we had been on the point of paying half an hour before. After a trip to a supermarket, where Adi bought vegetables while I caught up on my diary, we found a group of campsites in a leafy, park-like area in the middle of the town. All traffic noise died away, muted by trees, shrubs and flowers. We headed straight for the one recommended by the Rough Guide and gamely swallowed our disbelief when the receptionist told us the price.

'I bloody hate being fleeced,' Adi growled as we cycled around the campsite looking for a pitch.

'Me too.'

We went scowling through the usual pitch selection process: ants, shade in the morning, shade in the evening, proximity to showers, proximity to potentially noisy people (rare).

'You'd better let her know which one we've chosen,' Adi said as we grumpily started to unload the bikes.

The receptionist wasn't in her booth. I was spinning the bike round to come back to Adi when I thought - shall I just have a look?

Back to the mini-roundabout where we'd seen the signs for four campsites. I rode down the leafy lanes to each of them in turn. One of them was for members of some camping organisation only, one was closed for refurbishment, but the third one had clearly displayed prices out the front and they were reasonable! Less than half the cost of our site! I quickly recce'd the facilities I could see from the gate. Pleasant bar with no obvious degenerates, no crackheads, no litter, just the usual monoculture of retired couples... I sped back to Adi, who was just about to thread the poles through the tent.

'We're moving!'

The receptionist, back on duty, frowned but was polite. How I love the pay-in-the-morning system.

The campsite manager and his chow were right: the showers were wonderful. It's one of the many lovely things I remember of that night, along with the huge-bellied, smiling Frenchman in the tiny pair of shorts who came over to chat to us, the fact that we were the only ones in a tent, and that we were one of only two who didn't come from France. (The other was the obligatory Dutch campervan.) And the hoopoe scavenging around the tent at dawn. You got a better class of scavenger down here.

CHAPTER SEVENTEEN

To Marseillan-plage

The morning's ride was long and hot but unexpectedly pleasing. With the Canal off limits we took a cycle path west along the promenade. Grande Motte faded away, leaving us cycling between sparsely occupied beaches and dusty dunes. This bit of sun-worshippers' holiday-land is on a long spit separating a series of lagoons south of Montpellier from the sea, and the calls of unfamiliar waders came from the lagoons to our right, accompanying the gentle lap of the sea on our left and the hum of our wheels.

If you'd asked me beforehand if I'd enjoy cycling on a flat cycle path through Mediterranean sun resorts you'd probably have been answered with a snort. (It does, I realise, raise the question of how I'd been persuaded to take that route at all. This is what happens when you cycle with a companion. You compromise, people!) I'd expected these Mediterranean days to be a sort of endurance test, something to be got through before our return to verdant, hilly regions, so it was a treat to find myself taking pleasure in it. The cycle track clung to the shore for miles, rising up a little at times so we could enjoy seeing as well as hearing the birdlife in the lagoons. Little terns, black-winged stilts, avocets and pink flamingos wading and feeding. No binoculars required - they were just there. The lovely stretches of beach and lagoon were punctuated by the ageing, unfashionable but somehow likeable resorts of Carnon-Plage and Palavas-les-Flots. Everything shone squintingly, bright, white and sand-coloured concrete and gleaming white boats. At this early stage of the season there were very few tourists, even by my introverted standards, and there was something lovely and airy about cycling along the promenades, in and out of shade.

After a pause for mid-morning tea (still no teapot) in Palavas-les-Flot, we continued on a minor road west along the diminishing spit. Sometimes we could see the Canal running parallel to us through the middle of the lagoon, which looked bizarre: a waterway through water. We were both in good spirits. The Legs had nothing to complain about and Bike was stoic as ever. I had to remind myself to drink frequently; the cycling was easy but it was still hot and we weren't dawdling.

The next couple of hours were full of sunshine and squabbles, the most acrimonious of which was witnessed by a woman who was completely nude except for a pair of blue-rimmed sunglasses. She watched our argument - she didn't have a choice, we had it in a patch of undergrowth right in front of her - on a narrow, vegetated spit that went tantalisingly in the direction we wanted to go, with even more tantalising tracks heading through it in the correct direction, towards Frontignan and Sète. We'd seen lots of people heading down here, singly and in pairs, when we'd paused for a short barefoot walk on the silky-sanded beach. Back at the bikes, Adi squinted into the sun and frowned at the map. Here, at the last beach café and stand of showers, the road swung inland.

'It's a right pain, you know. The road goes all the way around the back of the lagoons, before it comes out again further on. Look.'

He showed me the map. 'We could go along those tracks, look, there're people walking along them.'

'But there's no track marked.' The spit on the map, and right there in front of us, was only a narrow strip of dune and scrub.

'But those paths are going in the right direction.'

'But they're tiny.'

'We'll just try for a little,' said Adi, correctly interpreting my dubious expression, 'and if it deteriorates we'll turn back.'

For ten minutes our little path wiggled between the lagoons and the sea that we could hear just beyond the low brow of the scrubby dune. It got a little better and a little worse in turn, but with a perceptible slide down the average scale. The squabble ensued when I said I didn't want to do it anymore.

'But if it improves a bit it'll be fine.'

'But it already has improved and then dis-improved again, and it's just getting too hard.' It really was hard; I'd had to dismount twice already to shove the bike through puddles of sand, having come to a wallowing halt. With the sound of eyes very loudly not being rolled, Adi wheeled his bike round and set off back the way we'd come. There was a grim, hard-done-by set to his shoulders as he vanished into the shrubbery.

I floundered through a seven-point turn in a sandy patch, which was when I became aware of the nude lady, sitting with knees drawn up in front of her demurely. The low trees formed a little bower around her. You can't ignore someone in France, whatever the circumstances, so as I passed close to her, hauling my sand-drugged bike, I nodded and said, 'Bonjour, Madame.' She returned the greeting with a slight smile.

The suspicion that she wasn't alone, and a possible explanation for the number of people we'd seen disappearing in this direction, was confirmed in the form of an enormous, cheerful and entirely naked German man who I almost bumped into. He engaged me in conversation and we chatted in mutually broken French. All I can remember is him beaming when I said I was Irish. 'Irlande! Il pleut en Irlande!'

'Did you see any naked people?' I asked Adi a few minutes later. He was slightly huffily waiting for me back by the beach showers and the little ice-cream booth.

'Naked people?'

We watched some more people disappearing down the little paths into the undergrowth.

'Ah,' he said after a couple of minutes. 'They're not going walking, are they?'

We'd read about Le Cap d'Agde, a huge resort forty or so miles to the west, incorporating the colossal Village Naturist, the largest nudist colony in France. We'd stumbled on an outlier.

Friends again, we visited the restored Cathédrale de Maguelone on an island in the lagoons. Inside was huge and light and airy, supported by tall pillars of coralline limestone, holey and cheese-like. Gentle music, a harp and soprano, floated into the space. There's something wonderfully, achingly uplifting about being inside in a tall, narrow space. Another candle for my mother.

We rode inland, north along peaceful cycle paths up above the main road, through Villeneuve-lès-Maguelone, a big name for a little town. A community policeman who was shooing schoolchildren across the road spotted us as we had one of our frequent frowning-over-map breaks. He sprinted over to us.

'Wait! I finish five minutes.'

Schoolchildren safely escorted, he asked us where we wanted to go and then cycled with us, guiding us through the village. 'You enjoy La France? You see the, the Pink Floyd? Non, non, the, the oiseau - flamingo! You see the pink? Pink flamingo?'

He sent us on our way with re-filled water bottles and a photograph of the regional map that hung on the police station's reception wall. Adi pointed to the spit we'd attempted to go along earlier and said, 'There isn't a track there?'

The startled expression on the policeman's face and emphatic shake of the head was clear enough.

'I just wanted to be sure that there wasn't a lovely cycle track somewhere just out of our sight, winding its way between the nudist hotspots,' Adi said after we'd waved goodbye and cycled off. 'You never know. You have to ask.'

The cycle track took us for miles, all the way to Sète, squeezed between the sea and Mont Saint-Clair, a small green hill that had been on our horizon all day.

We glimpsed expensive boats, incongruous in the narrow waterways between tall, Moorish-looking buildings. Scooters buzzed and traffic idled as we approached the centre of the town, which we had caught in rush hour. As the streets narrowed and the traffic thickened, Adi and I got separated while I was distracted by my 'ciao' moment.

Everyone should have one. As I pedalled slowly in the line of traffic, a pink scooter kept pace beside me for a few moments. When I looked up, the young dark-haired man on the scooter grinned widely and said 'Ciao!' before the traffic pulled him ahead of me. I was charmed.

Adi and I found each other outside the tourist office. It was my turn to collect the intel, as we were now calling it by way of variation. I went in and found out that the nearest campsite was eight miles away. I came out to find the bikes locked up, alone. Adi was up the street, talking to a couple on touring bikes. He and the male half of the couple were holding a map out between them, with much pointing and nodding and shaking of heads. When he returned it was with a grin.

'Intel!'

The Dutch couple had just cycled along the Canal du Midi and had generously given Adi their map, barely holding together along the creases after ten days. We studied it over a slice of pizza on the square until the nutter-ometer klaxon started blaring.

'Vous aimez la nature?'

Given our experience on the beach, I didn't think this scruffy man was asking about our interest in birds. It was the only time I was impolite to someone. 'Nous allons.' Not even an au revoir. That told him.

'Those people said the Canal was bumpy in parts and great in others,' Adi said as we cycled out later, replete with pizza. 'It's good around the cities.'

'Bumpy's not bad. How bad can it be?' I was in cheerful mood, squabbles behind, sea on our left and a broad lagoon, the Bassin de Thau, visible across the road on our right.

The first campsite was too expensive, a resort all by itself out on the edge of the dunes, with barriers and a 'complex' look about it. We carried on. Camping Beau Séjour, at the end of a lane that ended by the beach in Marseillan-Plage, was much more our style, though we were slightly disturbed when the proprietress told us to make sure that our bikes were 'bien-attaché'.

We bien-attached them and erected the tent, all the while bothered by mosquitos, which were vying with the baked ground to make pitching troublesome. By the time we got the tent up my hands were scored with red pressure marks from pressing the tent pegs into the ground, and Adi's shoulders bore a scattering of bites.

Walloping his shoulders like a self-flagellation fanatic hadn't done much to dissuade them. They found him much more palatable than they did me.

Positioning our tablecloth and ourselves where we could watch the ant-highways without sitting on them, we ate dinner with the Mediterranean whispering over the dune behind us and examined our statistics. We'd cycled 54 miles that day, our longest of the trip, in baking sunshine, with a substantial break at rush hour, a visit to the cathedral and plenty of stops to see wildfowl and waterfall in the lagoons. Long bike rides and long hours spent exploring on foot - that was the way to satisfy both of us.

A walk on the beach in almost-darkness, fishermen silhouetted against an indigo sea. Sounds of good cheer from further down the beach, close enough to make us smile, far enough not to disturb. Breeze in the trees above. Swallows, and swifts, and bats.

CHAPTER EIGHTEEN

To Le Grau d'Agde

The day started beautifully, with harmless early clouds and a coolish breeze. I'd slept like a stone.

'The bikes are still there,' Adi reported, peeking out. We went for a walk on the beach before we did anything. No baking bodies on the sand, just a couple of other walkers and a small, shaggy dog paddling cautiously in the azure shallows.

But my contentment was to be rattled.

'We need to stop and do some laundry and tent repair.'

'But we're only just getting into a rhythm!' I protested.

'I know, I enjoyed yesterday too. But that zip's not going to hold together much longer.'

It was true we could do with some maintenance. The zip of our Vango Spirit 200+ was trying to part company from the tent fabric, as well as getting temperamental about actually closing the last few inches from the ground. There were some less than waterproof patches that could do with some attention. And we did need to wash everything again. Sweat makes for frequent laundry.

We decided to go to Le Grau d'Agde. It was barely ten miles.

'That really doesn't count as cycle touring,' I insisted. 'Can we make it longer?'

There weren't many options but we did go north to Marseillan, on the edge of the Bassin de Thau and around the back of the Étang de Bagnas, which gave our legs a little more exercise. After the long cycle yesterday they felt lively and eager for action.

'We'll go cycling without panniers tomorrow,' Adi promised as we sped along the D61 to Agde.

I scribbled up my diary outside a hardware store where Adi was searching for paraffin for our multi-fuel stove. After a couple of confusing conversations in camping shops - paraffin is 'pétrole' in French - Adi had found it shelved with cleaning products. After the first startled-looking store assistant attempted to dissuade him, he'd stopped telling them that he wanted to cook with it.

Approaching the centre of Agde gave us another thrilling, scary ride on busy roads. I was beginning to relish it now. Before we'd come over I'd twisted my brain trying to visualise cycling around roundabouts the wrong way round, certain that I would die on a roundabout on our first day. Then there was the old Priorité á Droite, which had been haunting me ever since I'd read about it. It's an old French road rule that gives priority to traffic coming from the right, even from an apparently minor road. It has largely disappeared now, but explains the signs warning that 'vous n'avez pas la priorité' when approaching roundabouts, as the Priorité á Droite is directly contrary to the roundabout rule.

Happily, it turns out the body is better at doing than the mind is at imaging, or at least better than my mind. Now, high on adrenaline and HGV fumes, I was enjoying roundabouts, in an edge-of-saddle terror sort of way. Provided you're confident, and indicate where you're going, and make eye contact, it's grand. The trick, I thought, scribbling outside the store, was not to get overwhelmed by the noise, the fumes and the cars approaching from all directions, but to ride the roundabout wave. I scribbled in this vein until Adi came out waving a container of paraffin in triumph.

We picked up a cycle track that brought us to the river Hérault, avoiding Agde's town centre. We turned left and followed the east bank along a well-shaded, pleasant cycle track.

Camping Romarins, halfway between Agde and Le Grau d'Agde at the river's mouth, was full of English campervanners and one pair of English campers. Roy and Beryl from Essex, in the neighbouring pitch, came to introduce themselves and indicated their two enormous tents.

'Kitchen and bedroom,' said Roy.

'We've got a king-sized blow-up bed in there,' said Beryl.

'And a cooker.'

'There's a scops owl here too.'

They were retired and had been here for a month already, with another month to play with before going back. Next to them was a Welsh couple who were out for the day; the red dragon waved on a flag on the caravan.

We spent an hour hand-washing the most urgent of the laundry, hung it up on our washing line of spare guy ropes, and rode down the river to check out Le Grau d'Agde.

'It's great,' said Roy. 'Everything's really cheap!'

After the tangle of channels of the Rhône's vast meeting with the sea, the Hérault's was satisfying geometric. One moment you were walking on a river bank, then you turned 90 degrees to the left and you were walking along the sea shore. Two short breakwaters guided the river neatly out a little way, then left it to fend for itself. A lighthouse (*phare* is such a lovely word) stood at the end of each. A tiny boat ferried people and a dog across the mouth of the river.

We quickly found what we needed to find - general shop, boulangerie, ice-cream, tourist information, a likely looking bar - and sat down to read for a while. It was hot enough to keep my fidgeting in check. I had an unseasonable but lovely hot chocolate, served by a barman who was very easy on the eye. The town - a big seaside village really - had a friendly, unglamorous feel.

'People live here,' Roy had said, after telling us where in the Super U to find the tap where you could fill up your container with wine. 'It's not like the Cap d'Agde up the road. You can hear the fishermen coming back early in the morning, taking the catch up to Agde.'

Dafydd and Glenda from south Wales came to make friends with us as we cooked dinner.

'Do you know about the scops owl?' they asked.

Adi was on form with the dinner that night. A short ride hadn't diminished our appetites; I almost inhaled the potato cake. The sauce, of beef tomatoes, Mexican spices, petit pois, white onion, aubergine and spinach with a splash of balsamic vinegar to bring everything out, was one of the best so far.

When we washed up it was almost that time of evening when the bats and the swifts are out together. We were watching a bat the size of a blackbird when another Englishman, James, came to say hello.

'Has anyone told you about the scops owl?'

At dusk we walked along the river, past the line of bars and the corner of the sea out to the nearer lighthouse. We stopped at the same bar as before, with wine this time. Same attractive barman. It was very quiet back at the campsite; we were definitely the last into bed. Midnight as I turned off my headtorch and stopped reading. And then we heard it: the digital beep of the scops owl, calling plaintively into the dark like a lonesome reversing lorry.

CHAPTER NINETEEN

Le Grau d'Agde

Y ou know, we're the only people I've noticed using these,' said Adi the next morning, as we scrubbed and slapped and rinsed and wrung our clothes and sleeping bag liners in the campsite's laundry sinks. They were outside the shower block, under a wooden roof, and it was a pleasant task in the slowly-strengthening sunshine. We'd commandeered three of the sinks and were processing everything except the sleeping bags and mats and the tent itself.

Roy came over and watched as we hung out our laundry and sewed up the tears threatening the zips in our tent. It wasn't yet noon and he was holding a tumbler of wine and sweating disturbingly. He told us again where to get wine ('In the super-U! You take in a container and you can just fill it up at taps - better than stuff you pay six or seven quid for at home! And it's cheap! Cheap!') I know he said many other things, interesting things, but in my memory I see him with the tumbler of wine in the sun, slightly unsteady on his legs, going 'Cheep! Cheap! Cheap!'

We cycled out not long after midday, up towards Agde and across the river to the round lock, the Écluse du Bassin Rond. It wasn't quite a perfect circle anymore following an expansion in the late 1970s to allow even longer boats through to one of the lock exits. There were three exits: one west to the Canal du Midi, one east to the last section of the Canal and the upper Hérault, and one south to a short waterway that joined the lower Hérault. We watched it at work, letting five boats in from the eastern canal side, equalising and letting them through the west.

I liked Adge: the whole town had a strong Latin-North African feel, with tiny narrow streets and buildings edged with black volcanic stone. A group of young men sat in a small square, one playing guitar and singing, and the Latin rhythms and accents followed us for a couple of streets. By a fountain a family played with the water, chasing each other with buckets. On the bridge across the Hérault, teenagers dared each other to jump in.

We visited the Cathédrale Saint-Étienne, an enormous black basalt block of a building, as much a fortress as a church, with a high vaulted ceiling. The massive marble altar piece was set disconcertingly off-centre. Someone got their measurements wrong. Oh, to be there when they realised the ordered, completed altar piece of intricately carved marble, thirty feet wide, was not going to fit.

'We did what you asked for!'

'It doesn't fit! It doesn't bloody fit! It's too bloody wide!'

Le Cap d'Agde couldn't have been more different. We went not in search of naturists but to find the beach of black sand, black from the basaltic plug of rock that forms this headland. After winding on cycle tracks and quiet roads we suddenly found ourselves on a marina, pleasant enough but far busier than anything we'd experienced so far. Jetties were lined with shiny yachts while crowds of groomed, tanned and squeakily-clean-looking people wearing a thousand minute variations on the rich-person-with-yacht uniform strolled between the boats and shops. Once in, we couldn't seem to get out. We were driven upwards, pushing our bikes now, via ramps and steps to more levels, past more horrible tat shops, blingy cafés and posh sailor garb. Claustrophobia pressed in.

My blood sugar levels abruptly plummeted, adding to my grumpy desperation.

'I can't go on.' I felt like a complete idiot but suddenly I couldn't move. 'Pathetic!' my brain shouted at my legs. 'Bugger off,' retorted The Legs. 'You go on if you want, Brains.'

I sank onto a bench and Adi ran to the rescue, entering animated discussion with a pretty girl at a stall. He returned with two paper bags, each containing some sort of savoury tartlet, a can of Coke and a sweet mini-tartlet (a tartletette?) 'She gave me the offer of the day, at least that's what I think she said. Pudding for 50 cent extra. Get that down you.'

Most of it already was down me.

'I think it's because we've underestimated what we're doing,' Adi said, when I lifted my head out of the nosebag. 'We're gradually doing more miles now, in heat we're not used to, and when we're off the bike we're not idle, we're wandering around. And camping uses lots of calories.'

It does. It's one of the things that I love about camping. Everything takes a little bit of effort. I've seen tents described on some adventure websites as 'a rubbish version of a house', which makes me fume. You can hear in a tent. You might not be sleeping under the stars in a bivvy bag but being in a tent doesn't make you a wimp. You might not be feeling the wind and the breath of the night and the light of the stars right upon you, but they are only separated from you by the thinnest of nylon skins, and you can hear everything: the rain, the owls, the flap of wind, the footsteps nearby, the traffic, the boats going up the river, the rustle of small, cautious mammals going about their business carefully in the deep of night. You feel the ground. It's not a rubbish version of a house, it's a cosy version of outside.

I waxed lyrical to Adi in this vein as we sat on the bench, drinking the Coke and nibbling the tiny, raspberry custard tartlet. Soon I was able to look around once more without murder in my heart.

'Ready to go on without screaming?' Adi asked.

We pushed our bikes up past more shops and people in sunglasses and pseudo-sailor clothes and finally made it to the war memorial high on a rocky plug overlooking the black beach. We regarded it for a moment in silence.

'It's not that black,' we said together, and grinned.

The view wasn't bad though. Somewhere out of sight to the east was the naturist village, but south and west were entirely satisfactory. Sea, bright and hard to look at. Distant rumpled mountains, the Pyrenees meeting the Mediterranean.

We wiggled back to Le Grau d'Agde, taking a long detour north to ensure we'd avoid the marina and the endless horrible shops. The weather reminded us not to take it for granted and threw a spitty shower at us. We bumped into a little group of middle aged cyclists, pot-bellied and grim-faced on super-expensive bikes all with matching tiny bar bags. In sun again we entered Le Grau from the east shore, past the boulodrome where old men and women were teaching grandchildren to play. In our favourite bar I sipped my hot chocolate (I can drink hot chocolate no matter the weather) and watched the friendly (and frankly, sexy) bartender doing his stuff with casual grace. A tray of drinks held on the fingers of his left hand, moving effortlessly through tables, his wrist relaxed so that the tray tilted and swayed gently, the glasses not moving, as if glued to it.

Back at the campsite I attacked my fringe with the scissors from the First Aid kit. The result was a shaggy mess, but there was nobody to care. After a long, slow dinner of salad and pizza at the campsite café, we covered the table with maps and bumph. Up the Canal du Midi, to springboard us towards Toulouse and north. In two days time we'd be in Carcassonne.

PART SEVEN

Turning North:
Le Grau d'Agde to
Olargues

CHAPTER TWENTY

To Capestang

On account of a big list to things to buy and tourist information to visit (why hadn't we done this on the day off?) we didn't leave Agde until after midday. As usual, this made me want to scream. As usual, I managed not to.

We cycled over the Hérault for the last time, up to the Écluse du Bassin Rond and westward along the canal. Calm water reflected the rows of plane trees that line the banks. Somewhat to our surprise, given the people we'd met who had either cycled it or intended to cycle it, there was no cycle track at all, just the unimproved towpath. At best, a bare ribbon of earth snaked between the grasses growing lushly on the bank; at worst it was deeply rutted and dry as concrete. I had my first fall within a couple of miles, though 'fall' doesn't quite do it justice. The bike slipped as I rode too fast along a rut. I felt it slipping out of my control and I sprang off the saddle, surprising myself, Adi and a group of ducks by leaping clear of the bike and landing unhurt in the long grass of the bank.

After that progress was frustratingly slow. A barge overtook us. A barge. Overtook us. Things improved a few kilometres before Béziers when the barely-there gave way to tarmac. We took a wrong turn and cycled up the river Orb, under some magnificent bridges. Ten minutes later we saw them from above as we cycled along an aqueduct. Friendly bike-track signage and a good, gravelled surface reassured us.

We sped up and quickly reached the Écluses de Fonsèranes, a spectacular set of nine locks climbing up a low hill. Even though we'd started late we had to stop for tea at the wooden-shack-style café by the lock, because this one served tea in teapots! Adi took a photograph of it: the first teapot for twenty days. A wedding party and tourists thronged the broad, grassy banks and the footbridge over the lock. Two men were having difficulty manoeuvring a particularly long barge into the bottom lock, their efforts watched with interest by tourists. Unnoticed by anyone but Adi and me, a beaver pottered about in the deep water at the bottom of the staircase locks, totally unfazed by the boat activity and people upstream.

We started again, eager to make progress on the good surface. A few yards beyond the spot where the ninth lock would have disappeared in our rearview mirrors, if we'd had rearview mirrors, the track reverted to the ribbon of rutted earth.

'I'm detecting a trend,' said Adi, catching up to me after a stop to take a ride-by photo. (There were many of these, which were less alarming than when he took overtook me shooting video while speeding downhill one-handed.) 'Town and tourists: good path. No-one but cyclists: mountain bike path.'

We left the Canal to cycle up to the Oppidum d'Ensérune. 'Ancient hill town' seems to be the closest translation of 'oppidum', the Latin root of oppèdes that we'd encountered in Provence. We cycled up the wooded zigzag road (our first hill since the Alpilles), parked and wandered around the remains of the buildings. The village was occupied for five centuries, from about 600 BC to 100 AD, which is remarkable enough, but the most striking feature that remains isn't on top of the hill, or from that era. In the thirteenth century, the large marsh edging the lake of Montady was drained to create agricultural fields. The drainage ditches radiated out from a depression in the centre of the marsh like spokes of a wheel, making a pattern of huge wedge-shaped fields: the same principle as ladder farms on hillsides, where each farm gets a field of the best, low-lying land as well as fields of progressively less fertile land. Eight centuries later, the ditches still function. It looked like a great disc pattern stamped upon the surface of the land by an agricultural god. Or a gigantic earth pizza.

The canal wound its way to Capestang on the ruts-in-dust track and we wound on it. Even a couple of days later one of the only two things I could remember about Capestang was the shocking showers in the campsite. One press of the push-button brought forth a two-second burst of lukewarm water.

Cycle touring makes you filthy. You lather yourself in sunscreen. You sweat. It rains. You sweat again. Bits of road, dust and fragments of unfortunate insects glue themselves to you. A crud forms on your skin.

It is vile.

Getting clean had become one of the great pleasures of the day. A routine had developed: once we'd erected the tent, Adi went for his shower while I sorted out the bedding, arranged the panniers in the awning (there was a strict order for these) and laid out my personal items - Kindle, notebook, camera - on my side of the bedchamber. Adi would return and sort out his side of the tent and make a start on dinner while I went for my shower.

I'd always promise 'Just a quick one tonight', but I was fooling no-one. My showers took ages.

I'd emerge from the now-homey tent, clutching my wash bag, my clean t-shirt and almost-clean trousers and knickers. I'd take off as much as I could, so that I was down to sweaty t-shirt and and cycling shorts, and run to the shower in my sandals.

First was the selection of the shower stall, with much frowning at the floor to see which was the cleanest. They were usually all spotless, as there was invariably one of those rubber-edged brush-type things in the corner of the washroom. We'd noticed that French people were conscientious about cleaning shower stalls after themselves, but there could have been a Brit who'd left a scud of suds and hair on the floor, so I'd check all the cubicles, just in case.

I'd make a provisional choice. Next, the water check. Still fully clothed, I'd push the button and dodge back, watching the flow for duration and strength. I'd wiggle a hand under it, testing for temperature. There is nothing worse than, having already divested yourself of your clothes, discovering that you've chosen a showerhead with a dribbly, lukewarm flow. If satisfied, I'd close the door and start to disrobe.

Rarely was there a shower curtain. The usual arrangement was simply a six-inch wide partial partition protecting a seat-cum-shelf and a single hook. This was not enough, but I learned to cope. I'd hang

up my clean clothes on the uppermost of the two
hooks, if there were two, in the reverse order in which
I'd put them on. Then I hung my wash bag on top of
them by the elastic hairbands that always hang from
the clip.

By the way, I should point out that 'clean' is a bit
of an exaggeration here. I had a set of cycling clothes
and a set of what I grandly called my evening clothes.
No ball gowns: my evening clothes consisted of a pair
of walking trousers with zip-off legs for fine evenings
and tops and t-shirts that I never allowed myself to
sweat in. After showering and changing I'd go to
extreme lengths to avoid a droplet of sweat forming in
my armpits, up to and including walking holding my
arms out like a penguin. I also had a long sleeved
merino wool zip-neck top and my cosy fleece. Add to
this a pair of trainers and a pair of socks that were
almost clean and you have my evening wear.

Yes, I did say *almost* clean socks. I could make
them last for days because, I reasoned, I only wore
them for a few hours in the evening.

All this took long enough (and was clearly proof of
the lengths to which rituals can become extended
without the normal time constraints that apply at
home), but was extended considerably by my total
aversion to getting a single droplet of water onto
newly cleaned and dried skin. It would send me into

the reddest of red misty rages. With a lot of hair and only one travel towel, I'm quite proud that I didn't succumb to the rage more than three or four times.

All this means that the dismal showers in Capestang did not bring forth feelings great joy. But the second of the only two things I can remember about the place redeemed it: an unexpectedly spectacular show that the bats and swifts put on at dusk.

CHAPTER TWENTY-ONE

To Bois-Bas

W e both slept well and were up early. We had no choice. A boules contest started in the park across the road at seven in the morning. It sounded as if the whole village was there, cheering and shouting. It was a Saturday. What were they all doing up on a Saturday at this hour?

We breakfasted quickly. (Entirely acceptable croissants, although they didn't make it into the league table.) The campsite was a municipal, staffed by a shy youth who looked as if he'd have been happy to let us away without paying if it meant he wouldn't have to speak to us. I finally cornered him, hiding in an unoccupied pitch and pretending to clip a hedge. When I got back, Adi was having a quick word with a couple of French cycle tourers.

'Today, Carcassonne,' they said.

'See you there,' we said.

That they were on mountain bikes should have given us a clue.

We left at nine. Just after eleven I picked myself up off the bumpy, rut-riven track that Bike had just fallen on and declared melodramatically, 'We're never going to make it to Carcassonne!'

Adi came over to help me lift Bike and secure a front pannier that had become detached. We were somewhere near Argeliers, west of Capestang. It had taken two hours to cycle eight miles. I can walk faster. The towpath was now unrelentingly bumpy and rutted, slow and tough on pannier racks and attachments.

'I can't see any countryside.' I complained.

'Hmm. It is pretty though,' said Adi, looking on the bright side.

The twin rows of plane trees, planted on the tops of the low banks that enclosed the water, made a peaceful, green tunnel and the canal wended its way gracefully beneath. But it is difficult to appreciate the loveliness when your attention is necessarily focussed on the next two bumpy, rutted metres in front. We realised how slow we were going when canal boats started to overtake us again.

We stopped in tiny Poilhes, an enchanting hamlet typical of Languedoc, with bleached ochre stucco plaster and deep green and orange shutters fastened against the sun. We descended from the canal by an 'escalier pour des vélos', a shallow-stepped stairway with a cobbled ramp alongside for the rolling of bicycles. As we paused at the foot a man came up to us and launched into a rhapsody on the wonders of Carcassonne. 'Elton John came to France, and where did he play? Paris - and Carcassonne! Someone else came, and where did they play their only two dates in Europe? London - and Carcassonne! But remember,' he admonished, 'when you go in the main gate of Narbonne, you must close your ears. It is too much, the sellers, the nonsense. For the first street, you must close your ears. But then, ah!' And he told us where to find toilets in Poilhes, to enjoy our holiday, tipped his hat to us - actually tipped his hat - and went on his way.

We pedalled on, under the leaves of the plane trees and over the roots of the plane trees, until Adi burst.

'I can't see *anything*!'

We leant our bikes up against the bank and climbed to the top. We were curving around the edge of low hills falling down to the wide Midi basin. Heat-hazed hills rose in the distance. Pyrenean foothills.

'Let's leave it for a bit,' I suggested. 'We can always come back.'

We rode south, through the lovely village of Sallèles-d'Aude, where another canal, Canal de la

Robine, met the river Cesse. Onward, roughly following the river Aude along quiet roads, with the hills to the north and the mountains away to the south folding in and out of view. Under the shade of plane trees in the Place de la République of St-Nazaire-d'Aude we discussed our plans.

'The canal isn't working.'

'It isn't,' I agreed, sadly. I'd been fantasising about a café day in Carcassonne, just me and my books over a hot chocolate. It sounds odd, but neither of us got much time to ourselves, except when we were separated by the usual fifty metres on the road, or when Adi was shopping and I was minding the bikes, catching up on my diary.

Our discussion escalated into a proper disagreement. Our different approaches to touring were beginning to rankle.

'You always want to rush on,' Adi said crossly. With some justification.

'Wanting to cycle more than twenty-five miles in a day isn't exactly rushing,' I said, hurt. 'We could easily cycle more miles without rushing if we didn't dawdle in the morning. And if you didn't have to spend half-an-hour in every shop you go into,' I added.

He ignored that. 'And I'd like to pitch up earlier in the evening.'

'Shouldn't be a problem if we don't dawdle over the boring stuff. Like shopping.'

Then he said he wanted to meet our friends on the Loire valley on June 22nd. I was speechless. How, I asked, trying not to snap, were we going to manage that if we never started cycling till eleven o'clock, he didn't want me to 'rush on' AND wanted to pitch up earlier in the day?

The two o'clock buzzing of scooters pulled us back to ourselves. We called a truce, agreed to forget the canal and Carcassonne, made up a route for today and decided to worry about tomorrow tomorrow.

I couldn't help feeling unsettled. A change of plan means more decisions. Decisions take time and effort, while life goes on happening while you're deliberating over your plans. John Lennon knew what he was talking about.

Tea at a little canal-side café in Argen-Minervois revived us both, even thought it was not in a pot. The pleasant proprietress brought cups of hot water and a tray full of a selection of teabags.

In Olonzac's helpful tourist office we picked up a list of campsites and decided to aim for one in a little hamlet not far away called Bois Bas, listed intriguingly as a 'camping participatif'. The road took us through Minerve, a ridiculously picturesque old village spanning two sides of a plunging gorge. Narrow lanes twisted down the canyon walls to the viaduct that linked the two halves of the village. I scribbled in my diary leaning on the wall of the viaduct while Adi searched for beer and wine. It was beautiful. It was sunny. The views were opening up again. We'd have a gentle ride up the hill to the campsite, then an early dinner.

'It's about ten kilometres,' Adi said. 'We'll be pitched up well within the hour.'

Adi and I walk in mountains; we cycle all over the country. We understand maps. We know what contour lines mean. Altitude. So we ought to have noticed that the road to Bois Bas crossed a few of them.

It was about 5.30 p.m. when we left Minerve. Up we went, up a couple of steep zigzags that levelled off. There was some excitement when we spotted campervans at the top of the zigzags - could it be there was a campsite the tourist office didn't know about? Would we be drinking wine in the next half hour? - but it turned out to be an unofficial campervan layby. We rode on in good spirits. The gradient was lessening. We must be coming to the top of the plateau.

We ought to have learned by then. The gradient lessened, steadied, settled down at about 5% and stayed there. And stayed and stayed. For eight kilometres. The sun was still shining and the tarmac that had baked under it all day was radiating it back upwards. Caught between sun and shimmering road, I discovered for the first time that sweat really stings when it runs into your eyes. Droplets ran down my arms and dripped from my elbows onto my slowly pistoning thighs. My handlebar grips were slick with sweat. I was being cooked.

While one part of my brain was cataloguing the physical challenges and another trying to calculate how far we could have ridden and how far could possibly be left, a third part was in heaven. For we were climbing up the long edge of the Montagne Noir. Vineyard-striped hillsides tumbled down to the fields around Minerve. The road slowly twisted and rose into woodland that fell and fell away from us as we climbed. Around one corner Adi was waiting for me by a dead, muscly-limbed olive tree and we saw through a fold in the woods distant mountains. The Pyrenees!

'Now that,' said Adi, handing me a glucose sweet, 'makes it worthwhile.'

We pedalled on higher, my brain singing a 'When will it end?' and 'Wow, this is one of the most beautiful views I've ever seen in my life' duet. No high ground across the wide Midi basin to block our view of the Pyrenees now. A long, jagged green ridge faded upwards into bleached stony teeth, gleaming against the blue sky, impossibly high and awe-inspiring even from this distance.

We kept climbing until the trees thinned and petered out at about 600 metres, opening into mountain pasture. Above the tree line! Even in my brain-melted state, this delighted me. A loose herd of pretty brown goats grazed tall grass and meadow flowers, bells clunking lazily in the still, mirage-hot air, and still we climbed, until finally, when my lungs were about to give up, we reached something that felt as if it was—

'Is this really level ground?' I asked. Adi was too far ahead to hear, he was slowing down to let me catch up, but The Legs answered me by suddenly revolving quicker. I clicked up the gears. That means it's levelling out. Oh god, we must be nearly there.

At that point we passed a junction with a thin little road that led to nowhere further upslope. The sign said: 'Bois Bas 4 km.'

'It can't be serious,' I said. 'Four more kilometres? I'll be a puddle.'

'Shush,' Adi said. 'It's pointing that way. Look at that.' He pointed at the road ahead of us. 'Downhill!'

The Legs cheered.

As we rolled along the gentle slope – oh, blissful feeling – he said, 'What do you think "Camping participatif" means?'

Guessing kept us occupied for the next few minutes. Would we have to wash up for the owners? Participate in ritual dances? Grimace through some impromptu immersive theatre? When we turned a bend and saw the sign for Bois Bas pointing down a rough track into a wooded nook of the hillside, we were past caring.

It turned out to be gorgeous. 'Hippy farm!' Adi correctly characterised it as we bumped down towards a cluster of stone and wooden buildings in a clearing, deep out of sight of the road above. A large white Pyrenean mountain dog appeared and loped gently towards us. A heartbeat-skip at his size was quickly quelled by his demeanour.

'He's fine,' Adi said, greeting him. 'Just a big chilled hippy dog, aren't you?'

A small group of friendly people welcomed us, glasses of cold water appearing as if by magic. One man showed us where we could pitch in a broad, gently sloping wood pasture, with holm oak and other small trees unfamiliar to us. The campsite wasn't actually open yet, but there was a Dutch girl here as well, in a campervan tucked into a corner of the woodland. As the camping showerblock wasn't yet open for the season we got to use the collective's showers and toilets. Hot, steamy water, with TAPS! I turned them on and off, squeaking with excitement, and ran in and out of the little washrooms, which also had TAPS! And then I had a shower so long I almost felt guilty. Sloughing off all that sweat and road dust: blissful.

After dinner – cooked on a huge flat rock under holm oaks – we joined the group sitting around tables in a grove near the farmhouse. Someone had put on some mellow tunes. We talked mainly with the first man who'd welcomed us, Ed, whose name sounded much less English when he said it. His English was slightly better than my French, so we got on okay in a mixture of both languages. The collective farmed sheep, goats and cattle, and had moved here five years ago from an Alpine farm at 1000 metres.

'The winters were too hard,' he explained. 'Here, the work is still hard but we can manage.'

His lovely daughter hopped in and out of the conversation from behind his back, dressed as a pirate.

Fell asleep to the sound of crickets, music and the sleepy chime of sheep bells. I woke in the middle of the night and went for a moonlit walk among mooncast shadows, tiny lights down in the plain winking through the trees.

CHAPTER TWENTY-TWO

To Olargues

S heep bells woke me. It was one of those gorgeous mornings, with the sort of happy-buzz you wake with when a fractious day before somehow ended in pleasure and beauty. Adi cooked potato cakes (using the very end of the flour at last) while I collapsed the tent. Sheep grazed in the wood pasture around us, the bells that some of them wore ringing as they butted each other and munched.

As we ate a girl on a bicycle appeared from the direction of the house. She hopped off, opened the field gate into the wood and came in, whistling and calling, 'Allez! Venez!' The sheep appeared to ignore her entirely but slowly coalesced into mini-herds, following the lead of the three or four chief sheep wearing the bells. When the chiefs decided it was time, the whole herd made for the girl, tearing mouthfuls of grass as they trotted. She grabbed her bike and cycled back the way she'd come with forty sheep clanking in pursuit. I've had less charming awakenings.

That morning was one of the most magical. We were on tiny lanes, no cars, no bicycles, lanes maybe that no-one travels on unless they live there. Overcast skies with a bit of a breeze, perfect for cycling. We wiggled along, taking a circuitous route to avoid losing too much height, dropping a little and climbing again, mostly staying on the tree line. We weaved between trees and meadows, past brown goats sunbathing in thick pillows of flower-strewn grass. Stunning views of hidden valleys lay around each twist of the road. Trees and flowers at this altitude were similar to home. Swathes of oak. Sweet chestnut. One whole slope of cherry, with ash down in the flushes by the stream. Elder and dog rose amongst the cherry. Petite black butterflies and enormous pink hummingbees flickered up from the flowers in the verge at our slow approach. We rounded bends where yet another, different yet still entirely lovely green view tumbled away below us. We dropped down to a river valley and climbed our way slowly out of it, surprising a gang of workmen pouring gravel on the road. After more than an hour of the road to ourselves we met two motorists, one of whom gave us a nod and a smile and from the other, my favourite seal of approval: the silent, solemn thumbs-up. Respect.

We cycled over our highest pass yet, over 700 metres. Our lane joined one of the main routes over the Montagne Noir, and we stopped shortly after for lunch in Rieussec, possibly the only village in France without a boulangerie or a bar-tabac. Lizards, quicksilver green, scuttled on the fountain as we ate the end of yesterday's baguette and cheese.

Another climb up over a pass and then we began a long drop down. We paused for a moment to take photos. As we stood and admired the view - rumpled spurs of forested hills disappearing into the distance - a cyclist appeared coming up the hill, wearing shrink-to fit lycra. As he passed he gave us the filthiest look in which disbelief and contempt were perfectly balanced. My sandals got a particularly nasty stare. Yes, Mr You Who Think You Are A Proper Cyclist: small women in sandals on big laden bikes can cycle up the same hills as you can. HAH.

But he was an anomaly. A couple of minutes later we got a cheery thumbs up and big grins from a man and woman in a campervan chugging up the hill. We went down, and down, and down. When it came to descents I was normally a big girly wuss but here there were no tight bends to frighten me. Twenty minutes without touching the pedals! It was our first really long descent since Provence, and it was just glorious.

Pity it had to end in St-Pons-de-Thomières. Nothing wrong with it, just nothing particularly right either. The market had just ended and the last few stallholders were clearing up. As we sipped tea and coffee we had to listen to a large, extremely angry woman shouting at her very skinny, silent husband as they packed away.

We rode east into a breeze (naturally) along an off-road route. The going was easy on a hard track topped with fine gravel, with only a couple of surprising inclines. It followed an old railway route for the most part and hugged the north bank of the river. A few miles before we reached it we caught glimpses of our destination, Olargues, showing itself for tantalising moments. This is one of the things I love about cycling, the way landmarks reveal themselves gradually. We crossed the river a couple of miles before we reached the village. It looked as lovely as promised in the guide books, perched picturesquely and built of honeyed stone, glowing warmly in the sun that had decided to come out and play again. To complete the picture-postcard effect the track brought us in over the thirteenth century Devil's Bridge.

We decided instantly to stay for two nights and to have a café and planning day. After all, it had been a whole two days since we'd had a two-nighter. But there was a more serious reason.

'My knee's hurting,' Adi had said earlier, as we cycled along the old railway track.

It had a long history, that knee, and had been operated on four years before to sort out the anterior cruciate ligament. Adi was careful with it, but crawling around in the tent that morning he'd said 'Ouch'.

'Couple of nights should help it out,' he said hopefully, as I came out of tourist information with a map of the town and directions to the campsite.

'Bit of rest for the old man.'

'That's it,' he agreed.

'The nice woman said there's a centre where we can use the internet. We could have a session and find out about more campsite options to the north.'

You've got to love a place where the campsite manager welcomes you with a bag of cherries. It was a charming municipal site, tucked into a nook between the perched town and the river, run by a lovely man and a stern terrier who oomphed quietly at us as we went up to the office. He gave us a dirty look when we emerged after looking over the showerblock. I know where you've been, he seemed to say. Don't think I don't have my eye on you, because I do.

After the routine – ant inspection, pitch selection, tent erection, showers, the placement of all those things that make our pitch our home – we explored the village. Olargues is perched above the River Jaur, at the southern end of the Massif Central and the northern extremity of what's understood as southern France. The whole village was clustered around the bell tower, which was once the old castle keep. Marble-fronted shops with overhanging upper stories almost touched each other across narrow cobbled streets. Cats watched us climbing up through covered passageways towards the bell tower. From the top of the village we could see olive groves and vineyards amongst the cherry and sweet chestnut woods on the hill slopes.

We found a well-stocked little shop and had a drink at a bar before dinner, where we realised to our dismay that everyone sitting outside was English. A single man was reading David Lodge by himself. We left quickly, for an early dinner for once. Over a pudding of cherries and chocolate we pored over maps and guide books.

'How's the knee?' I asked as we snuggled down. Adi doesn't complain, you have to ask him.

'It's there.'

Ominous.

CHAPTER TWENTY-THREE

Olargues

I didn't mind having a day off. We'd had three good days, making some decent (I thought) distances. We were in mountains again, in scenery that gladdens both of our hearts.

We woke to calls of blackbirds, hoopoes and distant cuckoos. The croissant and baguette ranked middling to good, and the showers were excellent. I indulged in an extensive moisturising session in an attempt to use up some of varied goops I had brought with me. I had been carting around eye cream, two face moisturisers, hand cream, foot cream, body moisturiser and aftersun. One face moisturiser and a good aftersun would probably have sufficed. I lathered myself in creams and went to join Adi.

We spent an hour on the computer in the community centre, searching for campsites to the northwest and marking them on the map. We surprised ourselves by being almost in one mind about where we wanted to go. On account of the Old Man Knee, we decided to go for an easy day on the track west, back through St-Pons, through a town called Mazamet and then north up into the hills, the western end of the Monts de Lacaune.

We put the map away and went for a more thorough mooch. Olargues was beautiful: lots of delicate, friendly little cats and tiny streets that wound up and down, reminding me of Robin Hood's Bay again. Amazing views from the bell tower to the mountains all around: jagged, wooded, clouds snagging on their crests. Back to the tent for another map-marking session and discussion, tea and coffee and half a baguette with goat's cheese.

I sorted out the accumulation of tourist bumph that we were carrying between us, noted interesting details in the back of my diary, then discarded the booklets and leaflets. I'd been carrying about a kilo in paper. A thunderstorm rolled in just after dinner, so we ate our cherries and chocolate in the awning of the tent, peeking out through a gap in the flap, watching the sheet lightning and counting the seconds between the rolls of thunder.

We were easy, relaxed. We talked about places we'd seen so far, where we'd like to go back to. We both loved Apt and Forcalquier. I favoured Beaumont-de-Pertuis, Gordes got a big thumbs up, and St-Rémy came out on top. Adi would have liked to stay longer in Saintes-Maries-de-la-Mer, at a different time of the year. I said he could keep it. Le Grau? Possibly.

'I liked the bar,' I said.

'You liked the waiter.'

Comfortable pause.

'How's the knee feeling?'

A twist of his mouth. 'Okay. I think.'

Canals, Hills and Knees: Olargues to Figeac

CHAPTER TWENTY-FOUR

To Mazamet

Naturally, the breeze that had been in our faces all the way as we cycled east had swung 180°, clearly in love with us and loathe to leave us cycling un-breezed for even a couple of minutes.

'I didn't say anything,' said Adi, when I caught him looking at the tree-tops dancing by the river as we ate breakfast.

I've never minded linear walks and rides, seeing views from the opposite direction and perspective. Craggy hills and mountains rose up behind lower, wooded slopes as we pedalled back to St-Pons. We spotted a pair of Bonelli's eagles soaring, plunging, levelling, plunging again. Later, during a café stop on the bike track near Courris, we saw three peregrine falcons jousting and mock-passing in the sky above.

The tunnel through the col west of St-Pons was unnerving. 810 metres doesn't sound very long, but that point where the light behind is very small and distant and the light ahead is non-existent seemed to last for a very long time. Motion-sensored lights lit up as we passed through it. As a fully paid up member of the let's-live-sustainably-on-this-planet-club, I fully approve of energy-saving lights like this, but it's got to be faced: it's really creepy. I pedalled so fast it felt as if an evil pool of light was chasing us.

The valley on the western side broadened. Folded wooded hillside with rounded summit was followed by folded wooded hillside. For only the second time since Wales, we saw cows, black and white milch cows. I had to take a photo. But that was as exciting as it got. As with the Canal du Midi, you don't get to go through the villages unless you get off the track; there were only two, and we missed both.

The last ten kilometres of the track to Mazamet took us right alongside the main road, fast and noisy. Mazamet itself seemed to be a gritty, functional sort of town. Also a noisy town. In our spin to the town centre everyone – cars, bikes, scooters - seemed to be faster, noisier, more abrupt than anywhere we'd been so far. Lots of beeping. (Not at us though.) Adi and I had a slightly fractious exchange on the narrow pavement of a street corner as we looked at the Rough Guide's map.

Adi: 'I have to look at the map and the street signs to work out where we are.' With much exasperation.

Me: 'Could you please do it –' (pause while I shifted my bike out of the way of an approaching pushchair) '– somewhere a bit more pretty and spacious, like at that town square just up there?' With equal exasperation.

The campsite, a mile or so from the centre, was the most municipal of municipals, with no atmosphere and a coded gate. This troubled us. Was Mazamet a hot-bed of camp-equipment thieves? It was near the edge of the town, set back from one of the main arterial roads in from the east. But on the plus side, the pitches were of grass and soil instead of bare, baked ground, and the tent pegs went in without the painful pushing and wiggling using the sole of my sandal (assisted with foot in the sandal if Adi wasn't looking. Yes, those bent pegs were my fault.) But I could still hear cicadas calling, and the showers were hot and powerful.

When I emerged from mine Adi, unusually, hadn't started on dinner.

'We're eating out. Put your glad rags on.'

A chance to wear the glad rags! Among the completely unnecessary items of off-bike clothing I'd brought were a pair of black linen trousers, which I'd worn exactly no times at all. I put them on and they promptly slid down off my hips.

'Look! Look!' I showed Adi delightedly.

Now, I know that losing weight is not the aim of the cycle tourer. Obsessing about weight is bad, everyone, bad. But I defy anyone, man or woman, not to do a happy little dance when they discover that, while dining amply on wine, croissants and chocolate as well as good healthy stuff, some excess poundage has magically sloughed away.

'Now we've just got to make you decent for the night,' said Adi when I'd finished the dance.

I was glad I'd also brought another unsuitable and unnecessary item of clothing, a favourite loose, linen top. No-one who saw me would have guessed that underneath it my trousers were held up with a bungee.

Adi's nose for somewhere good to eat is rarely wrong. He led me to a tiny, unprepossessing pizzeria, *Le Main á la Pâte* down the street from us. I was doubtful, but we went in off the noisy street and it was a different world, clean and cheerful and crowded with people of all ages, noisy with cheerful chatter. Two pizzas, a big salad, two puddings and half a litre of wine for €34. We waddled back up the street and in through the coded gate in great good cheer.

Pizza and cicadas. You can be happy anywhere, I thought profoundly as I dropped off, if you have had a good pizza and if cicadas are singing you to sleep.

CHAPTER TWENTY-FIVE

To Castres

Morning brought bad news from The Knee, which had achieved title-case status during the night. Adi had consumed the strongest painkillers he had with him but they were barely touching the pain and inflammation. He needed something stronger, or The Knee needed time to recover, or this wouldn't be a cycle tour any more. It would be a long one-legged pedal to St Malo, and time was wriggling away from us.

'I don't want to force it,' he said, miserably.

We took out the map and forced ourselves to look away from the tentative route we'd marked north through the hills. The cycle track that had led us to Mazamet continued along the abandoned railway track up through the towns of Castres and Albi.

'Albi has "the biggest brick-built cathedral in the world",' I read from the Rough Guide. 'And Castres has markets four days a week.'

'Railway tracks have steady gradients,' Adi said hopefully.

We decided to take a couple of very short, easy days and to enjoy Castres and Albi.

'If it's okay, then we can head up to the north through the Massif Central from Albi, taking the easiest roads possible all the time.'

'And if it isn't…' Adi looked really worried.

'Then we'll work something out.'

Now that we had an enemy in the form of The Knee I stopped getting irritable about the distances we cycled daily. It brought it home to me that this was about enjoying the country safely and happily. The wanderlust and fidgetiness would never leave me, but the main thing was letting us both cycle at a pace we could enjoy.

Markets were one of our favourite things about France. Back at home in North Wales, there's a great weekend festival of food in the autumn, called Conwy Feast. Conwy's lovely walled inner town and castle host stalls and marquees bulging with food and flowing with drink, with local and Welsh and quirky food produce, anything as long as it's interesting, local, or has some sort of feel-good foodie hook. It's a wonderful idea, and crowds flock to it. Here, almost every French town manages the equivalent at least once a week.

We wheeled out early, through the middle of Mazamet and out the other side where Adi had a most uncharacteristic navigation fail, bringing us onto the speedy D12 rather than the quieter D60 as he'd intended.

'I wouldn't have known. You didn't have to confess,' I said when he apologized, holding the map up to show me where we were.

He grinned. 'Happy to stay on it?'

We stayed on it; it was the sort of road classification I wouldn't have dared cycle on in the UK but it wasn't too busy. France's population is almost the same as the UK's but is spread across three times the land-area. This was wonderfully reflected in density of traffic on the roads. Even the busiest we had encountered were never as clogged as at home, and I was usually perfectly happy to cycle along the D-roads. Here there was a cycle verge of varying but usually comfortable width, and at one point I saw a sign from a side road indicating that it was part of a signed vélo route for Tarn. We made it to the centre of Castres, about fourteen miles, in just over an hour. Which, we decided, wasn't too bad for a couple on laden bikes, one of whom had a dodgy knee.

Castres charmed us from the start, a busy town, pretty but functional, with lovely old wooden-balconied houses lining the river Agout and squares opening out of narrow streets. We arrived just as the market was winding down, just in time for me to buy a sweet treat in celebration of my vanished hip-flesh. Not too sweet, yellowish and melt in the mouth buttery-moist, a bit like a holey brioche with chunks of dark bitter chocolate. Heaven.

'That looks evil.' Adi had bought sensible vegetables for the night's dinner, found the tourist office and acquired a map of the town, outskirts and campsite location while I was drooling around patisserie stalls.

'I did buy peaches as well,' I showed him. They were still quite hard but delicious. Hard peaches at home are always tasteless.

We only spent one day in Castres but it seemed much longer. Before we headed to the campsite we'd already had two tea stops (no teapots) and had wandered the back streets a little, finding gorgeous hotels we promised ourselves we'd come back to when we were old and rich and not able to cycle with panniers, if that day ever came. We wouldn't even have to be that rich. €60 for a double room in a house that used to be a town mansion for a rich merchant family! We found calm ornamental gardens beside the old Bishop's Palace, which housed the Musée Goya, the Hôtel de Ville and the gendarmerie, all tall and clean-lined buildings built in a lovely, light stone, surrounding a cool courtyard.

Adi declared the town tourist map to be rubbish, put it away and followed his nose to the campsite instead: along a small river, through a wood, through a park, along a cycle track then a footpath that, from the looks a group of chatting women gave us, might not be a cycle track anymore, to, finally, a bridge. With steps up to it. Giggling, we heaved the bikes up, and very carefully lifted them down the other side. Through more trees into a wide green space, past a couple of mansions and finally to the campsite, set in the middle of an enormous municipal leisure park. Of the two mansions we'd passed, one housed one of Castres's museums and the other was for running residential courses.

The usual picking of the perfect pitch ensued, with ant-free spots and strategic trees for the hanging out of the rinsed out shorts and t-shirts. It was eerily quiet, just a handful of retirees in caravans and motorhomes, until a few youth leaders turned up with a load of teenagers.

Another Adi Special for dinner, with savoury potatoes accompanied by marinated vegetables, tomatoes, onions, garlic, red peppers, mushrooms and petit pois. Afterwards, we walked out into the park. There were archery butts, a football field, crazy golf and huge open areas for any sort of ball kicking and throwing. We tested the swings and the scattered outdoor gym equipment - parallel bars, slalom, japanese balancing cubes. We tested everything as the light faded out of the evening, the swifts having their last scream of barrelling hooliganism and the bats just starting to come out. Best of all was an enormous double pyracord. From two tall central poles 12 metres high hung thick flexible ropes, attached to the ground to form two cone-shaped spider webs, attached to each other by tube-shaped web of cord. It took us twenty minutes to get from one side to the other. Neither of us has a good head for heights at the best of times, but it's wonderful what a warm dusk, a beakerful of the warm south and a sign saying 'Seulement pour des enfants' can do.

'How's The Knee?' I asked.

He grimaced. After a day on the flat. Not good.

As evening began to darken, we settled down in little baskets eight metres above the ground and wondered what to do.

'You need your knees when cycling. There really isn't any getting around that,' said Adi.

It's horrible when you're the one with the problem. It's okay if you're alone. You struggle on, or you change your plans. With a companion you feel bad for the effect on the other person's plans. I knew this, and also knew that saying it didn't matter wasn't making him feel any better. I said it anyway.

We watched the bats, whirring and feeding busily.

'Is there a train station in Albi?' I asked.

'Think so.'

We perched and thought. Albi was thirty miles away along a cycle track, level and easy going.

'Let's just get there tomorrow, taking it really steady, and have a nice day exploring. Then the next morning we'll find a doctor, get you some proper anti-inflammatories. Then we'll pick somewhere pretty four days' ride north, take a train there and have a rest for four days. I can go out on day rides; you can rest The Knee. Let the drugs kick in and recover, then we'll carry on.'

Adi cheered up a bit and we clambered slowly down and back to the tent for pudding. I was surprisingly happy. I just hate uncertainty, I decided. Strange how it took forty years for me to work that out. Curled up in my sleeping bag I wrote up my diary, listening with a sort of indulgent affection to the teenagers, who'd been really quiet earlier, now lustily singing 'Olé olé olé olé''. Ten minutes later I wished they'd shut up. I could hear some other adults getting irate, just as I wondered if I'd better just take out something to read. The last thing I remember was checking the guidebook. We would have a lovely time in – that was it – Figeac.

CHAPTER TWENTY-SIX

To Albi

Next morning was a bit of a low for both of us. Despite having a plan to cope with The Knee, Adi was still really worried about it. It was a Sunday, so I spent quarter of an hour searching Castres for the one open boulangerie. I found it by accosting a man with three baguettes protruding from his rucksack. He didn't give me directions; he took me by the arm and led me right to the door. Lovely man.

The cycle from Castres was easy but wet and cold. The weather had found us again. On the positive side, for once we were going into Sunday and Monday, the traditional shopkeepers' days off, with plenty of food in our panniers, thanks to Castres's wonderful market. The baguettes I'd eventually found ranked high in the charts.

The bike track surface became slow and draggy in the rain, but it ran through gentle, green farming country, and was punctuated with water points, picnic benches, and small, neat signs detailing everything anyone could wish to know about the countryside, the railway track, the animals and plants. The wildlife count included two black kites and a red squirrel. No day can be a bad day with a red squirrel in it.

Sunday afternoon isn't the best time to arrive in a town best known for its cathedral. Albi's cathedral of Saint Cecile was stuffed with tourists. I lasted two minutes. Adi followed me out into the sun, back to the bikes waiting patiently by a bench.

'Let's give it a try in the morning,' he suggested. 'It is amazing.'

It was. The square outside the cathedral was enormous, so broad that the huge cathedral looked rather squat until you noticed how tiny the human figures teeming around its doors were.

I love French tourist information. A helpful young man gave us the addresses of two general practice surgeries, marking both of them on a map for us with neat red crosses. He added the locations of five pharmacies with green crosses. 'In case,' he said, looking concerned. 'It will be the Monday tomorrow.' He also marked on the map exactly where to find the only grocery shop near Albi's centre that would be open on Sunday and Monday, and wrote down the opening times neatly in the margin of the map. He was a gem.

The campsite was a shock. It was raining again - we couldn't complain, we hadn't seen rain for days - and the resigned cheerfulness we'd worked ourselves into seeped away with the rainwater down the drains. Adi yelped angrily when a sudden nasty hill up to the campsite took The Knee by surprise. The vestiges of good cheer abandoned us altogether when the receptionist told us how much a pitch would cost.

'Twenty-four bloody euro!' I hissed as we followed the man on his little buggy as he led us to our pitch.

'I want to choose my own bloody pitch,' muttered Adi.

If it hadn't been raining, and The Knee had been happy, we'd have left. This price was half as much again as the second most expensive campsite we'd stayed at. But we were trapped. And, despite ourselves, fascinated. Someone had had a vision, and that vision was of grizzly bears stalking the green spaces of Albi. Shiny retro campervans, all rounded corners and gleaming chrome, squatted invitingly under what looked like baby sequoias. Luxury log cabins stood on stilts. 'Don't feed the bears' signs bore great claw marks.

'Fecking mad house. Fecking *expensive* madhouse.'

The campsite man found a couple of spots. He was about to drive away in the buggy when something seemed to occur to him.

'Alors.' He took us to another pitch slightly upslope and pointed to the log cabin on stilts next to it. 'There's no one in there tonight. If you stay here, maybe you can cook, you can sit underneath out of the rain.'

I forgave him everything. Fantastic showers helped - they shot to number one in our chart. And there was yummy dinner and chocolate. By the time we went to bed, having wandered around the campsite and checked the essentials (Dutch campervan) a breeze had picked up and the tent was drying out. As I went to sleep, for the first time I couldn't hear birdsong, frogs, cicadas or crickets. Just traffic. But on the other hand, Albi was much more lovely than expected, in brick and stone and wood. And tomorrow we would do something about our problem.

CHAPTER TWENTY-SEVEN

To Figeac

I get nervous in many, many situations, and top of the list must be explaining a medical condition in a second language. After we'd eaten and packed everything into the panniers, I sat under the cabin on stilts with a phrasebook and notebook and muttered to myself, in approximate French, all the questions a doctor examining a knee might ask. I translated Adi's medical history and muttered it over and over. I muttered and muttered until Adi said 'People are looking.'

We found the first of the surgeries the lovely young man at the tourist office had marked easily enough, in a residential area on the edge of a square lined with solicitors' offices. A young woman welcomed us and listened attentively to my explanation. She looked concerned when I explained that we were travelling onwards.

'Ah – there may be a wait.' I felt my face fall as I waited for her to say three days, four days. 'Could you wait for one hour?'

In the waiting room we grinned at each other after 'Bonjour-ing' to the other patients.

'One hour. I love this country,' said Adi.

My nerves increased as we waited. We could see the doctor, tall and rake thin, as he popped out from his consulting room to call each patient in with a bark. He looked like a mobile ironing board. My translation-anticipation peaked when he popped out and briskly called out Adi's name. He opened the door and ushered us in, waving us to the seats.

Then he sat down behind his desk and smiled the loveliest smile, and every tense, anxious muscle in my body relaxed. Sometimes you just know when someone is going to turn out to be lovely, and the Albi doctor was. I managed to communicated the necessary without too much garbled nonsense. He lay Adi down and asked questions and I managed to convey the answers. He was all smiles and politenesses. He wrote a prescription for some strong anti-inflammatories. He questioned us about how far we were going, approved our plan to rest for a few days, and gave Adi some advice for cooling down The Knee after cycling. He saw us out with great courtesy and a bow to me. 'Merci pour la traduction. Très bonne!' I was glowing.

'Paying the actual doctor feels a bit odd, doesn't it?' Adi remarked when we were out on the street. 'As if he's some under-the-counter struck-off person who does gunshot wounds for gangs.'

Relaxation flooded me. We tracked down a pharmacy - it being Monday the first open one we found was third on the Lovely Young Man's list - and then went to book train tickets. We had until three o'clock before our train left for Figeac, so we got in some more touristy activity.

The cathedral was much quieter this morning. I sat and gazed up at the biblical scenes on the ceiling and listened to the headphones on the self-guided tour. We locked the bikes up and found a walkway that overlooked the river Tarn on one side and the gardens of the Bishop's Palace on the other. A couple of gardeners worked far below, apparently trimming the shrubs by hand, leaf by leaf. Like the cathedral, the Bishop's Palace and the Gardens' walls were of a pinkish brick, bright in the sun. Close to the river, houses in scarlet brick and age-darkened wood leant across to meet each other.

And the friendliness! Three times people approached us to ask us if they could help, having noticed us looking at street signs. The sun shone and the river shone right back at it. It was impossible not to be cheerful. We had an armoury of drugs to sort the offending knee out and we were going to have a rest in a pretty place. All was good.

Bike and train travel in France is a wonderful thing. Even our one-carriage bucket to Rodez was equipped with a row of hanging bike racks. We had to eject a very cool young man and his laptop from underneath them. Crossing the Tarn we could see back over the Bishop's Gardens and Palace, warm in the afternoon sun, with the cathedral's enormous bell tower far above.

At the first stop a madman got on with a bar stool, which he placed on the doorway and sat on with a slight hurrumph. At the next stop he was joined by a man with a beer can. They swayed alarmingly with the train but never toppled. It was compulsive viewing, until Adi nudged me.

'You're staring. Look out of the window.'

It felt odd to be travelling at this speed after weeks of 10 miles an hour. Wheat and potatoes and ploughed fields flashed by. Copses of trees. Cows. It looked similar to parts of England, only much more wooded and with different vernacular architecture. The train rolled over a sudden, deeply-folded river valley and returned to the gently rippling plateau.

I checked the tickets - I always fear they'll evaporate in my pocket - and noticed that our second train, from Rodez to Figeac, was actually a bus. I had missed this entirely, though it clearly said 'autocar' on the ticket. A bloody bus. I panicked.

'They won't let us on with bikes,' I said to Adi. Unable to calm me down, he did the next best thing and started to wind me up instead.

'They'll look at us and shake their fingers at us. We'll be stuck in Rodez forever. FOREVER.'

I was bouncing with anxiety by the time we arrived. The receptionist in the ticket office didn't help, pulling a doubtful face when I explained we had bikes.

'Ask the driver,' she said. Feeling slightly sick, I mentally rehearsed arguments over a cup of tea in the station café. The heavens opened. Adi was still in tease-the-Madigan mode.

'Atmosphere. There'll be lightning next and the only place to stay will be the creepy castle on the hill.'

Glaring out of the window I spotted a bunch of likely looking coaches. Heedless of the downpour, I sprinted across and explained breathlessly to an impassive driver that we had 'des velos'. He shrugged gallicly.

'Bien sûr.' He opened the luggage compartment and waved at the vast space inside. I nearly kissed his feet.

Adi and I sat on the back seat of the massive, shiny bus, with its comfy seats and clean dark blue curtains.

There were five people onboard including the driver and us.

The scenery continued to be lovely, though glistening through rain now. Signs welcomed us to the Lot Département. 'Trés nature. Trés patrimoine. Trés Lot.' Dreadful regional slogans were clearly not the preserve of the UK and Ireland. In the nineties, Irish Rail's slogan 'We Go Further To Get You There' was a treasured, unintentionally literal strapline.

Figeac disappointed at first sight. I'd been expecting something like a Provençal perched village. Instead it was in a valley, something I ought to have expected as I knew from reading that the river Célé flowed through the town. Rivers do not flow through perched villages. The bus stopped at the train station and we were greeted by a pile of dog poo and a drunk who came over asking us where we wanted to go and saying he'd show us the campsite. My stomach turned. He was just like those horrible kids who spot backpackers in Lisdoonvarna during the matchmaking festival and rush up saying 'I'll show ya a grand campsite, c'mon c'mon, this way' and then expect a fiver for dancing along beside you irritating you along a path you were perfectly capable of taking all by yourself. We fixed our panniers on at double speed and cycled away quickly away from him.

The campsite was a mile or so out of the town along the river, past a small water sports and recreation park on the banks of a quiet backwater. My heart sank at the sight of expensive-looking boats; it looked as if another budget-smashing campsite awaited us. We were relieved to find it only moderately pricey. €16.60 per night was a great improvement on the Albi experience.

For the third night running, it was raining as we pitched up. It had been torrential the night before, waking me in the small hours with maniacal drumming on the tent which had done nothing for my pre-translation nerves. We'd managed to dry the tent's outer skin before we left Albi, but inner was still slightly damp, and there was a faint musty smell.

I slumped after we'd pitched up. It was partly translation tiredness; I'd had to concentrate hard with the doctor, and to a lesser extent with the pharmacist and the various staff at train stations throughout the day. And I was disappointed in Figeac. But on the positive side, we had pitched in a nice spot close to the river, and when I'd finished showering the rain had stopped. We hadn't bought enough dinner ingredients, so we grabbed the bikes and walked towards the back gate of the campsite, along a path by the edge of the backwater. And just by the edge of the path, before we'd even mounted our bikes, was a water vole! It flattened itself into the grass when we stopped to stare in delighted disbelief, then got up cautiously and made its way, unhurried but with purpose, towards the water. While I was staring at it, Adi called softly and pointed: there was an otter swimming under the branches on the far bank. A moment later we heard two large splashes, another otter jumping.

'That's totally made my day,' Adi said.

Much happier, we pedalled in. It was as if the water vole and the otters had flicked a switch. Figeac suddenly glowed with loveliness. Buildings of warm pinkish sandstone and light limestone gleamed cheerfully in the wet. We spun around the open-sided market hall in the central square, surrounded by pretty narrow streets and tall buildings with wooden, covered balconies four and five stories above.

I loved this time of day. When we had found our place for the night, had showered, when our pitch and tent was laid out with those little things that give us comfort and made it ours - before or after dinner, depending upon how hungry we were, we'd take the bikes out and ride around the village. My bike loved it too, this evening cycle; I could tell. Free of the panniers, the front wheel turned lightly, responsively. By this time my bike handling skills had improved simply because of time spent in the saddle, and I loved pedalling gently through narrow streets, nosing down alleys, slowing down to look in café windows, checking the opening times of the boulangerie, turning slow circles in narrow lanes. No rushing, just a slow, easeful pleasure in being on the bike. Every day I went through some sort of a challenge, whether physical (hills) or mental (comparisonitis; curbing my impatience) but these moments at day's end, riding slowly around streets, around new corners, finding things to point out to each other - cats, dogs, pubs - were full of a quiet delight.

We found a take-away pizzeria and perched on high stools as they we waited for them, leafing through the regional French newspaper. The weather forecast made depressing reading so we moved on to articles on cycling. It's great when a piece is on a topic you partly understand; it helps to deduce the meanings of words and phrases.

We ate the pizzas sitting on the steps of the market hall in Place Carnot, the central square. Back at the tent, darkness had fallen by ten thirty. The summer solstice was only ten days away.

Figeac Interlude

B ut we know we're staying for four nights.'
       'I know, but just in case.'

I'd woken late. Adi had already arrived back with the baguette and croissants (excellent: the croissants made it into the top five on the league table) and we were checking how much cash we had. Plenty to pay the campsite for the four nights we intended to stay but Adi insisted on only booking one day at a time. I let it go; there were more worthy matters to get upset about.

Like rain! I stayed in the inner, refusing to go out, while Adi passed me tea and croissants and hunks of fresh bread, perched on a pannier just outside in the awning. I stayed in the inner because there wasn't a dry surface to sit on. The footprint was damp. The grass was wet from the night's downpour. We needed heat or wind and we had neither.

On the plus side, it wasn't actually raining just then. I forced myself out for the second cup of tea, acknowledging that I was being melodramatic, but I'd reached some sort of tipping point. I didn't want to get wet whichever way I moved. I didn't want my knees to get damp through kneeling on the awning floor to reach for my nice dry trainers. I didn't want my nice dry trainers to get damp by walking through wet grass to the toilet. Wet wet wet. It was the south of bloody France in June.

'It's going to improve, then deteriorate again.' Adi had found a forecast. He shrugged. 'Let's enjoy this while we can. We'll just make sure that we get into town before the next shower.'

Half an hour later we were sitting in a café, dripping onto it's dry wooden floor, sodden. I had no dry clothes left to wear, nothing. We chinked our tea cup and coffee cup together.

'To good timing.'

I came across the word 'dunderdash' years ago in a Joyce Stranger novel. It's always stayed with me; it captures to perfection the hammering, windless, rain-god-wielding-a-giant-showerhead-on-full-power nature of the quintessential rainstorm. We had been caught in a dunderdash. It had poured on us as if it was personal. We smiled ruefully. There was nothing else to be done. We stretched out the tea and coffee and slowly dried.

You could do an awful lot worse than Figeac for an unplanned, enforced rest. We managed to while away five hours, dodging showers, following a heritage trail, drinking tea. We bumped into a retired English couple who'd been living in the Midi-Pyrenees southwest of Toulouse for six years now. They loved it. They were just beginning to explore beyond their immediate region. They said you needed some sort of an income to live here; they'd known a few couples, early retirees, who sold their houses in Putney or wherever, came out and bought lovely old farmhouses with their capital, but many of them had been forced to move back to England by falling interest rates and dwindling capital.

'If you can earn, and you don't have your heart set on an old house in the country, it's great,' said the woman. 'Do it!' They had both travelled when young, she had worked in France for a long time, and they'd renovated a house in Devon when they were younger, had raised and sent their children off on their own travels.

'We didn't have any real roots in England any more, except childhood memories,' she said, 'and that country's gone now, they do things differently there.'

A display in the tourist office informed us that we were on the eastern edge of Natural Park of the Causses de Quercy. Booklets were available at reception, said a sign. I asked for them. 'What natural park?' asked the woman on duty. A colleague looked over her shoulder and took over. I came away laden with booklets on the geology, wildlife and built heritage. It was the best guide to the landscape and wildlife of the natural parks we'd come across yet.

Hardly a day went by without our seeing a bird or a mammal we'd never see at home, or at least not in such abundance, but generally it had been difficult to find information on wildlife in the tourist offices. That being said, I don't know where I'd find all the information on natural parks and landscape and wildlife conservation in the UK if I didn't work in the sector. All the literature wildlife organisations produce in the hope of reaching the general public struggles to get noticed amongst the mountains of bumph for 'attractions' (horrible word). Theme parks, historic buildings, activity centres, any thing that you pay money to get in.

'The whole region is one of the least light-polluted areas in the country,' I informed Adi. 'Very popular with astronomers.'

'When the skies are clear, I presume. Clear of clouds, d'you hear?' He directed this last upwards.

'The region we'll be cycling through in a few days is made up almost entirely of limestone plateaus cut by the rivers Célé, Lot and Dordogne,' I went on. 'An arid, sheep-inhabited region of dry stone walls, it says.'

'Arid?'

We'd found a pub called the Kheops, with lots of old ads for Jameson whiskey and pennants with the rugby insignia of Munster and Leinster as well as Toulouse and Marseille. It was just around corner from the Champollion Museum. Champollion, a son of Figeac, began the decoding of the Rosetta Stone. Figeac can't be accused of going over the top to broadcast this fact. Apart from the museum, all we could find was the larger-than-life reproduction of the Rosetta Stone that formed the floor of a tiny square next to it, and a very modest amount of stylish Egyptian tat on sale in a couple of shops.

The pub was a lovely, dark welcoming place, only marred by being the twentieth eating or drinking establishment where we'd heard Gimme Gimme Gimme by Abba. Radio stations seemed to play an awful lot of eighties English music. Campsite bars were particular offenders. I know there's wonderful French music out there, I listen to Cerys Matthews on Sunday mornings - why weren't we hearing it?

'Maybe they think it's what English tourists want,' Adi wondered.

Distressingly, Abba was followed by You're In The Army Now.

'I don't care if it's raining. Time to go.'

We dodged showers back to the tent and had enough time before the next downpour for a short wildlife mooch. The water vole was beside the track again, munching. I took two photos, in which you can make out a furry dark grey blob, before it scented me and trotted, unhurried, down to the water's edge. I watched for a while through the binoculars as it hunched round-backed and full-cheeked, eating grasses and leaves. No sign of otters.

Adi went into town to give us an hour or so alone. I read in the tent in the gathering gloaming, and chatted with some cycle tourers who'd arrived during the day. They were all English, touring in the region for a couple of weeks. I was slightly distracted during the conversation, my eyes straying to the little chairs they were sitting on. I wanted little chairs to sit on; perfect for an evening like this, when the ground was wet but it wasn't actually raining.

Just before it got completely dark I went for another wildlife mooch without much hope. I was scanning the path edge for the water vole when I disturbed a heron. I hadn't noticed him, standing on the bund that separated the backwater and the little island from the river proper. His clatter disturbed an otter, which swam silently away from the bund and disappeared under an overhanging bush about thirty yards away. I went to bed happy, falling asleep to the sound of the river and crickets.

W e've all experienced it. You struggle on at work, looking forward to your holiday. Your holiday comes and then your body pounces upon you. 'Hah!' it says. 'Now I've got your attention!'

I felt like that on the second rest day, when we made the daft decision to get on a bus to Cahors, which the Rough Guide raved about. I don't know what we were thinking. We fumed all the way - a good hour's journey - after paying €50 for our tickets. Why didn't we just get off? Because the bus driver had already printed the tickets. Why hadn't we asked the price first? Because we're dense. We cursed our reserve, in between dozing and grumbling to each other about our ailments. The Knee might be improving but we both seemed to have been afflicted with muggy headaches and I had an aching shoulder that wasn't going anywhere.

'I bet the bikes will be nicked,' I said. We'd left them locked to a tree in Figeac station's car park.

'This had better be worth it,' Adi said grimly as we alighted in Cahors. Not the most positive frame of mind in which to go exploring. I set off with him looking for things to complain about.

And find them we did! I was churlishly pleased to see that the market wasn't as good as the ones in Apt or Castres, that it seemed to be full of Americans making no effort to speak in French, that many of the stall holders seemed tourist-jaded and that the one at the dried fruit stall assumed that I was a rich American and tried to sell me three times as much dried mango as I wanted. I was headachey and cross enough to waggle a finger at him like the best French housewife. 'Non,' I said, severely, and made him take most of the mangoes back. If I'd been in a good mood I'd have been too polite to say anything. The weather provided plenty of grumble-fodder: the temperature plummeted and it started to rain. 'June, in the south of France, and we're cold,' we muttered to each other over and over.

But there's only so much wallowing in pleasurable disgruntlement that you can do before you start to cheer up in spite of yourself. The café we chose was cosy when the waiter pulled the clear screens down against the rain, and the hot chocolates he served us were very hot and very chocolatey. True, compared to some of the places we had seen Cahors wasn't spectacular, but if we'd come straight from Bangor we'd probably have been raving about it. The sun peeped out and the temperature lifted a smidgeon as we walked down to the riverside to see the bridge, the Pont Valentré, with the little carved devil clinging to the uppermost stone on a corner of the central tower. On the return bus ride we were in good enough humour to appreciate the prettiness of the valley as the road curled underneath the limestone cliffs. The Lot and Célé were full, swollen and brown; in river meadows, trees stood half-submerged where we suspected they should be enjoying a drought by now. And the bus journey gave me time to read uninterrupted - something that there wasn't a great deal of time to do with the daily business of cycling, searching for tourist offices and campsites, shopping for food and performing all the routines that camping and cycling demand.

'They haven't been nicked!'

'The day just gets better!'

I felt a pang of affection for our bikes, waiting patiently while we'd abandoned them. While Adi went for a coffee I took Bike for a spin up out of the back of the town in search of a different view. On it went, gently zigzagging up, high enough after half an hour to look back south over the town. High enough to see rain clouds bearing down on Figeac. Bike and me sped down in five wild minutes, reaching the square at the same time as the rain. It hammered. We treated ourselves to a risotto in the bar we'd sheltered in.

Rain stopped as we cycled back, a moody mist over the river, tree-tops eerily floating on the mist, apparently trunkless. The sky cleared, turning the night cold. Snuggly sleeping clothes, sleeping bags zipped right up. With silk linings. In, as I have mentioned before, June, in the south of France. But I didn't care about the cold. I could hear crickets, and the river.

Next day I called the curse down upon us. My spin to buy the croissants was achieved without any dodging of rain showers. By nine o'clock it still hadn't rained and the sun was coming out. By noon I was lying on our table cloth in the sunshine, sunbathing. Actually sunbathing! I read while Adi made a foray into town for some fruit and vegetables and came back and made the most delicious salad, with tomatoes, apricots, goat's cheese and an olive oil and balsamic vinegar dressing. We sat in sunshine, digesting. A tiny bead of sweat formed in the hollow of my throat. Bliss.

'You know, what would make this even more perfect would be the tiniest, teensiest bit of a breeze,' I said, as we watched a mallard duck escort four tiny ducklings, scraps of feathers with pink feet, across the riverside grass and into a sheltered corner of the backwater. Oh, foolish woman.

We left the topic of the weather and talked about our next trip.

'Two months again.'

'Definitely.'

'We'll get the train all the way to Marseille, and hop on the ferry to Corsica.'

'Yes,' I agreed happily.

'Two weeks, maybe three—'

'Two and a half.'

'Or three, and we'll get the ferry back as close as we can to the Italian border. We could work our way west inland of the coast, revisit the Luberon, perhaps Mont Ventoux this time.'

'Yes! Definitely the Gorges of Verdon.'

'Definitely. And across the Rhône towards the Cevennes, curl around into Haut Langeudoc...'

We carried on planning and watching the ducklings. Even with our disagreements about what cycle touring actually is, and the fact that we were taking an enforced break because of a dodgy knee, we were both certain as granite that we wanted to do this again. Despite our differences, we were loving the life, the freedom, the freshness, the views around each new bend.

But I should have known better than to speak about the weather. You should always make it clear that any comments about weather are just that - comments. Not suggestions, not complaints. Because there are weather demons, and they are bored and mischievous, and they are listening - always listening.

PART NINE

Limestone and Rivers: Figeac to Meyronne

CHAPTER TWENTY-NINE

To Cabreret

The Figeac campsite lay between the river and the GR65, which also forms part of the pilgrimage routes to both Santiago de Compostela in northwest Spain and to Rocamadour, not far north of here. We'd seen plenty of backpack-laden, wiry, earnest sorts walking along the lane. The couple of lads that we saw one night cycling through the main square, one with a tent on his rear rack and one with a crate of beer, might have been among their number. I rather hoped so. Even pilgrims have to take care of the essentials.

We surprised ourselves by getting away quite early. Our route to St-Cirq-Lapopie (a name I couldn't stop chanting to myself - a lovely set of syllables to get your mouth around) wouldn't involve any hills, so Adi's mind was at rest. He'd been taking good care of The Knee, walking, stretching it gently and putting his floppy Ortlieb waterskin full of chilled water on top of it. The pain had receded drastically and after three rest days on the trot he was as eager to be on the road as I was. The fine weather held and there was high cloud and warmth in the air as we rode away down the north bank of the Célé.

The road was easy and very quiet, following the looping river under cliffs and through meadows. We paused for a short wander in tiny, lovely Espagnac. A beautiful carving in dark wood of a pilgrim, staff in hand. A stunning gîte d'étape. Our late morning tea and coffee stop was in Brengues, no more than a crossroads with a café and a little shop. It looked deserted except for the café dog, a black-and-white lurcher-ish creature who strolled out to us with his tail wagging and a big panting smile. It was a far warmer welcome than the one we received from the waitress, but we sat down anyway. Within minutes people had descended upon Brengues from all directions: a couple of walkers buying sandwiches, women popping into the café for a chat with the waitress, cars dropping into the little car park, engines running while the drivers bought bread for lunch.

We stopped for lunch outside Santiac-sur-Célé. There was a little pull-in, with a picnic bench occupied by some people travelling by car. Adi and I agreed, as we laid out our picnic, that it ought to be a rule of travel that motorists should give up picnic benches to walkers and cyclists. Still, we picked a lovely spot, right by the river in dappled shade, the cliffs curling around behind us.

Thanks to the pilgrimage routes, the whole area was well-equipped for walkers and cyclists. All the villages sported a board with a map of the Célé, the neighbouring villages and the facilities at each. In long gaps between villages there would be a picnic area by the river, with a small sign to say how far it was to the next area of repose (I loved that expression: aire de repose.) Our picnic spot had a little shed with two toilets, an outside sink with cold water and even an electric socket above the sink.

'How's The Knee?' I asked Adi.

'Okay.' He was sitting with his watercarrier on it. 'I can feel it having to work a bit.'

After four days with virtually no cycling, my own knees and quads were feeling it a bit too. But pleasantly.

At Cabrerets in the late afternoon we pitched up quietly at the unattended municipal campsite. We cycled unburdened up a hill south of the river to the caves at Pech-Merles, two miles above the village. We arrived in time for a look in the museum before the guided tour of the caves began. That itself was a treat, with a small selection of objects rather than a thousand flint arrowheads.

The accounts of the caves we'd read had raved about them. They didn't go far enough. We were led first through stunning galleries, pleasantly chilly, shining with spectacular formations of calcite. Enormous discs three meters in diameter, spiral stalagmites and pillars, tiered slabs like wedding cakes. Curtains of calcite rippled from the roof. The guide explained that the variety of the formations came from different stages of the caves' histories; the original, ancient structures were eroded and scoured by underground floods. The waters left, the caves drained and dried and the younger calcite structures formed, some of them utterly bizarre: a small, perfect spinning top, and a plate of pearls - totally natural, totally looking like a bag of spilt mints.

Then there were the paintings... The first were etched on a panel of calcite, in the 'Chapelle des Mammouths': horses and bison, heads down in full charge; whiskery, tusked mammoths sketched in manganese and iron oxide dust. Finger paintings on the ceilings in clouds of red paint. Bison, mammoths, aurochs, bears, the relief of the walls used to give substance to the animals. The carving of a long mammoth trunk. A deer's head, alone and black; the form of a woman thumbed out in clouds of red dust on a ceiling. A perfect, flint-etched bear's head. The huge, glorious, spotted horses. And most haunting of all, the hands: especially the first, lone hand, outlined in red. It's heart-twisting. A human brother, long ago, regarded his paintings, or those of father, brother, friends, looked at what they had depicted and thought, can I depict myself? Placed his hand on the rock, spread his fingers, held in his other palm the red paint dust and blew. There is my mark. I am here. I am here.

We were contentedly quiet afterwards. Back in the village I saw a water snake in the little stream outside the Spar. It came out from under a rock, slipped into a clump of plants and rested, head out of the water, little red jewelled eyes sparkling, before dipping into the stream again.

We wandered. Cabreret was impossibly pretty, with troglodyte houses, a cluster of steep russet roofs and white wooden shutters on a knoll around the church, and a crystal pure stream flowing to the Célé. A drink at the little restaurant-and-ice-cream shop, the best value yet: €4 for a large beer ('Almost a pint,' Adi noted, approvingly) and an overflowing glass of red wine.

Our pitch was one of the loveliest yet, under the tangled branches of the trees on the river bank. The campsite manager, Dutchman Will, showed up as the light fell and the swifts took themselves to bed. A chatty soul, he sat down with us for a while in the dark. He lived in a half-troglodyte house in which, he said, the atmosphere was at 97% humidity at the moment. He told us to be sure to fill up our water bottles at the tap just down the road, the source of the Chèvres Blancs. I fell asleep to the sound of crickets and the whirr of bats, my falling-dreams full of glinting-eyed little green snakes, white goats, mammoths and hand prints.

CHAPTER THIRTY

To Rocamadour

It surprised me how much of France is limestone. Here we were, cycling north through an enormous expanse of river-riddled limestone hills and plateaus cut with lovely valleys. Limestone is comforting to me. My grandmother lived in County Clare, and the Burren's grey, bare limestone hills, are in my earliest memories. For years now I've lived on a Carboniferous limestone headland on Anglesey and for three years I worked on that limestone almost-island, the Great Orme.

It was the Orme that came to mind now as we followed the charming Sagane, not much more than a stream, northwards through long-grassed, watery meadows lined with willow, under small limestone hills of a sunnier hue than the Burren's glinty grey. In places the hills steepened, became cliffs, wooded and lovely, with tall oak, poplar and willow everywhere. A family of ravens flew off a crag, parents watching from trees as the youngsters flew in big, stiff-winged arcs. Endearingly awkward creatures, cautiously turning, uncertain of steerage. Like me going down bendy descents on Bike.

Following the advice of Dutchman Will, who said St-Cirq-Lapopie was very touristy, we'd started the day by cycling along the river to the confluence of the Célé and the Lot, then upstream long the Lot for a short distance until we could admire St-Cirq from afar. A round-apsed church with both a square tower and a round tower, surrounded by a huddle of sunny stone houses and steep, nut-coloured roofs, perched atop cliffs above the peacefully flowing river. Woods softened the ridge of hills behind it. Satisfied, un-frazzled by tourists, we retraced our wheels back into Cabrerets and then up the river valley.

'Winters are tough here.' Adi pointed at an enormous wall of chopped wood against the gable of a farmhouse as we cycled by. A store of corded wood almost as big waited in the yard under a shelter. All of the few houses we'd passed had these enormous woodstores.

We were alone on the road. The only vehicle we met was an unexpected coach, negotiating the narrow lane with care. Crickets sang full-throated and swifts were out in screaming, hooligan abundance. Poppies bloomed in the riverside meadows; We paused for lunch in the shade of an old lavoir, sunk into the rock and covered with a sturdy wooden roof at the edge of Sabadel-Lauzé's village green, across from a war memorial and a painted wooden cart. Vivid green and blue damselflies darted round us.

The day went on in joyful, steady cycling. My mind went to sleep, back down to the essentials. Pedal. Gaze around in delight at trees, ravens, cliffs, poppies. Click down the gears for the hills. Pause for a sip of water, to point out a bird to Adi, for him to show me a lizard scuttling in the verge. Onward with steady pedalling. Nothing to think about but to pedal and breathe. Cycling quiets the mind.

In the afternoon we stopped for tea at Labastide-Murat, a small town up high on a broad plateau. We were excited to see Murphy's on the menu

'You've got to have that,' I said to Adi. I'm from Cork, the home of Murphy's stout, but I can't stand the stuff. Adi stepped in to do my patriotic duty.

We were disconcerted when it arrived. No stout this, it was some sort of bitter, the same colour as my tea. We stared at it. It was in a proper Murphy's glass and everything. I'd never seen anything like it.

'One of those "only for the foreigners" brands?' I watched Adi sipping tentatively.

The verdict: 'Quite nice, but it's not proper Murphy's.'

We looked around at the by-now baking square. Every time I moved, my thighs performed a sticky detach and re-attachment to the seat. Adi took another sip.

'Thinking about it, a pint of stout might be a bit heavy in this weather.'

We rolled off the plateau, over the valley and towards the next range of hills. To our left a wide gorge yawned. It was like the Yorkshire Dales around Malham Tarn, except covered in trees.

This was one of our favourite things. Adi, especially, loves trees and they were here in abundance. It brought it home to us how denuded the landscape of the British Isles is.

Down into a deep valley, round bends, through a miniscule village called Carlucet, where a campsite had been listed but which seemed to be hiding. The whole village seemed to be hiding from the world, perched on a bend where the road rose up from a small stream.

We carried on towards Rocamadour. This last section of the ride would be the first real challenge for The Knee since leaving Figeac. The morning's climbs had been steady and very, very gentle. Adi was taking it slow, which meant that I could keep up with him.

'I wouldn't go that far,' he corrected me when I commented on his happy state. 'There's not much to complain about yet, I'll say that.'

We rode high on the top of the lovely limestone plateau, heavily wooded with sheep and goat pastures opening up on the gently rolling tops, deeply cut again and again with dry valleys and river valleys. Drystone walls enclosed small fields, just like at home. We climbed three hills, not long but testing enough in the warm sun.

'Still not complaining?'

'Not yet.'

As we paused near a wrought-iron cross at a crossroads a herd of sheep passed us, the farmer employing the time-honoured method of droving by following them in his car, tooting the horn. We could hear him from miles away. Our neighbour back on Anglesey herded his sheep in exactly the same way, though he didn't usually employ a long stick out of the window for the prodding of stragglers.

The final gorge was breathtaking, plunging deeply with trees clinging to every tiny ledge that their roots could grab. 'I didn't think we were up high enough for a valley that deep,' I said, after the first slack-jawed gawp.

The cliffs weren't sheer but had huge undercuts and jutting ledges, swollen rock beds bulging and overhanging the drop. Our lane descended, clinging to the opposite gorge wall. Right to the bottom. Even though 99% of my mind was occupied with the gloriousness of the view, the other 1% was shouting, 'Ah, come on. Right to the bottom? *Again*?'

But the 99% won. Rocamadour, the old town of the Black Madonna, is literally driven into the side of the gorge. Its citadel and churches and clinging town houses look like facades slapped onto the openings of caves and holes in the cliff ledges. Houses tumbled and gripped, hanging over the valley bottom far below.

We gazed at it as we freewheeled dangerously all the way to the valley bottom and then chugged very slowly up the other side. The road zigzagged up past the side of the town. It's ridiculous to call it a town, it's a big village stuck onto the side of a cliff. Halfway up the cliff, a side road followed a ledge into the village. We followed it and endured three minutes of almost unendurable tourist tat while we searched for the tourist office, which turned out to be closed.

We carried on up the hill, having one of our regular mild disagreements about what to do if we couldn't find a campsite. Our approaches differed.

Adi: That green down at the bottom, I'm sure you can camp on that.

Me: There's a sign that says 'No Camping'. It's only for campervans.

Adi: Yes, but if we needed to.

Me: You go and ask them then. (Pedalling away from the conversation. Cows with big horns and conversations I don't want to have: these are the things that give The Legs wings.)

Adi: It'll be fine! (Winding me up now.)

Me: Let's just find the campsite! (Pedalling even further away.)

The village of Rocamadour L'Hospitalet, on the edge of the plateau, was built entirely to service pilgrims and, increasingly nowadays, tourists. There was a church, a tourist information office, a couple of campsites, a shop with a tired-looking but friendly man, and an enormous car park near the top of the zigzag footpath that led down the cliff to Rocamadour itself. We chose the first campsite we found. It was great, big and cheerful with large pitches, plenty of sun and shade, and lots of walkers and cyclists. We chatted to some cycle tourers from northern England in the neighbouring pitch. They'd caught the European Bike Express to Orange, and were in the middle of an 18-day tour, to be collected in Bordeaux and deposited 25 miles from their home.

I got excited about the campsite showers. Excitingly, the showerhead was mounted on the side wall of the cubicle, instead of on the back wall, so it wasn't pointing at the door, my clean dry clothes and towel. Of such small pleasures was our trip strung together.

CHAPTER THIRTY-ONE

To Carennac

We'd intended to have a little bit of a lie-in the next morning, but had not bargained for the fact that we would be waking in a place of pilgrimage on a Sunday morning. At seven o'clock the church bells rang out the hours, paused, rang out the hours again, paused, and then started ringing and kept on ringing. It sounded as if it was in our tent. 'Get up peasants!' yelled the bells. 'Get to Mass, ye sinners!'

We strolled down to Rocamadour by The Way of The Cross, an outdoor Stations Of The Cross path switchbacking down the side of the hill, a carved representation of a moment from Jesus's walk with his cross at each point of the zig or the zag. Our different attitudes to crowds showed through almost instantly.

Adi: It's quite nice to see people.

Me (with slight shudder): God, it's HEAVING.

But we were up early enough to beat most tourists. We visited some of the grottos, some no more than altars in caves. The porch of the tiny Church of Notre Dame de la Vierge Noire was stuffed with tourists, all taking photos. 'Silence' requested a sign at the door. I politely squeezed past to sit in one of the pews and look. The carved black walnut-wood statue of the Madonna is small, slender, and lovely, with a little golden light in Mary's crown. The altar below it is carved off the same dark wood, and the slim angels with spears topped with the same little golden light stood around. I loved it. I have no traditional faith now but I love old churches, and to me Madonnas are the most beautiful of the imagery, statuary and iconry.

Villages like this are complicated enough when on a horizontal plane; on the vertical it became cheerfully confusing. We got lost in arcaded passageways. A Bonelli's eagle floated above us as we searched our way slowly out.

Two shopkeepers stand out in my memory. I bought a headband of stripy muted oranges and creams from a smiling woman from Brittany. When I explained that I was Irish and that we lived in Wales she was delighted.

'We are cousins - Celts! See, the green eyes, the skin...' I could have taken half the contents of her shop away with me, being my kind of hippy-but-not-too-barefoot style. Hippy-light. 'You will come back with a car some day, yes?'

I would, I promised her.

The other was the tired-eyed custodian of the general shop in Rocamadour L'Hopitalet. 'Troisième fois!' he greeted us on our final visit, just before we left at midday. He had a lovely smile. We speculated on his life as we cycled off.

'He's been in that shop for years,' said Adi. 'But it's all part of The Plan. He's going to be there, 7 till 12, 4 till 8, every day for, say ten years, maybe twelve, putting up with the tourists and the boredom, but he's not spending a penny, and when it gets to ten years—'

'—Or maybe twelve—'

'—Or maybe twelve, whooosh, that's it, he's gone with all his savings to live somewhere cheap and lovely.'

'Where there's no tourists.'

'Or churches.'

We hoped he'd enjoy it.

We were heading for the Gouffre de Padirac, where we intended to be tourists again. A natural feature in the cavern and pothole-riddled limestone through which we were riding, it was one of the must-sees of the region, according to all our accumulated guidebooks and leaflets. Inevitably with a name like that my day's earworm morphed into 'This Old Man', knick-knacking and paddywhacking and giving a dog a bone as we rolled along. We rode through more sun-lush limestone countryside till we found the village of Mathieu and the Gouffre just outside it.

The Gouffre was impressive, a circular chasm more than thirty metres across. A metal stairway clung to the wall of the chasm and spiralled out of sight, more than seventy metres down. Below, we knew, were caves and an underground river. We peered through the wire fence surrounding it, and then at the queue. There were about forty people ahead of us. We both hate queueing. 'Nah,' we thought, and pedalled on. We'd live with our loss.

Much later we sat outside a bar in Carennac, one of the smallest and most picturesque villages we'd stumbled into. We both felt a bit off; Adi's stomach was slightly upset, probably a side effect of the anti-inflammatories he was on for The Knee (which was doing very well) and I just felt - off.

We were having a bit of a Discussion.

'I just want to know!' I said, reasonably, I thought. 'If we go left in the morning, then it has implications for the rest of the trip. If we go right, it has completely different implications. I'd just like to know where we are going!'

The late afternoon ride had been glorious, a long swoop down to the banks of the Dordogne River, through a teeny hamlet called Gimrac. The campsite we settled on was a bit scruffy, but friendly, and we met a pleasant retired English couple called John and Joan. We had a great, wide-ranging chat with them, about places we must go ('The Menin Gate: the most emotive thing you'll ever see') and then they disconcerted us when we were on ant patrol during our pitch-selection ritual by offering us a chemical to kill the ants. Our startled looks startled John in turn and he retreated with the carton of nasty stuff in a mutual flurry of apologies.

The final pitch was lovely (situated in between the major ant highways), and we could hear the river pouring over a weir close by under the plane trees. And so into Carennac after a relatively early dinner. Utterly beautiful, elevated on the river bank, everything hewn from pale, warm limestone filled in with narrow red bricks. Dark wooden beams and frames picked out the windows and doors. An arch led to a courtyard; homes and the tourist office and a church all opened into it. A mysterious waist-high Alice-in-Wonderland door tucked under the steps up to a proper door. Rock martins and house martins scythed the air, vying with the hooligan swifts.

From our seats on the narrow street outside the bar we could see the drop down to the river bank; narrow gardens bordered a backwater of the river, wooded and gentle.

I tried again to get an answer out of Adi, but he was in a good mood and didn't notice that I was getting slightly agitated, or was wisely deciding not to notice.

Until now, we had been adopting a 'vaguely north' approach. As long as three days of cycling averaged a net northward gain, even a tiny one, it didn't matter too much which road we took. Or so we had been thinking. This had not, unsurprisingly, resulted in much northwards progress. But Adi had agreed to try to reach our friends, staying somewhere on the Loire, on the 24th or 25th of June. It was now the 18th.

'We were always going to get a train through the dull bit,' Adi had said that morning as we discussed our general plans for the next few weeks.

'Were we?' This was news to me. 'I didn't know that!'

There was rather a long silence while we took in the fact that, in months of discussion and preparation, plus a month of actual travelling, we had each managed not to notice this spectacular discrepancy in our expectations. I'd had no idea that Adi intended to take a train at any stage. He'd had no idea that I'd want to cycle through the flatter lands north of the Dordogne river.

I did not want to take a train, but it had become clear that we would not cover the miles between Rocamadour and the Loire in a week. We could not rely on The Knee, and we would have a horrible week if we tried to rush.

'It's not the most exciting landscape for cycling anyway, everyone says. That's why I thought we'd be skipping at least some of it,' Adi said at last.

I didn't argue. I felt as if we were cheating, but it would have to be. Which was why I had the Rough Guide's map of the main train lines through France open in front of me, and was trying to get an answer out of Adi about which way to go in the morning.

'They're staying near Chinon, Jim says,' said Adi.

'The thing about going north here,' I said, 'is that there are rivers flowing east to west, and valleys and ranges of hills following them, which affects the roads, which affects what we can do, and all this means that if we turn left in the morning, we have one set of options for going north, and if we turn right, we have another, totally different set of options.'

But Adi was still not in the mood to make a decision, and I was still feeling off, so I gave up the non-argument and went to bed defeated. As well as feeling a bit feeble, I felt under-exercised. We'd been riding relatively short distances on account of The Knee. Would we just get lazier and lazier? There must be a word to describe our kind of cycle touring. Slow. Slow touring. The great P.E. teacher in the sky was shaking his head in disgust. I told him to get lost and fell asleep to the sound of the weir.

CHAPTER THIRTY-TWO

To Meyronne

D ownstream,' Adi said in the morning.
       'Sure?'
'Sure.'

We paused in Carennac and were rewarded by spotting a rock martin nest, alongside the swifts in a high eave of the courtyard. A few minutes after leaving the village, a pine marten ran across the road in front of Adi, cheering us both up enormously.

Looking back, these few days around the Dordogne were the most unsettled of the tour. Adi was still being careful of the knee (down to lower case now), so our daily distances were still small. We didn't have a pressing need to rush. The landscape was beautiful, but I wished we could just make up a route for a week and follow it and not have to think about it, leaving us with only two things to do: pedal and breathe. Instead, the very fact that we had so much time and freedom - even more now that I knew we were taking the train - meant more decisions about which way to go at a crossroads. Each and every crossroads.

Now, I dearly love Adi, but during this part of the journey I confess I was struggling a bit with the intangible but very real constraints imposed by travelling together. Adi, much later, said that he was struggling with the very real constraints of cycling with an obscurely discontented companion. As travellers, as cyclists and as two autonomous, independent people, we had our own unique opinions on where to stop and what to do. There were experiences I'd never have had if I was by myself, things I'd never have noticed. I flipped back and forth between wishing I could make my own decisions totally, to being oh-so-glad he was there. Pine marten moments. Sudden heart-stopping views round a bend. The meeting of eyes that understand exactly why you're smiling. It affirms the experience, deepens it, adds joy.

It was a quiet day, during which we spent more time than usual cycling apart, lost in our own thoughts, rolling slowly alongside the river. Vineyards and walnut plantations alternated with meadows and fields of barley. In Floirac, another ridiculously charming village, we stopped for lunch. We lit our camp stove, made tea and drank it on a stone bench built into the wall above the river. Next to us the steep, yellow-and-green lichened roof of a riverside house almost reached the ground. Half-arches of long-gone buildings showed in the walls of younger but still venerable houses. Upper stories bulged out on wooden corbels. Windows showed small, quaintly uneven. Turrets squeezed into corners. Worried-looking stone angels and knights sat in niches high up in gable walls. Roofs were steep and pointed, flaring out at the bottom.

We were getting used to the shuttered nature of the villages, another consequence of being somewhere where it is usually hot. Shuttered windows, wooden gates, paint peeling, looking as if they haven't been opened for a decade. Sneak a glance as someone goes in and there will be a small courtyard behind the gates, or a large one, with windows looking down upon it and flowers in tubs, a small garden, maybe some small trees for shade in planters or pushing up through stone slabbed ground. Life, turning inwards, away from the sun. The best time to be in a French village is at half past three or four o'clock. Shutters thrown back, windows opening, mopeds screeching out of the peeling courtyard doors, people beginning to wander towards the boulangerie, whose own shutters are rising.

We waited with a small group of other tourists outside the church's tower for someone to come and open it at two, as a sign promised. Half an hour later we left. The church was still unopened but we'd been entertained by largest horde of swifts yet, flying low with high-speed yobbishness. A neat colony of housemartins had built a ring of nests around the central corbel of the domed underside of the belfry. Two chicks were pulled, protesting, from the nest by parents for their first flying lessons. With the swifts screaming past it must have been like pulling out of your dad's drive for the first time and finding yourself in Monte Carlo in June.

After a funny sort of day the evening was one of the loveliest. Benevolent fates watched over us. Adi waited for me at a campsite entrance beside the river. Just across a bridge was Meyronne, the village.

'Shall we pitch up first?' Adi said.

'Let's get the bread and food first.'

So we rode over the bridge to find the boulangerie and the shop. Tucked under walnut and lime trees was another campsite, between the village and the river.

'Let's stay in this one,' said Adi. 'I have a feeling.'

It was magical: an ant-free, shady pitch right beside the rolling Dordogne. The friendly young couple who ran it had set up a tiny shack selling cold beer and soft drinks, which we took immediate advantage of. I put aside my recent resolve not to drink too much Coke. Most importantly, we could hear from our perfect pitch the distant strumming of a guitar from the campsite across the river. Much nicer than being in the same campsite as the guitarist, whose repertoire, it turned out as the evening progressed, was limited in the extreme. But floating over the river, the strumming sounded good-natured and peaceful, joining with the clack of boules and laughter from a group of English canoeists who'd arrived soon after us.

The eight canoeists, a gang in their twenties had hired the canoes upriver and were paddling downstream. They told us this, then looked at each other in a taut silence for a second until the girls exploded into giggles.

'They're laughing,' said one of the lads, 'because we haven't actually done a thing, just a bit of steering. The current's doing it all for us. So much for an active holiday!'

We watched with the rest of them as two of them got into the river for a swim to get some exercise. The current was so strong just five feet from the bank that their frantic breast-stroking just kept them in the same spot in the water. They might have been anchored in place. I abandoned my plans for a sneaky dip.

PART TEN

To The North: Meyronne to Orléans (With A Little Help From SNCF)

CHAPTER THIRTY-THREE

To La Roque-Gageac

By eight o'clock next morning I'd had a foot-numbing paddle in the river, packed everything except the tent, and collected the croissants from across the river.

'Excellent,' I said around a mouthful of melting buttery flakes.

'Number four, I think,' Adi said. 'Not quite top three material, but not much to complain about.'

We were the only ones up apart from the operator of a mini-digger, noisily excavating a path through the campsite past the glamping huts where the canoeists were sleeping, possibly with the aid of ear plugs. I love France. The Real Jobs - jobs where you do things, like make a fence or build a house - all seemed to start at the crack of dawn, so that the men - it was almost always men - could be nipping into the bar-tabac for their coffee/absinthe by 11.30.

By the time we'd drained our second mugs of tea and coffee we'd reached a consensus. We'd head to Les Eyzies-de-Tayac, treat ourselves to a luxury campsite where we'd wash EVERYTHING, then cycle to Périgueux or Brives and catch a train north to somewhere on the Loire. It looked as if Orléans was the place to aim for.

I couldn't help a slight feeling of dread at the thought of going to such a large city. With our 10 mph pace of life even Castres and Albi had left me slack-jawed with over-stimulation, like a country child coming up to Cork to see the Christmas lights for the first time. I chided myself. It was all part of the picture. Nevertheless, I made sure to drink in the walnut-groved, riverside-cliffed vistas while we were still amongst them.

Our moods had switched: I was the positive, cheerful one; Adi was more downbeat, greeting the road with a frown. A lot of it was down to the indigestion he was suffering from The Knee tablets. Despite doing everything right - taking them with food, at the correct intervals - they were clearly having a strong adverse effect, and it was beginning to get him down. I had a lovely morning while he pedalled on, not exactly suffering but dreading the mid-morning onset of cramps that had bothered him for the last few days.

In a teeny hamlet called Pinsac we bought Coke and apples, and drank and munched them at little tables outside. 'Mon Petit Marché' was lettered into the backs of the chairs. An Alsatian dozed on a blanket under the next table. I loved the way that grocery shops and bakeries often had chairs and tables outside them, especially in the tinier villages. There was always someone there, usually a man, with a newspaper and a tiny cup of something tar-like, lifting his head at intervals to join in the conversation at the back of the shop.

Ever more walnut groves. Up and over bluffs, with snatches of views through trees of unexpectedly dizzying drops to the river curving below. Hayfields cut and turned, golden wheat fields laced red and purple with poppies and vetch. Through Souillac, a noisy through-road of a town. Reading the guidebook later we realised we had completely missed its charms, though a quick ride around the back streets redeemed it somewhat, especially the sight of a calm-eyed cart-horse tied up behind the huge, double-domed cathedral.

We followed the river's north bank for a mile or so to the bridge that would carry us over to quieter roads on the south bank - and then there was one of those instances of perfect timing that would never work if you'd planned it. As we cycled over the bridge, a couple of canoes approached and passed underneath. A shout went up from one of them. Eight arms waved madly. Yep, the English canoeists. It would never have worked if we'd tried to time it.

It was a toilet obsession day for me. It started poorly with Souillac, with a shocking squat-style cubicle in a cobwebby shed on the edge of a car park. A tiny hamlet had the most immaculate little toilet in a shed beside their 'Aire de Camping-Cars', with a seat AND toilet paper AND hot water AND soap AND hand towels. Later, when we reached Sarlat-le-Canéda, we had leisure to enjoy the rather nice facility in the middle of the town. We knew they were nice because we each spent twenty minutes in there cleaning cycle-track-grit off our exposed skin, drying ourselves off and changing our clothes.

The rain had started late morning as we cycled a gentle road through the walnut groves, and it kept on coming: heavy, windless, inexorable. By the time we reached the cycle track along an old railway line to Sarlat-le-Canéda, we were thoroughly wet. By the time we rolled into Sarlat we couldn't have been wetter if we'd jumped in the river. I had to wring water out of my ponytails.

Adi was very down but his mood was restored by a picnic lunch in a charming, landscaped park looking down over the old town centre, and by the delicious sensation of sunshine on rain-chilled skin. There is nothing like getting wet and grumpy and having it all taken away by the simple pleasure of warm, dry, toasty clothes and a patch of sunshine on your knees. His mood lifted further when he realised that the town map from the tourist office was rubbish, which gave him something to complain about and a chance to exercise his navigational skills.

It was the most touristy place we'd visited since the Mediterranean. As we'd pushed our bikes through to the tourist office I'd got looks from some people that led me to believe they'd never seen a bicycle before, or a wet person. I've rarely felt more as if I was a different species. But Sarlat was gorgeous, the medieval centre full of buildings of a rich, yellow stone, glowing in the sunshine. All the lovelier to enjoy when clean and dry.

We wandered around, Adi chuntering contentedly at the rubbish map, me ignoring street signs altogether. We amused ourselves by ticking off the streets and squares you find in every French town. I found this immensely comforting. Somewhere there will be a Rue or a Place de la République, an Avenue Charles de Gaulle, a Rue Victor Hugo and a something de la Liberté. Rue Gambetta showed up as a popular fifth in many towns. We found four of the five - no Charles de

Gaulle! - and settled down at a café to decide the route for the afternoon.

'Excellent toilets,' said Adi on his return from them. Through a courtyard, small and dark of carved stone and enormous etched beams of wood.

'Today's winner,' I agreed.

An English couple in late middle age sat not far from us. We couldn't help hearing their discussion.

'Do they have chips?' the woman wondered. The menu had pictures on it, one of them of a bowl of chips, but she got up and went to find a waiter. She met one, a pleasant young man, coming out of the door to take their order. She wore an expression that I understand well, as I wear it myself whenever I have to ask a question that's outside the everyday conversations and transactions. It is the expression I wear when concentrating hard on what I want to say and also on what the possible answers might be, so I can latch onto the critical words in the reply and get the gist, if not the detail. Good on her, I thought, she's going to have a go.

She opened her mouth and said: 'Do you do chips?'

Loudly.

In English.

The small, generous part of me felt I should go and help them out but the louder, less charitable part, was rolling its eyes and thinking, 'For God's sake learn a few words of the language.' How hard is it to learn the French for 'Do you do chips?' and 'Yes' and 'No'?

Too hard for some.

'Frites?' said the waiter.

'Chips?'

'Frites?'

'Feesh? Fish and chips?'

He escorted her to her table and showed her and her husband the pictures on the menu. After a few seconds' contemplation she looked at him and said, very loudly and slowly, 'What can you have with it?'

He didn't thump her as I would have done, just politely indicated the pictures on the menu.

'Can you have chicken?'

'Poulet?'

'Chicken? Chicken?'

At which point Adi and I silently put our payment down on the table and left, afraid that they might discover we were English speakers and try to talk to us. Probably about the French. I know I am being unkind, and I did feel a little sorry for them. They probably had a load of friends at home who'd told them, 'Oh, you don't need to speak French, everyone speaks English.' And then they come over and find out that while they may be understood most of the time provided their wants are basic, in the majority of

France, even in quite touristy areas, most people's spoken English is about as good as our French would be if the French had been holidaying and buying second homes in England for fifty years and loudly going around saying 'Avez vous des frites?' and refusing to try English.

There was so much to please the eye in Sarlat, with the mellow hue of the stone giving the whole town a glow. We counted three knife shops; we'd noticed that there were a lot of knife shops in France, with windows full of decorative stuff, the sort of thing people collect and hang on their living room walls in slightly unsettling displays. In one shop stood a man at a whirring grindstone, wearing a leather apron and sharpening knives one after the other. I approached him and hesitantly explained that we were travelling on bikes and had a camping knife that was now far from sharp. Would it be possible…?

He held our knife to the wheel, a peaceful expression on his face as he moved it along the spinning whetstone. He didn't even look at it: just held it and moved it, adjusting its position and angle, running his fingers over the blade to test it, holding it to the wheel again to sharpen it just a little more. He eventually handed it back to me with a gentle smile, refusing to take any payment. That evening it almost took our fingers off.

'That,' declared Adi, 'is the sharpest knife we have ever owned.'

We rode on south to find the Dordogne again, and followed it downstream to La Roque-Gageac. What with the lovely cycling, the knife-sharpening cheer and the dry clothes - oh, simple pleasures! - Adi had thoroughly cheered up. Which was fortunate, because the campsite we eventually found was...

'There's something not right about it,' Adi said, frowning around. Most of it wasn't yet open.

'Well, we're here now,' I said. 'Showers, tent up, back into the village for a look. It'll be grand.'

We cycled back into La Roque-Gageac. It was like Rocamadour in miniature and without the pilgrims, slapped up against the river cliff. The location was gorgeous, but it just didn't do anything for us, especially when everything was closed except for one bar. It was just Adi's turn for grumps, that's all. I'd have been grumpy if my stomach was acting up whilst cycling 50 miles in rain and considerable heat. We were a little cheered by our mileage, which we had accomplished without racing and including the three-hour stop in Sarlat.

Fortunately, we had already bought a bottle of wine. It was a wine-needing sort of evening. Mildly inebriated after dinner, we went through the recent wildlife tally. Lots of green woodpeckers over the last few days, all along the Dordogne and the Célé, sometimes glimpses, more often just hearing their yaffling call. Swifts were our constant companions. The further north we wriggled the more swallows we saw, parents swooping with fledgelings low over the fields, adults darting in and out of barns. But swifts were clearly still in charge, in terms of numbers and sheer brio.

We heard, over dinner, a call that we'd heard a couple of times but never so loudly. We thought it was a type of duck but stalking the river banks after dinner revealed nothing. Yet the noise was everywhere, like a huge colony of invisible ducks with throat infections. Despite staring until our eyes hurt we couldn't see what could be making it. It kept rattling, long into the night, keeping me awake long enough that I switched on my torch and got my diary out again to scribble a rant about them.

'Fecking Roque-Gageac,' said Adi into the dark, 'and its fecking invisible ducks.'

CHAPTER THIRTY-FOUR

To Les Eyzies

In the morning the collared doves were calling away - you can't really call it singing - joined by wood pigeons, which had been increasingly adding to the soundscape since Figeac. The birdsong wasn't quite enough to cheer us when we realised that wretched little La Roque (I had come around to Adi's dismissive view of the village) didn't have an open shop. The epicerie wouldn't open until 8 a.m. The boulangerie was closed today. We shook the dust of La Roque off our wheels and cycled away, to find a sparkling little village two miles down the road, with everything open and a picturesque campsite tucked into a curve of the river.

'We should have stayed here!' Adi wailed.

'Next time,' I promised. We munched delicious croissants and half a baguette on the wall in Baynac, watching lizards scrapping on a rock as the sun burnt the last of the mist off the river. The wide Dordogne curled peacefully while lorries rattled noisily on the road squeezed between the river and the village. Baynac was another one of those lovely warm-tinted villages that spread improbably upwards, clinging to the cliffs.

Leaving aside the downpour that had soaked us on the way into Sarlat-le-Canéda, the weather had been beautiful for the last couple of days. The application of sunscreen had become a daily ritual and my left leg and arm were slowly turning brown. Adi was in much better form, having purchased some antacids. Stomach under control, he and The Knee were in flying form, speeding along the road with the rattling lorries, me in dogged pursuit fifty metres behind. At St-Cyprien we waved goodbye to the Dordogne and took a lane into the hills. Wolf country, farms and trees and rolling limestone views. I was in limestone heaven.

It took us less than three hours to reach Les Eyzies-de-Tayac, where Adi came out of the tourist office with more campsite bumph than any couple should need in a week. We went straight to a café, picked a table on the edge of the sun and shade and ate an ice-cream while he studied it intently. My impatience is such that any joint decision follows this pattern. He examines everything, makes a shortlist, and I join in with the final selection process.

Les Eyzies sits at the junction of three valleys. The north-eastern valley of the river Vézère has long been branded for tourism purposes as 'Le Vallée d'Homme', a fact it is impossible not to notice when browsing the postcard racks. Oiled, muscular male bodies superimposed against the backdrop of the Vézère river in a profusion of poses: it doesn't exactly elevate the tone. The moniker comes from the region's abundance of sites with evidence of human occupation for tens of millennia, from skeletons of Cro-Magnon people - the earliest anatomically modern humans - to the remains of settlements in caves and, often, extensive wall drawings. Most famous are the caves at Lascaux, not actually in this valley and not actually open to the public anymore, owing to the danger to the cave paintings caused by atmospheric changes from the breath of thousands of visitors. Lascaux II has been open since 1983, a faithful replica of a portion of the original caves. I thought this was completely over the top when I first heard this but now I find it touching that so many of us want to see something of our ancestors, people like us but not us. Any way of experiencing that connection without jeopardising the paintings is worth the immense trouble.

If we hadn't already experienced the magical Pech-Merles we'd have treated ourselves to some more caves, but today we had more prosaic matters on our minds than 40,000-year-old caves and paintings.

We chose a very fine campsite but nearly came to blows because on a sunny afternoon I was glued to a screen, looking up things I really didn't want to know. Adi wanted to compare the benefits of trains from Les Eyzies via Périgueux versus those via Brives, to a variety of towns on the Loire. I'd thought we'd decided on Orléans but Adi, ever wary of commitment, didn't want to narrow us down. The wifi was slow so we couldn't use our phones; the computer wasn't much faster, loading web pages in a leisurely fashion until I was ready to put my foot through it. Every time I found out one small fact, such as that you can get to Paris from Brives with three changes, Adi would ask 'What about this instead? Or that?', starting off another cycle of sluggish page-loading. After half an hour I had a fit and cycled off to the local train station to get a paper timetable and a price from the ticket master there.

'How much is it to Brives?' I asked.

I have forgotten the answer because it was shockingly expensive.

'Let's cycle to Périgueux in the morning,' I said, when we had dismissed the idea of taking a train from Les Eyzies. 'It's only twenty-five miles, we can get there in a couple of hours.'

We went for a short cycle up the valley, constantly being overtaken by coaches that immediately pulled in across us to one of the car parks outside the caves and grottoes. We'd forgotten to take into account that unless you are planning to visit a museum or one of the caves or grottoes, there isn't really much to do in Les Eyzies other than laugh at the awful postcards and shudder at the photos of geese being force fed. Foie gras and porn-star postcards. The best of Les Eyzies was definitely underground.

Last time we were here we'd visited an excavation of a settlement under a curved overhang in the river cliff, inhabited for thousands of years continuously. The hearth remains were clearly visible, preserved in the layers of river sands and soils deposited since. We and the six other English speakers were furnished with sheets in English, summarising what the guides were saying at each point, but that all faded beside the enthusiastic archaeology student with a mop of short dreadlocks who took us aside at each point after his colleague had finished her spiel. 'Now, now!' he would say, before launching into his talk, with a proper taking-the-piss-out-of-the-French accent, his dreads bouncing wildly. He was absolutely brilliant. I cherish the memory of him excitedly pointing out the remains of the hearth, a wide black strip in the soil horizon.

'And here zey sit around in ze evening, zey talk, zey 'ave ze tea, ze coffee...'

Having decided on a sort of a plan Adi and I made friends again. We did manage to launder and dry almost all our clothes and the sleeping liners. The sun shone all afternoon, and there was time too for reading, lying on soft grass with a glass of wine at my elbow.

'Do you feel as if you're cheating?' I asked as we looked at the map again after dinner. 'Not cycling all the way?'

'No. We were always going to get a train through this lot.' Adi waved a finger over the middle of France.

'I didn't bloody know that till three days ago!'

There was a short silence.

'But it's all right.'

But I did secretly feel like a cheat.

CHAPTER THIRTY-FIVE

To Orléans

We cycled the twenty-five miles to Périgueux in two hours along high classification roads, where we were treated with respect by everyone except British motorhomes. Pedalling my usual ten to fifty metres behind Adi, I was in the perfect position to see the couple of UK-registered campervans clearly unable to understand why he wasn't cycling in the gutter.

All we saw of Périgueux was the tourist office, the train station, and a brief swing around the cathedral. It seems in retrospect that we should have paid a little more attention to the largest town of the region we'd been touring for the last week, but our minds were already north. I've always hated in-between stages. I just wanted to get north and start enjoying the next phase.

Discussion with the man at the ticket office was protracted. A USSR-style queue had grown behind us by the time we had established that it was possible to reach Orléans that day in three hops. I handed over my credit card with a wince; the price for both of us came to €128, which was not expensive for a last-minute journey halfway up the country, but it was an expense we hadn't taken into account when budgeting. The man explained carefully which carriages our seats would be on, and where our bicycles would have to go on the second leg, where there would be a separate bicycle compartment. Separate bicycle compartment!

The first train would be leaving shortly so we went straight to the platform, wheeling our bikes carefully down the ramps. And there the tension started. It's nerve-wracking, waiting for a train while you have a bicycle laden with panniers. You position yourself in the middle of the platform, and as the train approaches you tense up and turn your eyes into lasers, looking out for the little bike symbol over the door. If you see it glide past you follow it maniacally, only a vestige of decency preventing you from doing what you really want to do which is hurl everyone else who might want the bike space - wheelchair users, pushchairs, prams, mobility scooters - out of the way. Because bikes go at the bottom of the list, folks, even if you were there first and you have a ticket for your bike.

So you rush down the platform and find the correct door. There are people alighting, people waiting. You pull off your front panniers and maybe a rear one as well, because there's no way you can lift the bike otherwise. When there's a gap in the crowds you heave it on and quickly shove it into the bike space. You wriggle through the people still getting on and go to retrieve the rest of the panniers from the platform, hoping some evil opportunist hasn't made off with them. And then you do the same for your partner and his bike, while all the time unladen passengers swirl around you.

It is the most anxious-making, sweat-making cycling experience there is. It should be easy - bikes and trains should go together! Our experience from Albi to Rodez had eased our minds somewhat, but it was our much more fraught experiences on UK trains that were uppermost in my mind.

Our departure time came and went with no sign of our train. More passengers arrived until the platform, which had been relatively empty at the actual departure time, was stuffed with people. To my fevered eyes it looked as if about half them had greater claim to the bike space: wheelchairs, pushchairs, other bikes (No! No!) and scores of people with enormous rucksacks and oversized suitcases on wheels. As the departure time of our connecting train came and went I relaxed into something past despair, watching €128 go down the drain.

I zinged into life again when Adi nudged me.

'It's coming!'

All over the platform, people were shuffling into alertness. The train slid in; the bike symbol glided past and stopped only a few yards away. We leapt into action, flinging off the front panniers and the tent. Adi helped me lift Bike on and I found the bike racks. Hanging ones. Curses. I shouted out to Adi that he'd have to remove his rear panniers, and started fumbling with mine in the train aisle while he removed his, adding to the pile of luggage on the platform.

At this point the surrounding atmosphere began to get through to me. It was - amazingly - calm. Two ladies helped me to hang my bike up while another held Adi's bike in the aisle. As Adi flung the last of the panniers into the train, a guard walked by with a big smile, making shushing gestures with his hands. 'Tranquille, m'sieur, tranquille! This train isn't going anywhere.'

And it didn't. The kind women helped me lift Adi's bike into place beside mine and to stow the panniers neatly. We were seated and breathing out sighs of relief before the train moved.

'That wasn't too awful.' Adi-speak for wonderful and uncomplicated.

One of the women who'd helped us sat next to us. She asked questions about where we'd been, and when an announcement about onward journeys for those who had missed connections came through the intercom she made certain that I had understood the time and number of the replacement train we'd need to find in Limoges. She departed with a smile, wishing us a pleasant journey.

When we changed at Limoges, a second helpful woman came over to do some pannier lifting and showed us where the lifts to the platforms were. She was there to help us load our bikes into the bike compartment half an hour later. It turned out to be a spacious area at the end of one of the second-class carriages, with oodles of space. When we'd secured them, Adi and I made to leave to find our designated seats down in third class, as instructed by the man in the ticket office, but the woman, whose name was Pascale, wouldn't hear of it.

'It is not an obligation,' she explained as she ushered us into her second class compartment. My qualms - I am an natural obeyer of rules - were laid to rest when she explained that she worked for SNCF, the national train company, and that she was a cyclist as well, so she understood better than most how they worked both separately and together.

The journey flew as we chatted with her, mostly in French. My brain experienced that painful-but-pleasant stretching sensation that it always does when I'm trying to converse in a second language beyond the boundaries of my comfort zone. Except for a few, short conversations about where we were from ('Irlande! Il pleut toujours en Irlande!' was a phrase that come up often) we hadn't often spoken about our lives, our homes, our jobs. Trying to describe the complicated quango, charity and private landowning beast that is landscape and nature conservation in the UK, and how Adi and I fit into it as contractors, is difficult enough in English. Most of my friends and relatives have only the haziest idea of what we do. In French it was mind-frazzling. Synapses snapped and buzzed. It was like being back in the kitchen with the farmer and the old woman in Beaumont-de-Pertuis.

Pascale was lovely, curious and attentive, with plenty to say for herself as well. She showed us pictures of her grandfather's farm just outside Les Eyzies, where she'd spent the weekend with a dozen members of her extended family. She lived in Paris now, and made us a promise to get in touch if ever we visited. When we parted on the platform at Châteauroux it was with three kisses - three for friends - and her email address.

We'd only known her for a couple of hours but after Pascale had gone the colour seemed to fade out of the day. We caused a blockage getting on the third train. We'd clearly run through our day's allowance of helpful people. Everyone seemed to want to use the door behind two people with bikes and a feck-load of luggage and stared, patiently but unhelpfully, as Adi and I struggled. The train was already moving before we'd de-panniered the bikes. We managed, with much swaying, to hang them, squashed the panniers in and then collapsed.

'This lot have got to be Parisians,' Adi said when he returned from a coffee-and-loos reconnoitre. 'They all look miserable.'

I didn't follow the logic, but couldn't think. Maybe they just all felt as suddenly zonked as I did. I stared out of the window, stupefied, at a landscape ironed flat and dull, dull, dull. The happy anticipation had left me entirely.

When our carriage almost emptied a couple of stops later, Adi nudged me. 'I know how to wake us up.' We excavated our evening clothes and wash kits from the depths of our panniers and transformed ourselves. On with the unsuitable, brightly coloured wrap-around skirt.

We fell out into Orléans as if from another country, another age. We walked out of the airy, white station onto a broad boulevard and the sound of music hit us at the same time as the strong, warm wind. I found a clip and pinned my skirt down while Adi checked the name of the boulevard against the Rough Guide's town map.

'We'll find the campsite no problem, even after a glass of wine,' he said confidently, and headed into the middle of town, me pedalling behind him with one hand grabbing my unsuitable but cheerful-coloured skirt.

The Rue de Bourgogne had once been the Gallo-Roman main street and was now, according to the Rough Guide, the lively heart of the city, and the place to find cafés and food. We rolled across a huge open space in front of the Cathédrale Sainte-Croix, huge and gleaming in the early evening light, and paused again to get bearings. The sound of music was louder now.

'Down there. Leads straight to it.' I followed again, then paused behind him as our narrow back street intersected with the Rue de Bourgogne.

'Lively?' said Adi.

I just stared. A thick river of people filled the narrow street from wall to wall, moving ketchup-slow. The crowd stopped just the right side of body-crushing. Opposite the side street where we locked our bikes, an amped-up teenage threesome was playing and singing with more enthusiasm than tunefulness.

304 | MARIE MADIGAN

From further up and down the street came the clashing strains of more voices, instruments and drumbeats. The whole town was buzzing, and this street was the buzzing, humming heart.

We squeezed in to join the throng. Every 20 metres or so there was either a band, a choir or music pumping out of a speaker. The bass notes of dance music layered with chatter and laughter with a top note of swift screams - they were still there, whirling above. Banging dance music, a brass band, lads playing in groups, a gospel choir, a fire-eater.

We sat outside a bar with a glass of wine and asked the barman if it was always like this.

'Not always,' he smiled. 'We celebrate this weekend the start of summer.'

June 21st! Aha!

Over the fire eater a window opened and a hand with a camera emerged, filming the life below. We retrieved our bikes and pushed them through the street - something I would never have done at home, and probably not there if I hadn't already seen a couple of people actually cycling down the street, attracting not a single disapproving glance. Every age and type of people were out: families, oldies, cool types, couples, wanderers like us. Warm breeze, lively faces.

We found a pizzeria in an open area at the end of the street and locked up the bikes opposite, where we could see them from our table. While we ate a troupe of breakdancers threw down a slab of cardboard and did their crazy thing, spinning on heads, bouncing from hands to feet. As we waited for our bill they were replaced by a bunch of flamenco dancers, swirling and spinning and stamping and snapping with our bikes as a backdrop.

'This,' said Adi, 'is surreal.'

I nodded lazily in agreement. Light was fading from the sky and deep down inside me a tiny balloon of anxiety about the campsite was trying, with not much success, to break through my wine-and-pizza happy-buzz. During a break in the flamenco performance we whisked in and liberated the bikes. We found the river, examined the map once more and strapped our lamps on for the last cycle of the day.

Nearly eleven o'clock by now and still people were pouring in across the bridge over the Loire - friends, groups, couples elderly and young. We left them behind, sped out into the western suburbs under a moon on sliver-setting to find the campsite. Fifteen minutes of back and forth ensued before we found it and the big sign that said it was - surprise surprise - closed until July.

The great thing about leaving important things like where you're going to sleep so ridiculously late is that it leaves time for the anaesthetic effect of food and alcohol to take hold. I felt almost excited about the thought of pitching up on some municipal bit of green - a roundabout or a strip of lawn around a suburban terrace. Fortunately, Adi's brain is more resistant to alcohol than mine and he was studying the map with the benefit of functioning neurones.

'I know what we're going to do.' He pointed out that we were within a couple of kilometres of a major motorway junction. 'And what do you find just off motorway junctions near big cities?'

Within half-an-hour we were squashed in a tiny lift surrounded by a tower of panniers, holding the bikes like rearing ponies up on their rear wheels, ascending to a little room on the second floor of a cheap motorway hotel. We'd paid with a credit card at an ATM-like machine outside the door, which had toyed with us by refusing Adi's card but had no problem with mine. In the foyer, another fright when the room number 207, printed on the receipt the machine had spat out at me, didn't appear on the plan of the hotel fixed to the lobby wall. Panic. Would we be sleeping in the corridor? Then I spotted that the plans of both the first and second floors listed room numbers 100-167. Could some idiot have just copied the first floor plan twice?

Some idiot had. We got into the lift, fell out of it at room 207, whose door opened and where we fell into our twin beds and slept deeply, surrounded by bikes and baggage.

PART ELEVEN

Along The Loire: Orléans to Neuil-sous-Faye

CHAPTER THIRTY-SIX

To Blois

On a list of things I didn't expect to see the next day, little terns would have been close to the top.

'Terns!'

'Seriously?'

Binoculars out, we paused and examined the sandbank in the river. I'd been aware of the harsh call of black-headed gulls since leaving Orléans, but it wasn't until we paused for a nibble of food that we noticed something funny about some of them. That croaking, scratchy call, the shape of the black on the head, not so much a black head as a black cap.

'They are! They're little terns!'

The Collins Bird Guide to Britain and Europe (a brick of a book but so much better than a soulless app) confirmed it. A thick blue line ran from the west coast inland along the Loire, showing the range where little terns are resident.

Breakfast had been a muted, slightly hungover, all-you-can-eat-for-€5 affair. We stowed croissants and pains-au-chocolat about our persons as we worked our way through it, chatting to a pleasant Englishman in his early sixties who was not eating quite as much as we were. He was driving from his home in southwest London down to Barcelona, to see some classical concerts and visit the Dalí museum in Figueres. A few minutes later he looked startled as we rolled our bikes from the lift out through the lobby, unlike the receptionist, who didn't even blink.

It was one of those not-leaving-till-after-midday days but I was too tired and mellow to care. I loved the cathedral: the central aisle was narrow-ribbed and immensely tall, austere and light. High above, arrays of narrow windows let soft light flow in. An altar to Jeanne d'Arc on the left of the main aisle. It was the only garishly painted altar. Outside in the sunny square was a simple,carved block of stone on the spot where she was burned, a thought to bring shivers of horror on a bright sunny day.

A more cheerful sculpture was the simple but lovely figure, cast in dark metal, of a girl holding a basket overflowing with sheaves of wheat, vegetables and fruits, the personification of the Loire.

Our first food foray showed that the quality of the fresh produce had leapt up. The standard of the fruit and vegetables had declined slowly over the past couple of weeks, especially in the shops. The markets still provided excellent fresh produce, but it was not as mouthwateringly toothsome as in Provence. Except for apples. I hadn't had a good apple since leaving home. I really missed tangy, crunchy apples.

We left Orléans on the south bank, following the Loire á Vélo cycle track, part of the Eurovélo Route 6. It wasn't difficult to follow. Easy, well-signed, flat, on quiet roads or well-surfaced cycle lanes beside or close to the river. Pretty enough in its own way but just a tiny bit dull. I chided myself: this would be easy on The Knee. But we'd grown used to lumpy, buckled landscapes, the view changing all the time, new horizons opening out or closing in. I kept my thoughts to myself, until we paused for a nibble of squashed pain-au-chocolat.

'Bit dull, isn't it?' Adi said after a moment.

'It is.'

Then we spotted the little terns, and satisfaction was restored. I love this about cycling - there is always something to see, and if it is a pleasant something you can stop and see it more closely. Or you can just ride on madly as fast as you can through the duller landscapes.

We went on, smiling. It's a great thing to be easily pleased: just the sight of these harsh-voiced, graceful little birds with their shaggy black caps and their pointed wings and tails put us in a good mood.

Wildlife made up for the relative ordinariness of the landscape. Dozens of swallows and martins hawked for insects over the river banks. Yellowhammers yammered, sedge and reed warblers rattled in the reeds and bushes by the river's edge. Linnets and sparrows yelled. Lapwings fed on sandy islets. A kingfisher flashed electric blue in front of Adi. The river widened and narrowed, always with sandy banks and islets and fringes of reedbeds.

We covered the 52 miles to Blois easily in the afternoon, despite a headwind. The warm breeze that had blown my skirt up yesterday hadn't let up, had increased if anything, but we'd felt strong, eating up the miles. The bikes felt strong too, as if eager to get on. The only niggle was Adi's stomach. He'd finished the anti-inflammatory tablets yesterday and from crampy indigestion his insides had gone into meltdown. It seemed unfair that having endured the side-effects stoically he now had to suffer apparent withdrawal symptoms. He'd been great with the indigestion, just carried on, never complaining - not about the indigestion anyway - just munching antacid tablets and being really careful about food.

We camped just outside Blois, a small city whose name had entertained us for the last couple of hours.

For some reason, the French 'oi' sound, so easy to make when saying the word 'Loire', was much more difficult with a B stuck in front of it. The campsite was cheap and a bit scruffy, on the south side of the river, adjacent to a canoe/boat/leisure place and within earshot of a busy road. Our time in the south had spoiled us; we'd rarely heard traffic at night. The campsite bar was pumping out banging tunes, which competed with the traffic noise, but the calls of swifts and little terns were still winning. And something else.

'Is that those ducks again?' Adi wondered.

We went for a walk in search of the source of the croaking as dusk darkened. No ducks to be seen, but there it was, that rasping sound, impossibly loud.

'Frogs!' Adi said, and burst out laughing.

And we call ourselves nature conservationists. Tiny tree frogs made the hugest noise as they discussed the day's events on the river bank.

For once I cooked, a peasant dish of mashed potatoes fried with onions, accompanied by an elegant side-salad of lolla rossa, cheese, onions, tomato and apricots, all courtesy of a market stall on the quays of Blois. We fell asleep replete, the frogs still conversing by the river.

CHAPTER THIRTY-SEVEN

To Ballan-Miré

That morning I realised with a shock that it was June 23rd.

'We've only got three and a half weeks left!' I panicked for a second, then heard myself and laughed. Ages left! But something shifted, a slight sense of urgency. We had less time ahead of us than behind us.

'The best is yet to come!' Adi said, adding rather grimly, 'It bloody better be.'

We left Blois on time (for us), with only a pause to pick up a baguette.

Never let Adi into a boulangerie by himself. Instead of a baguette, he came out with a slab of fougasse covered in melted Roquefort cheese. Despite my arteries shuddering at the first taste of it, it was delicious. We weren't eating meat, or sampling real French cooking; because of our budget and our vegetarianism, on the few occasions we ate out we played safe and looked for an Italian, where we could have a risotto or a pizza. Thus we, and I really mean me, felt we should sample as many French breads and pastries as possible to redress the balance.

The landscape was much more interesting during the morning, with the cycle route going into and out of the river bank and even, thrillingly, going up and down some little hills. We were leaving the flat lands of the Île de France behind and entering a gently rolling world, passing fields of sweetcorn, wheat and barley, of cucumbers and other marrows with big plump green leaves full of promise.

In the middle of the day we passed a milestone: 1,000 miles from Avignon. Adi stopped and waited for me to catch up, then showed me the numbers on the screen of his bike computer.

'Wow!' I said. And then I tried to work out how far a day that was.

'Stop it!' He recognized the furrowed brow that indicated Madigan struggling with mental arithmetic. 'It's about spending two months in a country on a bike, remember? Not eating up miles.'

'It is,' I agreed

'Anyway,' he said, getting ready to cycle into the one thousand and oneth mile, 'some days we rode much more than the average.'

Of course he was right. It wasn't a competition. We'd explored. We'd walked. We'd got to know shape of the country, the jigsaw of its landscapes, how it was put together. 1,000 miles of countryside in one holiday.

'One thousand miles of headwind,' Adi said when I caught up to him a moment later.

'We haven't had headwind all the time.'

'We've got it now.'

We had. The warm wind that had greeted us in Orléans had waxed and waned, but had never dropped below a muscular breeze.

We hoped to camp near Tours that night, which would mean an easy ride to Chinon the following day, to meet our friends Jim and Christine.

We paused for lunch in Amboise. We'd been through here years ago when we drove up through France in our Landrover. I recognised the hill down which is the mansion house of Clos-Lucé, where Leonardo da Vinci lived and which houses sketches and models of brilliant imaginings of machines of varying degrees of impracticability. Very Jules Verne-esque.

Over lunch we discussed the advantages and disadvantages of following cycle routes. I love them from time to time because it eliminates the need to waste time at crossroads checking our route. This always seemed (to me) to take longer than necessary because Adi, Map Man, didn't approve of the map case that came with his bar bag and was supposed to sit on the lid. The attachments did not meet Adi's stringent construction standards, so the map was either in the bag, where it had to be brought out and unfolded at every doubtful junction, or pinned to the top of his handlebars with a big red butterfly clip. This, of course, did not work in the rain. I do not have a patient disposition and in delicate moods the unclipping of the bar bag lid, the removal of the map, the unfolding and the 'Let's see where we are now' sent my nerves twanging. Signed cycle routes were a pleasant respite from that.

Adi's irritation with the Loire track stemmed from the fact that it kept sending us in little loops instead of the most direct way. 'It's not that irritating,' I said, though it clearly was to him. Usually the loops took us through villages rather than past them, which he agreed was fair enough - directing tourists to the middle of villages served both the tourists and the shops, and keeps money coming into the area to justify spending money on nice surfaces on cycle tracks, for example.

We compromised in the afternoon by sometimes ignoring the signs and bypassing villages, only to find that the time spent searching for the route on the far side of the bypassed village just about equalled the time we saved by going through. I mentioned this after our second diversion from the signs, but The Stomach was playing with Adi's good humour. His temper rapidly declined, and we pedalled mostly in silence, me keeping back.

In a nature reserve a few miles before Tours I found the first compost toilet I'd seen in France. Looking back, I can see that it was naïve of me to expect that this news would cheer Adi up.

'Great.'

It was in a lovely spot, with nature walks and bird hides and woods and views over the river, but the morning's cheerfulness was gone.

The roads into Tours would have been challenging at the best of times, half of them being scooped out for new tramlines, but with a roiling stomach it nearly led to an accident. I was a couple of cars behind Adi at a set of lights when his impatience led him to nip dangerously between two moving cars. In the UK that sort of cycling would have led to a blare of horns from all sides; there, the cars just stopped and let him go through. Not a pip of a horn, which only made me more embarrassed at his aggressive cycling.

It took a few minutes to catch up with him, in the middle of an enormous square. I was still shaky with nerves, and left him to find the tourist office while I soothed myself with a golden-brown brioche-au-chocolat. Cake: it's nearly as good as stationery for soothing the nerves.

Adi returned forty minutes later in much better humour. To further cheer us, a young man who had just made himself a sandwich with a fresh baguette gave us half of the bread.

'This is enough for me. I'll only throw it away,' he said.

We cycled out in almost-reconciled silence with the aid of an excellent set of town maps. Tours straddles the Loire and the Cher where they run parallel to each other for a few miles upstream of their confluence, and spills out onto the banks of both. This explained the number of bridges in Tours. We found our way through the suburbs, riding around the back of a little park where the end of a festival was taking place. Folk music was playing and a lot of tiny children wearing enormous ladybird outfits were running around, brandishing oversized daisies. We were charmed.

There was never a bad day that didn't end up being redeemed somehow. After navigational interludes at crossroads (no more signs) we finally found our campsite, and it was just lovely, outside tiny Ballac-Miré. A pleasant sloping field with terraced pitches caught the evening sun. It was full of families. A couple of boys, less than twelve years old, wished us

'Bon appetit' as they walked past. When Adi replied 'Bonsoir' they clearly went on to discuss whether or not the English people had understood, because when they walked back past us they said, 'Good eating', in English.

After dinner, we went to a bar just down the road, where we ate ice-creams from a freezer, dispensed by the entirely spherical barman. Navigational discussion ensued. Adi and Jim had finally managed to speak to each other, and it turned out that he and Christine were not staying on the Loire, somewhere near Chinon. They were staying in a gîte south of Richelieu, more than twenty miles south of the river, and adding to our proposed ride by at about 15 miles.

'It's not that much extra,' Adi said.

'And it means we can eat more croissants.' I cheered up; for once I'd not been relishing the thought of a longish ride.

'And it will take us out of the direct headwind,' Adi said..

CHAPTER THIRTY-EIGHT

To Neuil-sous-Faye

The entire village population and everyone for miles around was in Ballan-Miré in the morning. A café-bar formed one entire side of the tiny square and was already full of elderly men watching the goings-on at the market, glasses of pastis and rosé in front of them. 'Attends les parents!' a young man called across the square to his friends. We picked up oranges and a bag of tiny, delicious apricots which, when we ate them later that morning, caused me to drool and make embarrassing noises.

We wriggled along lanes southwards, crossing a motorway, leaving the Loire and the Cher behind. We picked up a lovely road along the river Indre, another Loire tributary, flowing between banks of soft limestone. More troglodyte dwellings dug into the low cliffs. Troglodyte: it's a guttural word that doesn't capture the charm of these homes, the doors and walls and windows built into carefully-cut rock faces.

Only a little later we had stopped again, because it's not possible to cycle past a bric-à-brac barn and café built into a cave in the side of a cliff. I had to stifle more moans when drinking the apple juice, juice made from Pink Lady apples grown and squeezed and bottled right there. Exquisite surroundings: the warm, honey-tinted stone of the cliff formed two walls of the courtyard, a small wooden café the third, the road wall and open iron gates the fourth. A wooden barn door opened directly into the cliff, underneath the lumpy, irregular surface. Tiny windows were cut into it, and tin tubs and containers hung from the cliff wall, matching the ones in the courtyard filled with flowers and young fruit trees.

We turned gradually south, cycling through the Forest of Chinon towards the Vienne, another Loire tributary. Miles of conifers and, close to the river, fields of sunflowers, asparagus and wheat chequered the gently undulating landscape.

That day's picnic lunch was one of the best, in a field of stiff competition. By the side of the river Vienne in L'Île Bouchard, we had a full spread: baguette stuffed with Camembert and apple slices, apricots and oranges from the morning's market AND tea and coffee brewed on our stove, on a picnic table by the river spread with our wonderful multi-purpose table cloth from Arles.

'We've got the best-looking picnic table on the river,' Adi said. It was so perfect that he didn't even swear much when the wind attempted to lift everything off. Digesting happily afterwards, I took in the sounds: little girls at the next table; a scooter like a wasp on the road behind; wind in the weeping willows; the water's surface rippling; frogs on the river bank.

On the long straight road south to Richelieu the inevitable happened.

Adi waited for me in a layby, staring at a field of sunflowers, bending their heads northwards. Towards us. The wind had found us. I didn't need showing. I'd been fighting it for an hour, clicking down the gears.

'Just think about the gîte that's waiting for us,' I said.

We wouldn't be camping for four days. I wasn't quite sure how I felt about this. I mentioned this to Adi, who confessed he felt the same.

'But just think about it: turning taps in the shower.'

That would do.

We paused for a moment in a blink of a village called Brizay, where I assessed the toilets, half-hidden beside the Mairie. Excellent, only half a mark taken off, and that was for the rather bleachy smell. Yes, I was aware that I was becoming a bit toilet obsessed, but such matters assume great importance when on the road.

'Just try not to tell anyone else about them,' Adi grinned.

Then it was on down south to Richelieu, with its enormous square and charming sprawl of parkland. The last leg into a knackering headwind towards the tiny village of Neuil-sous-Faye where Jim and Christine were competing in a local boules tournament. The boulodrome was bigger than the village. Good cheer, bric-à-brac stalls, rosé in tiny glasses and dancing in traditional black dresses and bonnets (to the most appalling music), and then there were Jim and Christine, waiting for their names to be called for the last pairing of the tournament. And then it was luxury in a gîte for three nights while I turned from forty to forty-one.

The Headwind Is Winning: Neuil-sous-Faye to Nantes

CHAPTER THIRTY-NINE

To Montsoreau

After three days of rest, Adi was itching just as much as I was to get moving again. Even though we lacked the flinty-eyed focus and impressive (lunatic) daily distances of many a 'proper' tourer, we were still living an active life: cycling, parking the bikes, lifting the bikes, lifting panniers on and off the bikes, walking and cycling everywhere. It's amazing how many calories camping burns. Without noticing, we'd become accustomed to it, and we missed the physicality of the cycling touring life. More than that, we missed the simple state of being on the road. In nearly six weeks we'd hardly rounded a single bend in the road twice. That state of constant freshness, of the world unfolding around and under us, was enormously seductive, and we missed it.

And we missed our routines. Plotting our route, putting up the tent, and all the other on-road customs we'd fallen into over the last five weeks. We were ready to go.

Though I had enjoyed the showers with turning taps.

We waved goodbye and cycled back towards the Loire, northwest into a headwind that had clearly missed us and changed its direction to greet us.

'The weather back home's been awful,' Christine had told us. They live in Derbyshire. 'We've hardly seen the sun since the start of May. It must be worse in Wales.'

It was a small consolation but a consolation nonetheless as we put our heads down and stolidly pumped the pedals across the expanse of rather featureless countryside that lay between us and the confluence of the Loire and the Vienne. There would have been shouting if Britain had been enjoying a heatwave. I felt strong and content, and eager to get rid of the little roll of belly fat that's an inevitable consequence of spending any time in the vicinity of Jim's cooking.

It had been a bit of a shock to the system; over the last few weeks, the restrictions posed upon our diet by our lifestyle had become habits - waist-minimising habits, as it turned out. No butter on anything, far less cheese, no milk, and regular eating times: breakfast, snack, lunch, snack, snack, dinner, chocolate before bed. That was our luxury, never, ever missed, and we were becoming connoisseurs of slabs of dark, bitter chocolate.

The weather was cool, just warm enough for a tee-shirt when cycling at a steady pace. My legs were constantly exposed now; the last time we'd been genuinely chilly had been in Figeac. In spite of the almost permanent cloud since Orléans, my legs and arms were turning a toasty brown. Adi's fair hair was bleached white-blonde; two inches long now, the headwind brushed it up dramatically; I thought he looked like a Viking.

Long vistas of barely undulating fields of wheat and vegetables. Few villages, identical, sleepy and apparently barely habited. Silence reigned, apart from the whirr of our tyres and the rush of headwind in our ears. Even the swifts were muted.

Life returned when we reached the rivers, broad and lovely, with sand banks, islets, waterside meadows and wooded banks. A few people were rowing in the traditional flat-bottomed wooden boats, negotiating the sandbanks just under the surface with care. Because of these and the treacherously shifting channels, there was very little traffic on the Loire. Happily, this leaves plenty of undisturbed feeding and nesting places for the little terns, herons, lapwings and all the other birds taking full advantage of this long wildlife haven.

We spent the first night in Montsoreau, just beyond the confluence of the Vienne and the Loire. The campsite was full of retired Britons, mostly friendly but completely taken aback when we arrived and set about erecting our home. Two of the men came over and questioned us about how we managed. A fair enough question, but he asked it in the manner of an anthropologist. 'Fascinating,' he kept saying. 'Fascinating.' I felt like a specimen. Then he shocked us by not knowing what time the boulangerie opened, or even what it was. He'd been there for six weeks. Adi and I couldn't stop muttering in amazement to each other when he'd gone out of earshot.

'Six fecking weeks!'

'And he doesn't know what the "boulangerie" is!'

'He hasn't even been IN IT!'

This was beyond our comprehension.

It was European Championship time, Spain playing Portugal. All the English took the indoor seats at the campsite bar so we sat outside, Adi and the French watching the match through the plate glass windows while I wrote up my diary. Later, we went for a walk with another young couple along the bank of the river. We didn't understand each other's language but our common aim was clear: we were going to spot a frog before we went to sleep. It took half an hour of determined staring, all the while with the crazy croaking going non-stop. The swifts had gone to bed before Adi spotted one, tiny on a broad blade of green. It took a full five minutes before I could make it out. They were still sawing away as I fell asleep.

CHAPTER FORTY

To Gennes

I had one of those days next day. All cyclists get them. You've eaten enough, slept well enough, even stretched before starting off, but your legs are dead weights. You are starving all the time. Your legs feel hungry. The dreaded bonk looms from the moment you wake up. There's nothing to do but persuade your legs to just turn the pedals, stuff your bar bag with bread and chocolate and nibble continuously. Fortunately, this is quite easy to do on the flat.

I couldn't think about anything but food as I pedalled. The scenery was charming, but I was unmoved. Even the little terns grabbed only a quarter second of my attention before I fell to wondering when I could justify my next biscuit. Five minutes? Two?

We stopped at the Greenwich Meridian for a photo, which should have felt more meaningful but which to me was just an excuse to eat more bread and honey.

Despite regular nibbling I was still tired and truculent by the time we reached Saumur and had bought lunch ingredients. Left to myself I'd have sat on the pavement and guzzled them there and then but Adi persuaded me, with heroic persistence, to wait five minutes while we rolled the bikes upwards in search of the ideal picnic setting. It was worth it; we had the most scenic lunch spot in the city, high up behind the chateau in a patch of parkland, looking down on the river below. Once again, good humour was restored by good views and good food. But mostly by food.

We are not chateau buffs, and, as mentioned, our budget did not extend to many trips to museums and the like, but we had visited the Chateau Villandry on my birthday. The gardens had lured me: medieval monastic gardens recreated in loving detail in the nineteenth century. Walking into the winter garden, full of hues of white and pale blue in fluffy sprays, had a cooling effect despite the heat of the day. (True to form, we had good weather when we weren't cycling.) The summer garden was full of yellows and oranges, nothing garish, just warm and lovely.

But that was the extent of our experience of one of the Loire's greatest draws. The chateau itself had raised my Irish peasant hackles, and there was plenty more raising of hackles to be had as we pedalled along. Every town of any size and many a village of no size at all was dominated by at least one chateau, situated for maximum effect overlooking the river. Very pretty to look at and great for shouting anti-feudal slogans at.

From Saumur the route followed a cycle track that clung to the south bank of the Loire. Occasionally unladen cyclists would pass us, a finger raised from the handlebars in greeting. A couple on a tandem came the opposite way, pulling a trailer in which a small, shaggy terrier was standing up, nose to the wind. The river was almost freakishly calm, satiny and silent, only the gentlest of ripples on the shelving banks. It stretched away, reflecting pewter clouds, to the far, tree-clothed bank, and the barely-rippling landscape stretched away behind. The sky was huge. We cycled past slipways with small fleets of wooden boats moored up, with sometimes a little hamlet of houses nearby. We'd stop and have a quick look around before moving on. Peace reigned. Little things stayed with me: the beaten metal sculpture of a heron in the act of plunging his neck to catch an unwary fish.

A rain shower overtook us but the headwind had dried us out before we reached Gennes. One silver lining of headwinds. Tiny Gennes was a beautiful village with a gem of a campsite. We claimed The Best Pitch On The Loire, right by the river, furnished with - luxury! - a picnic bench. To our excitement, we realised that our pitch and the other riverside pitches were ONLY accessible to hikers and cyclists! Tiny low hedges prevented car and campervan campers from occupying them. A NO CAR ZONE! The shower block was wonderful with special bike-parking fences outside it. There was one outside reception too: little fences that ONLY existed for cyclists to lean their bikes against them! AND it was less than €10! I shot a short video, running around to show all these wonderful features. My commentary ranges from excited to unhinged. I even captured Adi saying something you don't often hear Adi say:

'I'm struggling to find anything to complain about.' Even the wind had dropped to a gentle, non-dinner-threatening breeze. Frogs in the river islets croaked a soundtrack throughout the evening rituals of chopping, cooking, eating, washing up, checking for Dutch campers, walking, reading and retiring. I loved these days. Dodgy starts, perfect endings.

CHAPTER FORTY-ONE

To St-Florian-le-Vieil

I knew it was eight o'clock as we finished breakfast because the church bell on our side of the river rang the hours twice, and then the church on the far side of the river rang them twice, leaving us in no doubt.

Since we'd arrived on the Loire we'd been averaging 60 miles a day but were still managing plenty of exploring. Our routine had streamlined and settled into a rhythm that suited us both.

Our mornings went like this:

I'd wake up sometime between six and seven and get up no later than seven. I'd go for a shower, then snatch a few moments to read or catch up on my diary while Adi was in the shower. There'd be a discussion about whose turn it was to collect the baguette and croissants. This turned out to be my task more often than Adi's, as he was the magician who understood the

335

MSR stove, a device which needed coaxing and a very gentle touch of the hand on the fuel outlet tap.

I'd speed off to the boulangerie or shop we'd identified the previous evening, braving traffic and queues of locals. I loved this, seeing people walking and cycling off with paper bags full of yummy breads, and ordering my own bread and cycling back with it protruding from my bar bag. If tea and coffee weren't quite ready when I got back I'd finish tidying inside the tent: rolling and packing the sleeping bags, liners, mats and pillows, and moving all the panniers outside to sit more or less neatly beside the bikes. If it was dry and warm we'd hang the sleeping bags up on a line for a few minutes and lie the sleeping mats on the ground to get some sun on them.

After breakfast one of us would wash up while the other finished packing the sleeping gear and anything else we'd had loose in the tent. By this stage all the panniers would be standing neatly, almost ready to be clipped shut. Washing up finished, we'd collapse the tent together. One last look at the maps to finalise where we would aim for lunch, although no matter how definite we were, this almost always changed. A last visit to the shower block for the brushing of teeth and the application of sunscreen, and we were off. There was always a moment when I'd look at the tent-shaped patch of flattened grass and marvel. I found it, and still find it, amazing, that you can make somewhere your home for the night, your own personal little patch, and move on the next day, leaving only faint and transient traces.

We spent the morning playing leap-frog with a lone British cycle tourer and a small peleton of lightly-laden Loire-à-Vélo-ists. We'd noticed more and more people cycling in groups on day rides, and more and more cycle tourers like ourselves. When we'd overtaken the solo guy for the third time and got no more of a grunt from him than we had the first time, we discussed our riding style compared to his. He was clearly cycling more slowly than we were, but we'd probably take the same amount of time to reach the same destination, the difference being that we would have got off our bikes and nosed around on foot a little. Most of the nosing today involved trying to get a glimpse of the frogs whose throaty song once again formed the soundtrack to the day.

We paused in Montjean-sur-Loire, a fact Adi told me around a mouthful of the massive chocolate and coffee ice-cream he was eating. It was the first afternoon break we'd had for some time, and it was sweet to sit there in patchy sunlight. Adi's stomach seemed to be settling down; the grumps were away, bothering some other couple. We counted up the wildlife tally for the day. Frogs, frogs, frogs, especially in still places on the river; a hobby; lapwings, cormorants, little egrets; more little terns. Hirondelles galore: swifts, swallows, house martins and sand martins.

At some point we crossed to the southern bank and ate up the miles, rolling steadily into the headwind on quiet lanes. Though the roads were flat, there was some relief in the surrounding landscape, with some high bluffs overlooking the river. We overtook some cyclists and were overtaken by others, sometimes being leapfrogged when we stopped to look for frogs. My favourite was a stout couple of middle age, slowly and inexorably pedalling in jeans and thick cotton shirts. Least favourite was the British man, who eventually did respond to our greetings during a pause. He was cycling north to meet friends on the north coast but they were taking their time, he said, rather disapprovingly, and he was 'running out of France'. What on earth did that mean? I bit my lip on my lecture about how to explore instead of race through a country.

'New département,' said Adi with satisfaction as we cycled north across the river to St-Florian-le-Vieil's campsite. 'We are now in Loire-Atlantique. Or Historic Brittany, if you prefer.'

The campsite was basic but nice, cheap and clean, and full of tents. Tents outnumbered caravans and campervans, the first time this had happened. Cars with tents, cyclists with tents, walkers with tents. We waved hello to the jeans-clad couple we'd seen earlier and smiled as they went through the same ritual as we'd just been through - carefully walking over a selection of pitches, checking for ants.

Many of the campers were here for the oriental festival, we guessed, when we went for a walk up to the top of the old cité, perched on a bluff on the southern bank. A huge double marquee stood ready on the square, equipped with a stage and loudspeakers. There was even a sound system set up in the church - a tall, lovely structure in pretty white tufa stone. An 'oriental' (read 'vaguely hippy festival-ish') market lined the edges of the square against the battlements overlooking the river. The new town, down beside the bridge, was a mess of converging roads, evilly channelled with a set of junctions apparently designed to generate maximum disorder. But there was a lovely boulangerie where we picked up a bag of 'madeleines' - sort of a cross between a fairy cake and a miniature brioche. I inhaled a couple before Adi noticed and confiscated the rest for pudding.

CHAPTER FORTY-TWO

To Nantes

Two weeks and three days to go exactly,' Adi reported at breakfast. I'd known we were well over the half-way point but it was a jolt to realise we were almost at three-quarters.

Something in my outlook had begun to change after Orléans, and took more definite shape after our break with Jim and Christine. It had been a wrench to give up our routine and our independence, lovely though the company and the creature comforts (turning taps!) were. It made me realise that, in spite of my incessant internal self-criticism and the fact that Adi and I were dependent on each other in a way that I found constraining sometimes, we enjoyed an independence that most people only dream of. This is hardly an original observation, and one that I seem to come to anew with every cycle tour, and I'm a bit embarrassed that this time it took more than five weeks of cycling and four days in a gîte for me to work it out. But it was a small, personal revelation to me nonetheless. That, and the limited time we had left, made it feel as if we truly were a team. We were a unit. Indivisible. Marie and Adi, cycling through France.

I spent every day in a reverie, either lost in thought, or lost in my surroundings, or simply lost in the rhythm of the pedals. And we were seeing such things: a whole new country, a new countryside. This state of being is seductive. On the bike all day, the big and small questions that occupied my mind most of the time at home - Have I got enough work lined up for the next month? Did I remember to pick up milk? Is there enough chocolate in the house? - faded away, leaving two basic questions. Where are we heading for today? And how are we going to get there? After that, it was just the two of us, Adi and me, The Legs, and Bike.

(Although the chocolate question did tend to hang around.)

As I pedalled beside Adi that morning, I pondered my feelings about going home. I wasn't sure whether I was looking forward to it or not. In a way we'd just found our rhythm. We'd fallen into a routine that satisfied each of us. Lots of wandering and nosy exploring for both of us. Relaxed mooching around for Adi. Lots of miles on the bike for me. Plenty of tea-stops and sweet boulangerie treats for both of us. France was enchanting to me, familiar yet unfailingly foreign, and so, so beautiful.

So it was a pity that the last section of our Loire ride was the dullest by far, alongside dusty fields already harvested and bare, beside long sheds of an industrial-agricultural nature. It went on forever but finally the track became a tree-shaded path between a park and the river. A red squirrel scooted across the path in front of us, and a plump ten-year-old boy was practising skidding on his bike. Like all cool-dudes-in-training, he made sure that we couldn't avoid noticing his prowess by skidding across our path, shouting 'Bonjour!' as he whipped the bike round at the end of the skid. 'Bonjour,' we replied, stony-faced.

The hopes we'd had about the weather getting better and the wind - the wretched headwind! - dying off came to nothing. The heavens opened when we reached Nantes's outskirts. On with the jackets for a last spray-flinging, drenching ride on the north embankment. We followed the bike track to a busy interchange beside a bridge and turned up into the city, losing the track in a mess of traffic lanes.

'This'll do,' said Adi, as we lashed our bikes to a bench and shook the rain out of our jackets and hair.

The traffic had conveniently swept us up into the heart of the town. Beside us was the enormous

Chateau des Ducs, home to the last rulers of an independent Brittany in the 1500s, separated from the equally enormous cathedral by a small square and the chateau's moat.

We'd long ago earmarked Nantes as our next rest day. This jarred a little with my new-found contentment, but any impatience was put to rest almost instantly. It was impossible not to be charmed by Nantes; it was such a lively, light city, with a great sense of airiness. The old centre of narrow streets huddled close the cathedral and the chateau, while wide boulevards opened out to the west. It isn't the capital of Brittany any more, but it still felt like the gateway to the region. There was certainly something Atlantic in the weather.

We did the tourist office ritual, then cycled out to the campsite, a couple of miles along one of the tram lines towards the northern suburbs. The facilities were wonderful and once again we were in a pitch designed specifically for people on foot or on bikes. Another manic session with the camera ensued before pitching up. I only stopped when a friendly man called Olivier offered to share coffee with us.

Olivier was a dote. We sat on a bench under a wooden shelter, considerately placed in the middle of the no-car pitches, and chatted about cycling culture in Wales and France until his three-year-old son Raphael demanded a bike ride. When Adi and I left for the city centre we saw them going round and round the footpaths, Olivier on his tiny-wheeled 'vélo-de-camping' with a hand on Raphael's head, gently steering the toddler as he pedalled his little green three-wheeler with fierce concentration.

We passed the afternoon exploring, wandering in the old town streets, reading and drinking tea. The headwind had been tiring me more than I realised; I found myself grateful for the rest and the chance to just roam around on foot and unladen bike.

We treated ourselves to dinner in a restaurant.

'Not much of it, is there?' Adi said, looking at his plate.

We'd rather foolishly chosen a crêperie. A crêpe is not a meal, no matter what Brittany has managed to convince the world. What there was of it was delicious, but I could have eaten ten of them. It might explain why my half of the bottle of wine went straight to my head. I have confused memories of a tiny bar with very cool patrons and a minute bathroom painted in chequerboard squares in shades of turquoise. While waiting for the tram I bought and inhaled two bags of chips from a Turkish fast food stall to soak up the excess of wine. Crêpes, I philosophised drunkenly at Adi, are not a good way to soak up alcohol.

CHAPTER FORTY-THREE

Nantes

I didn't wake the next morning so much as come round. Adi'd already been for the baguette and wordlessly handed a big wodge of fresh bread, a bottle of water and two ibuprofen through the flap of the inner tent, careful not to let daylight touch my slitted eyes.

We had a lovely day, if a bit desiccated. Dim memories faded mercifully as the sun came out. (Sun! On a non-cycling day *again*.) We rolled easily into town down the gentle hill and mooched around on the bikes in the wide open spaces west of the tangle of old-town streets. An early lunch (soakage) at a fast food outlet, tasty hot paninis and tartlet puddings we'd have paid a fortune for at home. I loved the way that most fast food in France was nicely presented. Food is important, is the message you get across all kinds and levels of eateries. Food is very important.

We cycled through the medieval streets and squares to the nineteenth century town, with broader boulevards and open spaces and crossed the main channel of the Loire to the Île de Nantes. This is one of the last actual islands; after World War II five of the seven sinuous channels of the Loire were filled in, mostly using the labour of German prisoners of war. Most of the old warehouses and port buildings on the island are given over to artistic and innovative projects, and we'd come to see one of them.

We wandered towards the entrance of a huge, glass-covered hangar and joined the small crowd taking photographs. Five metres high, the Great Elephant stood at rest, eyelashes closed, trunk hanging straight down. This is the most famous of the fantastical creatures and structures created by the wonderful Company of the Machines, partly inspired by the works of Jules Verne, part homage to Leonardo da Vinci's inventions. We bought tickets and joined the queue of forty people climbing up the stairs to a gallery in the hangar to enter the elephant's belly.

Immense, incredible, intricate. It was one of those experiences where words fail. Trying to describe it to others afterwards I could only fall back on 'Magical! Magical!' and a huge smile. Upwards of forty people from one to sixty milled in and out, onto the little platforms over the legs, up into the howdah on the elephant's back - two stories high - and through the cavern of its belly.

You can see how it works, which adds to rather than takes away from the wonder. The mechanical engine that drives it along is clearly visible, as is the little cockpit under the chest where the driver sits. I stayed in the belly for ages, staring at the rollers and articulations moving its legs, watching the little labels on the controls jiggling. Pure steampunk. A guide explained to a little boy how to make it roar, and then let him pull the lever.

Out on the balconies over the legs I watched her tail twitching - I had decided she was a she - and her legs striding. The movement was beautifully realistic, cogs and pistons instead of bone and muscle rolling smoothly under a skin of polished tulipwood. It turned its head, blinked its gorgeous, long-lashed eyes, opened and flapped its great leather ears. and swung its trunk to spray water at the delighted entourage following its progress along the esplanade, past other old warehouses and port buildings. Close by was the Manège d'Andréa, a fairground carousel of toads, birds and unidentifiable creatures from the magical natural history books.

When we dismounted we couldn't leave the elephant alone. Its return journey took it behind the warehouses to enter the hangar from the other end.

Everyone wore smiles so big they hurt. A small boy's face, unable to hold any more wonder, eyes huge and smile huger, open-mouthed. The air rang with the elephant's trumpets and shrieks from soaked pedestrians who'd been too dazzled to dodge the spraying trunk. The driver of the elephant in his little cab beneath the head, operating the trunk, was laughing his head off.

We followed it back, around the great open space behind the Compagnie des Machines and the Chantiers de Nantes, into the huge, light, girdered and green-glassed space. The elephant marched slowly up the bright aisle, huge and lovely, still spraying. Up on the balcony we got an unexpected dousing, perfectly timed. Hysterical drenched giggling from all.

We weaved along the old quays on our bikes, between two old cranes, yellow and grey, relics of Nantes' past, between pedestrians and myriad cyclists: tiny cyclists, steady cyclists, cool cyclists, family cyclists. Roller bladers and skate-boarders. Lads on jumping bikes - I don't know what else to call them (no saddles! No seatposts!) - jumping from standing starts on the ground to the tops of walls.

The afternoon melted into early evening. A DJ had installed himself on a small podium on the grassy bank river bank, next to a small bar in a tent. People fanned out on the grass, lots of couples gay and straight, lots of families, some people dancing with very cool and minimalist moves, others clearly too cool to dance. On the fringe, others milled around a merry-go-round with crazy creatures; I can still see the little girl in yellow pedalling a bespectacled ostrich like mad. It was all very French: organised but relaxed, the sort of small musical event that French towns and villages seem to excel at.

We watched the last half hour of the Spain and Italy football match while Spain smashed Italy 4-0 and the Irish bar cheered, all except for the pretty, disconsolate Italian woman just behind us. We ate pizza outside a tiny pizza house, narrow as a ginnel, next to a woman eating alone while reading an academic textbook on sociology. One last peep on the ride out to the campsite into the lovely airy, stubbornly surviving cathedral.

'That,' said Adi as we snuggled into our sleeping bags after the lovely ride home, 'was the best rest day ever.'

I had to agree.

Canal And Ocean: Nantes To Guidel

CHAPTER FORTY-FOUR

To Blain

It was drizzling.

'Of course it is!' Adi said, handing me my mug of tea. 'Rest days, good weather. Almost always.'

'True. It's lifting though.' The mellow day yesterday led me to look on the drizzle almost affectionately. Though there was still that disturbing wind coming from the west.

I pushed the thought away. Even though I've lived all my life on west coasts of wet countries, I still cherished the conviction that further west, there would be sunshine.

We packed everything away but the tent, leaving it up to give it a chance to dry out as the drizzle lightened. We brewed an extra tea and coffee and sat at the sheltered picnic table (oh lovely, lovely campsite) with the middle-aged couple we'd met a couple of nights ago at St-Florian-le-Vieil. They'd turned up late last night, still in their jeans. Their post-rain tent-drying ritual was longer and more complicated even than ours. They were lovely, from north-east France, and had toured on their bikes all over Europe, including Scotland. Like us, they intended to head towards the Canal de Nantes à Brest.

I passed an hour swapping circus skills with Olivier's lovely wife. Five seconds after picking up my hula hoop she was spinning gracefully. An hour after playing with her magic contact balls I was only dropping them every ten seconds instead of instantly. The sun came out, we said goodbye and on we went. We left with the memory of a couple of days of friendly conversations, and kindness and courtesy.

Adi and I had had some long and not very conclusive discussions on how to spend the rest of our limited time. South coast of Brittany, I thought, but Adi doubted we could make it all the way to the furthest point of Finistère. 'I think we can,' I'd said. It wasn't that far on the map, and we could always shave bits of the coast off. Finistère is such a lovely word, redolent of wildness and the end of things. I badly wanted to get there. We would have to crack on, though. We had yet to reach the coast.

This is probably one of the reasons why the contentment I'd found on the Loire took a bit of a battering that day. Because of the drizzle it was after eleven before we left. By midday we'd had our first disagreement.

One of the differences between Adi and me is the way we perceive the passage of time. Take shopping. Adi can go into a shop with a list of three items and take twenty-five minutes, because he examines all the other shelves to see if there is anything interesting. If I'm the one shopping, I will go in and buy the three items. If something catches my eye whilst I am searching for those items, I might examine it, maybe even buy it, but I don't browse. (Unless I'm in a bookshop. Bookshops don't count as shopping.) I was no longer allowed to go shopping for food with him any more, because I bounced up and down beside him and irritated him.

Normally I swallowed my impatience, because this was his holiday too and it's no fun having your beloved fizzing impatiently at your shoulder, but I had noticed that much of my diary writing tended to take place outside shops, while I waited for Adi to come out with three items. I tried to keep my impatience in check but sometimes it won.

Like this morning. We followed the cycle tracks in the road along the river Erdre north out of Nantes. He stopped to go into a shop. By the time he came out I'd read a chapter of my book. I started to put my Kindle away until I noticed that he was sitting down on a bench, peeling a banana.

'Are you hungry already?' I was trying very, very hard not to say, 'You can't be hungry, we've only just had breakfast'.

'Breakfast was a while ago.'

Surely then we should be making tracks, I thought, but did not say out loud.

Adi ate the banana slowly while I read, watching for any bike-directed movement out of the corner of my eye. He put the banana in a bin and sat down again. I kept reading. Finally he went towards his bike. I tentatively closed my Kindle. Then he looked at his bike computer and turned to me in astonishment.

'It's five to twelve!'

I snapped. My voice wobbled. I held my arms out wide.

'My life is wasting away outside shops!' I think I was actually declaiming.

'What?'

'What time did you think it would be?'

'Well I don't know, I was just buying stuff for us to eat and having a banana. Stuff for us to eat,' he repeated crossly.

'How long were you in there?' I demanded. 'Go on, tell me.'

'I don't know, ten minutes?'

'Twenty five. And it's nearly another ten since you came out.'

It was a silent ride. We often rode apart because I was slower almost all the time, even when the knee had been troublesome, but this time we were Riding Apart. I was genuinely ashamed of my outburst - Adi is really tolerant and even-tempered, not given to outbursts except towards camping stoves and other inanimate objects - but on the other hand I really was tired of waiting outside shops. It was my holiday too, and we were running out of it.

We stopped for lunch by a little village. Pontoons poked out into a calm nook of the river. I shivered and put my fleece on. When the wind stopped, or we found somewhere sheltered from it, the air was mild, but the breeze was cool. 'We could be beside a Scottish loch,' Adi said, breaking the hour-long silence

The Canal de Nantes à Brest intersected with the river in a few miles. We found handy cycle route signs guiding us towards it, which we followed gratefully until one went missing. Fifteen minutes of fruitless back-and-forthing, Adi cursing, me scowling, before Adi chose a direction at random. We found the signs, and shortly afterwards found the Canal, and spent the rest of the afternoon on a well-surfaced track along the old towpath.

Far, far better than the Canal du Midi: a good fine-gravelled surface, with calm water on one side of us, trees on another. A red squirrel scooted up a trunk and paused, limbs splayed and claws clinging, to watch us pass. Other notable sights included a very long man leaning over a very low bike, speeding along in a blur of stringy grey hair and stringy brown calves, and a young couple touring with a couple of huge furry cats in a bike trailer. This surely took feline compliance to previously unrecorded levels. I've never known a cat who'd have suffered such a thing. When we passed them for the second time they were having a picnic with the cats on leads. The cats didn't look particularly happy.

More and more cycle tourists; like the Loire cycle route, the Canal is one of those routes that lots of people 'do'.

We swiftly erected the tent in the municipal campsite of a little village called Blain, and cycled into the village to find the boulangerie and a café. Rain threatened and the forecast was awful, but my feet were warm as we sat in the little bar by the river, drawing out our hot chocolates, and the proprietress's smile as she shook hands and introduced herself would have cheered grumpier hearts than Adi's and mine. I loved places like this: really basic, formica everywhere, but a welcoming atmosphere, with staff taking the serving of food and drink as seriously as in an upmarket restaurant. Michelle served us with the same attention and courtesy that she served people eating their three-course meals at the tables around the corner.

Back at the campsite rain had started falling, but we had dinner in the dry, always a positive thing. A municipal costing €7.50 (a cheap campsite always cheered us up), it was equipped with covered areas next to reception: a tiny cupboard-sized room stuffed with books in an assortment of languages, and a large room with notice boards and a map of Brittany on the wall etched in wood, and a large table. We cooked and ate in there, sheltered from the rain.

Our humour was restored. No matter what happened, we were still cycling, still out in the world riding around new bends, seeing new things, no matter now fast or how slowly. We were still doing what we wanted to do. And we were doing it together. I grinned at Adi as we washed up. He asked me why, grinning back. No reason, I said, still grinning.

Back in the shelter after washing up, Adi had just spread all the maps and tourist office bumph out on the table when the light went out. There was a resigned sigh but no cursing. I didn't mind; I felt all bumphed out and listened to a mistle thrush singing into the dusk, so intensely that it sounded almost like a nightingale.

We weren't the only cycle tourers here. There was an English couple we'd spoken to this morning in Nantes and another couple on a tandem with a trailer. The tandem pair were slightly older than us but serious about mileage; they'd only left Orléans four days ago. There was also a lone person in a tiny one-man tent who was snoring loudly.

'What's the betting he's gone before we wake?' Adi said.

I didn't take him up on it. He'd be gone by dawn. The snoring stopped suddenly. Maybe someone poked him with a long stick.

Adi fetched our candle lantern and we had a quick look at the map. We would go to Redon for lunch tomorrow and think about the onwards route then. Adi continued to frown over the Rough Guide.

'Redon sounds lovely,' he said. 'We could stay there, maybe?'

I looked at the map. Redon was only 30 miles up the road.

'Why don't we aim there for lunch, have a good two or three hours exploring, then carry on,' I suggested. 'It's not huge, we could probably see most of its sights in a few hours, and get a nice ride onward in the afternoon as well.'

He thought.

'If we want to get as far as Finistère we'll have to think about how to combine our sightseeing and our cycling,' I said, sneakily.

And so it was agreed. I hugged him suddenly. A compromise! I vowed not to have hysterics outside little shops again. Looking at the snoring solo tourer's padded shorts hanging damply from his handlebars in the dusk, I thought how miserable it would be now if I was alone. Independence isn't everything..

CHAPTER FORTY-FIVE

To St Martin-sur-Oust

We'd been right about the lone cyclist. He was gone, vanished, not a trace left behind when I peeped out of the tent just before six. Such a feat of organisation was utterly beyond me. How did he have time for a good breakfast? How had he managed to pack away his books so quickly?

We got chatting to the English couple, Denis and Anne. They'd spent a couple of weeks touring around Normandy last summer and got hooked. This time they'd cycled straight down from the ferry at St-Malo to Vannes, worked their way along the coast to Nantes and were now following the canal for a while before heading back to St-Malo.

It was lovely cycling beside the canal, under a pewter sky and a sprinkly rain. We cycled by still water, bedecked with lily pads and lilies in flower, past trees and fields and crisply painted lock gates guarded by neat lock cottages with gardens full of flowers. At Guenrouet we paused to nibble our baguette (a céréale stuffed with seeds, excellent, from Blain's unpromising-looking boulangerie).

I'm always surprised when canals aren't straight. I think of them as great feats of engineering, which they are, but in my mind they cut through the countryside like Roman roads. Not the case: canals, like railways, are constrained by the contours of the land. Thus the pleasant, sinuous ribbon of the Canal de Nantes à Brest.

It beat the Canal du Midi hands down. The surface was good enough that we didn't have to keep our eyes peeled for the tree roots and ruts that had slowed us so devastatingly on the Canal du Midi. We couldn't race along it but we were able to maintain a steady average of 13 mph all morning while enjoying the treed and meadowed banks. Wildlife abounded, with cormorants, a hoopoe in full crazy crest mode, a huge, low-flying heron doing his pterodactyl impression and frogs creak-croaking in little ponds bordering the track. And we could actually see the countryside we were cycling through: not jaw-droppingly spectacular but green and lovely, a proper step up from the scenery around the Loire. The trees usually only lined one bank at a time, giving us simultaneous views of woodland and meadows. The canal narrowed and widened within its curving, inclined banks, wavelets rippling gently in the slight breeze.

That was another thing. We whispered it to each other, for fear of awakening the weather demon again. The wind was the lowest it had been since Orléans.

With a lack of antagonistic forces - Knee, Stomach, Wind or Grumps - we covered the 30 miles to Redon comfortably. Lunch was eaten sitting on what I can only describe as a small stone thing in the middle of a small square. Adi had made a monster sandwich with the twin of this morning's baguette, some cheese and an apple. We'd arrived just in time to quiz the tourist office about interesting things to see and campsites in a westerly direction. We discussed our onward options over lunch, and afterwards in a little bar-tabac. The Beatles 'Help' was playing on the radio as we waited for our tea and coffee, and then something something wonderful happened. I was served tea IN A TEAPOT. WITH THE TEABAG INSIDE THE POT. NOT ON THE SIDE.

'That's only the second time this has happened on the entire trip!' I told Adi. He was taking a photo of it. The first had been beside the staircase lock near Narbonne, clearly an aberration. Tea was usually served with hot water in the teapot - if there was a pot at all - with the tea bag on the side or waiting in the cup. The service had always been so courteous that I'd

364 | MARIE MADIGAN

never been able to bring myself to ask why? Why do you do it like that? I made no comment on this teapot, just gave the barman the biggest smile I could fit on my face.

On tea generally, I had noticed that the infusions were very mild. I'm an Earl Grey drinker at home, I don't drink milk, and find most normal British and Irish teas (with the exception of Barry's Tea, from Cork, of course) are harsh on the stomach. Not a problem in France. Even the Tetley's was clearly blended specially for the foreign market.

Redon was a pretty town, its heritage as a meeting of three waterways - the Canal and the rivers Oust and La Vilaine - reflected in the mix of styles in the buildings. Half-timbered and sloping, slate roofs, solid granite stone next to rosy sandstone, plastered and painted, balconied and unadorned, tipping gently towards each other down the old, narrow high street and looking sedately at each other across the canal, the river and the locks.

The cycle track confused us when we left, with a total change in the style of the signs.

'This is what happens when you start following signs. You turn off your brain!' Adi said. He spotted the change, and stopped and called me back - I'd been riding on regardless - and checked the maps. 'That way.'

We followed the Oust for a while. Beautiful, with indented banks and gentle fields, rising land to the left and some bare bluffs of rock. The track joined the canal again just past a high ropes adventure playground, with signs advertising 'Location Poneys Shetland', which tickled me. There were fewer locks along this section; the one just before the village where we camped was one of the prettiest, with a lovely weir alongside.

We tried a municipal campsite which should have been the right place. The location, on the south bank of the canal, was perfectly lovely, but it was unnervingly empty, with a soulless look about the office. 'Pay at the Mairie' said a handwritten note on the door.

'There's something not right about this place,' Adi said. He didn't have to say it twice; we were back on the bike track riding away within seconds. A few miles later at St-Martin-sur-Oust we found another campsite, also unattended but with a more kempt air about it. A few campervans and motorhomes were scattered around what looked like a large, tended lawn.

'Bonsoir!' A lady, another camper, came over to tell us everything about the campsite and the village. By the time she left the tent was up and we knew everything there was to know, and she knew everything about us that it was in my power to tell her.

'The boulangerie will be closed tomorrow,' she said, waving a finger, 'so to be sure to get your bread for breakfast this evening.'

People were always very kind about this, eager to make sure we knew when the shops would be closed, which was helpful as we'd been having a bit of trouble finding small shops and epiceries over the last two days; they were either difficult to find or closed, our passage through happening to coincide with lunchtime or the day off.

A blur of positive impressions of St-Martin: excellent showers, really hot and powerful; a little roundabout with impish figures in flowers, one of them playing a green piano; a wonderful boulangerie where I bought on impulse a tiny sweet pastry, a little mound of brioche-flavoured airy space, encrusted with sugar. 'I won't have too many more chances to sample stuff like this,' I justified to Adi's raised eyebrows.

We did like to spread our money around these little villages, so we went in search of a cup of tea and a beer. The pleasant-looking bar tucked beside the bridge looked just the job.

It was the worst we'd been in. The elderly lady who ran it greeted us with waving arms and an anxious wittering. She nearly had a canary when she saw Adi looking for somewhere to lean his bike, eyeing up her flower tubs. My order of tea disconcerted her. When it came, was in a dirty cup. The beer, Adi reported, was horrible. As we sat out in the picturesque surroundings with our nasty drinks we caught glimpses of her looking at us out through the windows; the laser-like anxiety of her gaze cut through the glass.

'Not a natural in the hospitality industry, then,' Adi said.

We had pitched strategically beside the swings (you're never too old for swings, especially when camping) and a picnic table. Proper seats! A table! Of such things are pleasure made. The wind did its usual Adi-and-Marie's-dinnertime gusting but we were ready for it; all corners and the middle pinned down and stable. Adi got experimental, lightly frying thin slices of potato to accompany herby sauce of tomatoes, onions and peppers.

We'd formulated a plan over the old lady's nasty tea and beer. We'd take the D-roads towards Vannes on the coast if they weren't too scary traffic-wise, and deviate onto a little road that looked as if it would get us to the centre. Then we'd carry on, aiming for Carnac. We were in the mood for ocean. It had been lovely to see the interior of the country - France has a lot of interior - but we missed the sea.

Adi complained slightly of a sniffle as he cooked. 'Three days since there was something wrong with me. Must be the nose's turn.'

I wrote my diary while waiting for the chips to cook, smelling authentically chip-like in the evening air. I was wearing trousers, my woollen Icebreaker t-shirt and my thick, 250 Icebreaker long-sleeved winter top, with socks and trainers for the first time in ages, and I was STILL COLD! There's a sort of pathetic resignation in the tone of my diary entry. What did you expect, the pessimistic part of my brain said. You brought it with you! Scottish weather!

A walk around the campsite fringes, down to the bridge in the village and back, telling ourselves how cold it was in a companionable sort of way. We wondered about Anne and Denis, how far they'd made it today, if they'd gone further. Adi disturbed a tiny frog as we looked at the river; he hopped away lightly, minutely, and the croaks of his extended family kept me company as I drifted off to sleep.

CHAPTER FORTY-SIX

To Vannes

I wrote my first diary entry of the day sitting on a pannier inside the outer of the tent while rain pattered down on the skin. The rest of the baggage was packed up, waiting outside in the rain. It was like sitting in a small green aircraft hangar. A blobby mist and a tiny breeze hung around outside. The slow morning had allowed for a long breakfast, with two rounds of tea and coffee, the end of yesterday's bread, juice and yoghurt, the last two fetched by Adi from the village store (open when the boulangerie is shut). And a tiny bit of cheese made in the village, with a handwritten weight and date on the package.

The drizzle lifted as we cycled away just after ten o'clock. It took the worst of the cold away with it; I was back in my sandals, and riding along I felt damp but cheerful, which is probably something you don't want to say in public.

It wasn't far to Vannes by the roads we intended to follow, a southwesterly ride towards the Gulf of Morbihan. I was thoroughly in the mood for ocean.

I didn't get to use the maps often, as I'm sure I've mentioned. Adi is Map Man. I don't mind this, he gets more out of them than I do, but when I realised that today's section was represented on two maps of different scale, I requested one of them.

'Does this mean you're going to be challenging my authority?'

After the scuffle I took the smaller scale one, covering all of Brittany, while Adi took the Finistère-Morbihan map at 1 cm to 1.5 km.

'It means we won't spend hours at every cross roads!' I retorted.

We paused for an early lunch on the outskirts of Sulniac, where there was a bench surrounded by a pretty flower bed and a bus shelter within sprinting distance if rained again. Soon after lunch, it did. As if we were in any doubt that we were approaching the Atlantic with all its glorious Celtic weather, the drizzle thickened and was hurled into our faces by the stiffening breeze as we rode, exaggerated by the downhill swoop towards Questembert. Slit-eyed, fringe in wet whips stinging my eyes, freewheeling on slippery tarmac, I felt well and truly welcomed into weather systems I know and lo— well, know and understand.

Questembert, where we stopped for a quick food shop, boasted a confusing one-way system around the outside of the town, a magnificent open-sided timbered market hall dating from the 1550s, and an impressive collection of drunks of various ages, unaggressive but unnerving.

By half-past three we'd been through the tourist office routine in Vannes and were having a good-natured argument about whether or not we'd been here before. Adi was convinced that we had; I couldn't remember a thing about it. We carried on the discussion - these sorts of discussions tended to go on for a while - in a café overlooking the port.

We were on the cusp of the high season now. Irish and Scottish schools had already broken up, and from the accents from the number of families wandering around Vannes, it looked as if they'd shot south as fast as they could before the English and Welsh arrived in their hordes. It was a cheerful place, lots of people strolling past the yachts and catamarans moored in their hundreds off the promenade. The sky was silvery but warm, the merest hint of drizzle and the faintest promise of sun.

To my horror I was charged €3.10 for my pot of tea.

'Back to the bar-tabacs,' said Adi.

Bar-tabacs and PMU bars: you can't beat them. PMU bars are run by a betting group, and there was usually a room to the side devoted to watching the sports results come in. They were often in some of the older buildings, with 'Café de France' or 'Café de Paris' lettered in gilt above the entrance. They were never, ever pretentious, there were hardly ever any tourists in them, they were always the cheapest places to drink, and I'd often had the best wine from them.

The tiny voice that had been bravely assuring me that we would reach sunshine again once we got to the coast - Brittany's Riviera, I was sure I'd read somewhere - had piped down as we'd cycled through that lush, well-watered countryside after Nantes. It faded out altogether as I pottered around Vannes' tourist shops. Postcards with such legends as 'In Brittany it only rains twice a week: once for three days and once for four days!' didn't suggest we were entering balmy climes.

We picked up some bread and fresh food in the pleasant old town centre and saddled up again quickly. I had trouble keeping up with Adi, who had the tourist map. Despite the onset of a virus, he was riding along powerfully, happy to be out on the roads. The canal had been beautiful, but there is something energising about being out on the thoroughfares, jostling with other traffic. It was nice too to see broader vistas again, and to feel the land roll in long gentle waves. The shape of it was familiar: if it hadn't been for the amount of tree cover, the fields of sweetcorn and the total lack of sheep, we could have been in mid-Wales.

Not much later we had chosen our pitch and everything was lying on the grass drying in the sun - finally, again, sun! - before erecting the tent. Camping Le Conleau was terraced into the side of a low hill south of the town. The polite but infinitely dozy young receptionist had taken forty minutes to book us in, but that couldn't bring me down - I was writing my diary in the sun! While Adi went out for a recce I hung everything - bedding, cycling clothes and as many other clothes as I could - on spare guy-lines strung between the trees that shaded us.

Dinner that night had a high-ranking view. From our pitch we could see down to one of the inlets of the Gulf of Morbihan. Afterwards, we went for a ride further south onto the tiny Île Conleau and the Île de Baëdic, linked to each other and the mainland by causeways. Adi led me towards a bustling bar that he'd found earlier.

'I don't believe it.'

It was now shuttered and looked as if it hadn't been open for years. We found an open café-bar that met Adi's standards and sat down and discussed the different attitudes to commerce between the UK and Ireland on the one hand and France on the other. Adi had been mildly irritated that the bar was closed. This discussion followed on from one we'd had a few nights before, when he was expressing his annoyance that the shop in the village was closed. I liked this difference. I like not being treated as a voracious, insatiable consumer. I liked the fact that in a little village like St-Martin-sur-Oust the three shops - boucherie, boulangerie, epicerie - rotated their days off so that each proprietor could have their one day off a week in addition to Sunday.

Hurdy-gurdy music played while we talked and drank small glasses of mild cider and sorted out the problems of the UK economy and the attitude to work-life balance. The café was wooden-floored, with small, red-clothed tables and red, white and blue streamers hanging in bunches from the walls. Outside, a bunch of Frenchmen of varying ages were leaning back in their chairs and smoking, perhaps sorting out the French economy. Inside, a middle-aged couple sat with a small and hairy dog lying across both their feet. A pair of very handsome young men were seated facing each other, talking animatedly over a beer and a coffee. Actually, I could only see the back of the head of one of them; the other one, though, was handsome enough for two.

CHAPTER FORTY-SEVEN

To Carnac

We'd pitched on a slightly sideways slope so I woke repeatedly during the night, sliding down towards Adi. From five o'clock onwards two teams of wood pigeons competed against each other in a boring birdsong contest. Not surprising then that it took us both a while to get going. Also, the powdered Lemsip-equivalent that Adi had bought and taken yesterday for his looming head cold turned out to be unexpectedly strong.

'This could knock a bull out,' he said over breakfast, trying to blink the doziness out of his eyes. The coffee was made extra strong.

We rolled down the little track and out past the queue already forming at the polite-but-dozy receptionist's desk. (During the long check-in yesterday we'd made the prescient decision to insist on paying there and then rather than on leaving. A good call.)

Just east of Vannes a thick pincer of land curls first south and then west, narrowing to a headland that almost meets a smaller, mirroring peninsula that begins just west of Auray. Together they enclose the Gulf of Morbihan, in effect a vast sea-lake strewn with islands and pierced by littler narrower peninsulas.

Our route took us along a minor road, discarded by most motorists in favour of the dual carriageway linking the two towns in a straight line. We cycled in an arc linking villages perched at the head of or alongside other inlets of the gulf, starting with a quiet (apart from the joggers) cycle track winding along the fringes of a reed-edged inlet. All morning we had glimpses of water; rush-lined lakes, rivers opening out, sudden views of exposed mudflats and tree-rimmed pools. Lovely calm water, lapwings resting unconcerned at our passing, unfolding views of more water and tiny isolated houses. A bridge over a tributary of the Auray gave a view of the photogenic riverside village of Bono, with tall yachts moored up in ranks, ready to go out into the gulf to practise some safe ocean sailing. We got the impression that a lot of sailing teaching went on within the relative safety of those protective limbs of land.

Despite the low cloud and the forecast (dire), we were cheerful. I had one of my munchies mornings. On the way I ate a pain au chocolat and two chouqettes (bought from a boulangerie on the outskirts of Vannes with displays to die for: wonderful trays of smoothly risen, golden brioche that made me drool and that I resisted only because there was no way I could hide my piggery from Adi).

I was still starving when we reached Auray's outskirts, so when weather forced an early lunch there were no complaints from me. We'd been cycling past a complex of apartments and business offices with a couple of pedestrian walkways linking the car park and the courtyard when the first raindrops fell. They felt like drops that meant business so we swiftly pulled in and took shelter in the walkways. By the time the heavy shower had passed it was nearly noon (and I'd eaten all the food), so we locked up the bikes and went exploring.

Auray turned out to be a pretty, busy place, with an upper town on a bluff high above the river d'Auray, connected by steep cobbled streets to a picturesque lower town. A pretty stone bridge crossed the river, the last crossing before it opened into another inlet of the Gulf.

I'd noticed a little dog motif since Nantes, on lamp posts, drain covers and other sorts of municipal hardware: a small hound with a cape, marked with a cross, tied around its neck flying back in the wind.

'It looks like Welsh, doesn't it?' said Adi as we tried to decipher an interpretation board written in French and Breton.

We tried to remember how many regional languages we had seen since we'd arrived in France. Provençal; Occitan; we were sure there had been something else in the middle. Breton was definitely the third, if not the fourth. And it was reminiscent of Welsh, though with fewer double consonants and added z's. I started to take photos of road signs and village names.

The afternoon was a short, salty ride out to Carnac. The village is renowned for the concentration of megalithic stones in its environs: some solitary, some in spectacular alignments, in serried ranks stretching across fields. I knew my mother and my father's stone-cutter cousin Frances would love hearing about this, so it had been on my list of must-sees from the beginning.

Our first touch of the coast proper was at La Trinité-sur-Mer, boats and yachts and ocean-going catamarans glinting in the emerging sunshine, huge stork-like creatures tilted sideways at rest on two of their three hulls. We paused for an ice-cream then carried on to Carnac-plage, under sun and cloud and blue sky and light rain. Bikes locked up by the tourist office, we went for a walk, admiring more yachts and ocean-going catamarans moored on the ranks of pontoons jutting out into the sea.

Carnac-plage was a strip of holiday-land stretching for a couple of miles along the south-facing shore, looking into the Bay of Quiberon. Squinting, we could just make out Quiberon itself, a virtual island at the end of a low-lying peninsula extending south for miles into the Atlantic. As with the Mediterranean coast, it was brilliantly set up for cyclists, with plenty of off-road cycle lanes. Not that on-road cycling was discouraged. The whole place felt almost terminally relaxed. If I tell you that a mild traffic jam was caused by three girls pedalling a sort of seated, hooded, pedal-powered old car, you'll understand that it wasn't a very aggressive little town. Cars idled patiently behind the giggling girls as they tried to co-ordinate their efforts. It would never happen in Menai Bridge.

Our pleasure at reaching our campsite in sunshine with a dry tent was slightly tarnished by the cost: €19 for the night. We hadn't paid that much since Albi. But we were mollified by its location, the fabulousness of its showers, the friendliness of our neighbours and the fact that we erected the tent just before a rain shower: always a reason for the dance of joy. It was a mile outside Carnac-ville, a couple of miles inland from Carnac-plage, and the road back into the village took us past one of the largest fields of the alignments: rows and rows of megaliths, enormous squat stones that have been standing there since before 3000 BC.

After pitching up and showering we cycled back into the village via the alignments and the Maison des Monuments, where we found out that the only English-language guided tour took place on Wednesdays. It was not Wednesday. A scale model of the alignments nearby and further afield help us make a bit of sense of the area. There were lots of expensive books to browse with some utterly beautiful photographs of the megaliths in different conditions: sun, mist, pearlescent cloudy backdrops.

In the village a mini-market was in full swing, with stalls set out along the narrow streets and the square. We spoke to a writer who was selling copies of his crime novels. They were set in Oban! I had to buy one.

In the main market hall (I love the French word 'halle') musicians were playing traditional music: one excellent accordion player, an indifferent violinist and gifted wind player, switching from flute to clarinet. Tragically, they were soon replaced by a pair of youngsters, a lad on uilleann pipes and a girl playing the flute. There was no getting away from the sound. You've got to admire bagpipes and uilleann pipes and their attitude: a great loud instrument that says, 'YOU WILL LISTEN TO ME! YOU HAVE NO CHOICE!'

Shops and stalls were still open at half-past ten. We rode back past the megaliths in the half-light, made our plans for the next day by torchlight, and slept.

CHAPTER FORTY-EIGHT

To Guidel

By now I was the veteran of many early morning rides to boulangeries for the breakfast baguette and croissants, but that morning in Carnac was the most memorable: mist hanging over the fields, a low sun silvering slatey clouds, droplets gleaming on long meadow grasses between the megaliths, the myriad stones gleaming wetly and the church across a meadow, silhouetted on its little mound, two plain windows and one slim tower glinting. I wouldn't have missed it for anything.

Our plan was to camp on the south coast tonight, then ride west along it until lunchtime the following day, when we'd turn north to cross the interior. We aimed to hit the north coast somewhere near Morlaix in the next three or four days and have a week cycling with the wind on our backs all the way to St-Malo. Always assuming it didn't change direction.

This was a difficult decision. We'd both have loved to reach 'the end of the world'. We hadn't ever concluded whether we'd aim for the Pointe du Raz, the western tip of the Finistère's more southerly finger, or for the Pointe de Kermovan, the tiny and actually most westerly point of France's mainland, projecting out of the more northerly, blunter finger of Brittany, but we'd always assumed, all the way, that we would stand with our bikes on a windy headland, looking out into the Atlantic.

'I'd really love to make it out there,' said Adi.

'Me too. But…' I trailed off.

'We'd have to leather it out there and back, and might not enjoy it.' He looked around. 'Leather it into the headwind, too. It's gone for now, but it'll be back.'

I felt a twist in my heart at the thought of the coasts we wouldn't see. I knew Adi felt the same. We just wanted to keep plodding on, with the sea on our left. But it was not to be this time.

We spent some time on the internet in the Espace Culturel, booking a festival in Suffolk in August, sorting out some money affairs and checking out camping options on the road ahead. It was late when we cycled out, and not long after that when we paused for lunch. This was one of our best picnic spots: sitting atop a horizontal megalith in a shady, dappled grove, one of the stones that forms the alignments of Kerzelio, outside Erdeven.

One of my favourite pastimes was chalking up the number of 'villages historiques' or 'un des plus beaux villages' we cycled through in a day. These designations were announced on the welcome signs into the villages. Way back - I forget where - one had advised us that we were about to cycle through a 'village sur surveillance vidéo' - thankfully a unique experience. Almost all of the signs also announced which town or village they were twinned with. Usually, the twin was in another region of France. It had only been a couple of weeks since I'd noticed the first one twinned with a foreign town, in Germany. In the last couple of days we'd seen a few twinned with towns in Britain, and when we paused for a water-refill break in a village called Plouhinec I was charmed to see that it was twinned with Kilkee, down the road from where my father is from in County Clare.

It was a day of contrasts. The traffic disappeared after the main road swung away north towards Lorient. Following a chance mention in the Rough Guide, and a blue dotted line on the map, we made our way to Port-Louis, on the eastern bank of the estuary of the rivers Scorff and Blavé. It was reminiscent of the entrance to Cork harbour, one of the biggest natural harbours in the world, I'll have you know. There was a lovely homey feel to the villages leading up to Port-Louis, left in peace by the road taking all the through traffic northwards.

Port-Louis was lovely and sleepy, a town enclosed on the landward side within a semicircle of ramparts, with an ancient central square and a church completely dressed in scaffolding. Off to the seaward side was an imposing citadel, housing four museums. We needed to get on, so we found the tourist office near the harbour. The views were that odd but pleasing mix of industrial and rural, with Lorient's port buildings on the skyline across the estuary, trees along the inlet's near shore and dozy boats bobbing in tranquil water.

The young woman in the tourist office near the harbour was wonderful. She sold us tickets for the ferry crossing, which cost €1.30 each, with bikes going free. As well as a town plan for Port-Louis, she gave us detailed maps for the district across the inlet where the ferry would deposit us, and for the coast further south and west. She also came to the door and pointed out exactly where the ferry would dock.

The sun was out and there was high passing cloud, and the breeze was slightly cool, but there was no rain, not a drop, and it was lovely sitting on the decking outside the ticket office, waiting for the ferry to come in. We could have done with another half-hour to look around the town - we'd only seen the barest glimpse of it - but sometimes that's better. It was a cheerful glimpse.

There's no word for the Breton seaman who helped us on with our bikes other than 'burly'. He looked as if he could have run with them tucked under his arms. They stood in the prow, loaded and awkward and lovely, back in their element, resting against the sides. As most of our cycle touring to date had been in Scotland they were seasoned sailors, and I always think they look completely at home leaning against the side of a boat with backdrop of glinting sea.

We disembarked into a totally different world, in the southern suburbs of Lorient. We had much cause to sing loudly the praises of that brilliant young woman in Port-Louis as we negotiated, with her map, the dockland world of old cobbled port streets. We were surrounded by huge warehouses and sprawling industrial units, some with names in a language I can only describe as English-ish. We stocked up on food in a Géant Casino - our favourite of the supermarket chains - and rode onward, making our way south with the aid of the second map, still singing her praises. The phrase 'We'd be lost without this map' chanted around in my head as I pedalled in Adi's wake.

It chanted even louder when I found myself alone, without the map and without Adi. It's surprising that it was only the second time we'd become separated from each other. In Périgueux we'd known that we were heading for the train station; this time I only knew we were heading to the sea. Adi was normally great at waiting for me anywhere potentially confusing, and mishaps had only occurred when I hadn't been quick enough to see where he'd gone, or when I'd been slowed down by something he couldn't see, so that I wasn't as close behind as he'd thought.

This time he hadn't realised how fast he was cycling. On the hill up to that last roundabout there was, just ahead of Adi, a lycra-clad cyclist. I could tell that Adi had the bit between his teeth. He was going to reel that cyclist in. By the time I reached the roundabout they'd both vanished. I pedalled around it three times, increasingly wild-eyed. Polite drivers kept their distance. I chose an exit based on the position of the sun in the sky and guessing where the sea was. Actually, that's a lie. I chose an exit at random. When I reached a second roundabout and he wasn't waiting for me, I stopped and rooted out my despised Blackberry. I laid Bike down, walked around the large and rather scary roundabout, and texted Adi all the road numbers and town names I could see on the signs. Ten minutes later he'd found me.

'Tell me you overtook him,' I said. He grinned.

'I didn't want to embarrass him so I just sat behind him.'

We found the correct road to the coast and recommenced singing the praises of the map maiden of Port-Louis as the sea came into view. By the time we reached the coast road the sun was shining and the Atlantic was rolling onto the shore, blue-grey and windblown, which is exactly what the Atlantic should look like. Heath on one side of the road, sweetcorn on another. Proper breakers surged onto long, curving beaches punctuated by small, rocky headlands. Surfers, wind surfers and VW campervans; the first village we cycled through could have been on the west coast of Anglesey.

We passed a couple of campsites but cycled on, thinking there would be plenty more. The Legs agreed, slightly goose-bumped but perfectly happy. The wind coming straight off the ocean was invigorating rather than draining. But Sod's Law prevailed, and by the time we were in the mood to stop the campsites had run out. We found one and examined its prices: very expensive, and there were no nearby shops. Where would we get our bread?

We carried on, tiring rapidly. It happens quite suddenly sometimes. You're absolutely fine, then half an hour later it's almost dusk, you need nibbles of bread and honey every five minutes and The Legs have lost their good cheer. Abruptly, the level bike track we'd been cycling on ended at the mouth of a river. The only road onward led up a hill.

I like hills, but not at the wrong time. This hill led from Guidel-plage - not even a hamlet - up into lands unseen. The slope looked vertical to my tired eyes, Yorkshire-style with no wimpy zigzagging to lessen the incline, and there was an ominous chevron on the map. We had no information on campsites this far west. We could go back to the expensive one or we could cycle up the hill (weeping) and see what Guidel-ville had to offer in the way of accommodation. There must be something, we reasoned, looking round at the few surfers towelling themselves off beside their VWs.

'Back on the flat or up the hill?' Adi said.

'I hate being fleeced.'

'Me too.'

Sometimes just being tight-fisted lends power to your tired body. Bike and The Legs and I all girded our loins and pedalled, incredibly slowly, up the hill behind Adi. Within a mile he was waiting for me with a grin at a crossroads, beside - hurrah! - signs for two campsites. The four-star one was closest.

'Let's have some luxury,' said Adi. So we did.

Dinner was a curry with pasta followed by squares of truffle-filled chocolate for pudding. I was making plans for stashing a hundred bars of this chocolate about my person for the journey home.

Chocolate was becoming a bit of a habit. We had each lost a bit of weight through exercise and the fact that our on-the-bike lifestyle precluded lots of fatty foods. On my part, there was also the fact that it's difficult to hide what you are eating when you are almost always in the company of the other. Years of not particularly mindful eating habits had changed out of necessity, and we'd been on the road long enough, with these constraints, for those good habits to become ingrained. They say it takes 21 days to form a new habit. Make it 30 days, a month, to be sure. This was our fifty-third night on the road.

Our one luxury was chocolate. We had chocolate every night for pudding, at least 100 grammes. Our favourites were the 150 gramme mint or truffle. Considering the low amount of fat in our diet otherwise, and the fact that it was good stuff - dark and nutty, none of your vegelate - we weren't too worried about it. The downside of was that we now had a new chocolate-every-night habit. But we'd worry about that when we got home.

We were in great good humour after dinner. Adi's snuffles seemed to have been beaten into submission by the Lemsip-on-speed powder, while mine had vanished merely by waving a sachet of the stuff in front of my nose. We'd arrived in time to hang our bags and liners up for an airing in a patch of sunlight.

The showers were excellent and really hot, we felt clean and full and, best of all, there was really hot water in the dish washing sinks!

We had noticed very early on in the trip that the presence of a blue or a red dot on a push-button tap on a sink meant nothing; the same not-quite-lukewarm water came out of both, and it might come out in a dribble or in a geyser. (Don't get me started on the water pressure.) Sometimes a sink would have taps with red buttons on both, next to a sink with blue buttons on both. Mystifyingly, some taps had green buttons, which seemed to mean 'Don't ask me, I'm only a tap, what do I know?' Which made sinks with taps that provided really hot water really, really special! To top it off the shower units were piping music, which for once wasn't Genesis And The Worst Of The Eighties but was actually really good, very funky.

We wandered over to the bar and had a drink outside, between the kids on the playground and the disco dancing competition inside. It was the first week of French school holidays. No longer were we with with a monoculture of early retirees in campervans and caravans, with occasional childless couples like us, or very young families. Now there were families with young kids, couples, school-age children, groups of friends - we found ourselves really enjoying the buzz of people of all ages around. There were a few midges about, and it was cold enough to need my fleece, but it was cheerful and lively, and some of the teenage girls in the competition (it's always the girls) were excellent. We cheered them on with everyone else. All part of the tapestry.

PART THIRTEEN

Turning North: Guidel To Loguilvy de la Mer

CHAPTER FORTY-NINE

To Scaër

'Twinned with Carrigaline!'

'With where?'

'Carrigaline! County Cork! A bit west of the city, on the harbour.'

Adi was rooting in his bar bag for his wallet. 'Oh. Is it nice?'

'No, no, well I don't know, you always just drive past it, there's a bypass, it's one of those places. Look, we're on Rue de Carrigaline!'

He smiled indulgently at me and went into the shop in Guidel-ville, leaving me to look at the street name in wonder for another moment.

This would be our last day on the south coast. Adi had worked out that, time-wise, we could afford to ride along the coast until lunchtime and then turn north, cycling overland for a couple of nights.

'Are you going to want to be racing?' he asked me as we went through the ritual stashing [Move this earlier]of the purchased comestibles in the panniers, with all the horse-trading that goes with it. ('Can you take the juice?' 'I'll take the juice if you've got space for the onion.' 'Only next to the sleeping bags.' 'Oh no, look, I'll swap you the onion for an apple and the bag of muesli.' 'Only if you take your shoes back.')

'No,' I said, quite unjustifiably insulted.

'Let's look around here first.'

The woman in the tourist office couldn't have been nicer. She furnished us with a great map of the southern part of Finistère - not actually her region - and told us everything we needed to know - campsites, tourist offices, and the best place to aim for that night. 'Scaër. I would go there,' she said.

We went out for the look around.

I hadn't noticed this routine developing. Somewhere along the road I'd become a bit less fidgety and impatient to be gone, Adi had become a bit more eager to get going and less likely to want to spend forever in shops examining every single shelf. I realised that, to be completely fair, the banana-eating episode outside Nantes had been a blip. We were converging.

We found the war memorial with a Breton inscription to Guidel's dead. We found the statue of La

France, the Rue de la République and the Avenue Charles de Gaulle. It's hard to say it without sounding painfully earnest but these reminders, every day, gave me shudders, a shiver of gratitude for my great good fortune in being born where and when I was, in a place and time where no matter what sort of crap the governments and other institutions and life throws at me, I've got my freedom. Here we were on our bikes, cycling around a neighbouring but still-foreign country, nobody to tell us what to believe and what to think and where we could or couldn't go. Not in fear for our lives.

Joy gripped me as we rode over the bridge across the river Laïta, the waterway that had forced us up the hill last night. According to the map it flowed into the Anse du Pouldu, which gave us giggles of the most immature kind as we deliberately misread it.

We cycled in a triangle north, west and finally slightly south-east towards the village of Pouldu which, after an hour of cycling, was about a mile west of where we'd pitched last night. Too late, we remembered the handy ferry at the bottom of last night's hill. But it was a good ride, with rested, contented Legs. Pouldu's beach was absolutely lovely; I stood leaning into the breeze off the ocean while Adi visited the shop for something or other. The rain held off and everything, sky, sea and long-grassed fields, was rendered in hues of greeny-blue. *Glas.* The wind was there, of course, blowing the green-blue grass into swoopy waves. Knowing we were about to leave the coast made it feel prettier. Maybe it really was prettier.

'Not as good as Scotland,' said Adi when we stopped at the end of a dead-end lane to look over a meadow-edged little bay, ending in low cliffs of ancient rock, 'but pretty good.'

Placid cows gazed at us as we rolled past, each apparently surrounded by an acre each of lush grass. Inland a little, then down to the sea again at the small harbour of Doëlan, a notch in the coastline, a indented cove of steep rocks, white-painted houses and protected moorings. We cycled towards the small green-and-white lighthouse on the eastern cliff, then down over the bridge to the fishery buildings and the piers and the matching red-and-white lighthouse on the other side. Real fishing boats were moored next to a few small yachts. The boats and the whole village were pretty and slightly scruffy.

From Pouldu the landscape was just beautiful, simply rural and coastal, low Celtic cliffs so like West Cork and small roads, dead ends all over the place, ending in houses or hamlets mostly called Ker-something. Was that like 'kirk' in northern England, we wondered, the Norse and the Celtic meeting here? Ker, ker, ker all over the map.

Breton names and phrases confused the language centres in my brain; there were teasing glimpses of Welsh, French and Irish, with the added fun of all those z's and h's. No prizes for guessing what Pouldu means if you have a smattering of Welsh, Irish or Scots Gaelic: black pool. Pays de Lorient became 'Bro an Orient' in Breton, like a Welsh 'bro' and Irish 'an'. Patrimoine Naturelle became 'Glad Natur'. Almost-Welsh and total-Welsh. Translation-wise, Doëlan stumped us entirely, but I couldn't help thinking of Doolin on the west coast of County Clare, a tiny hamlet where the Burren meets the Atlantic, consisting almost entirely of pubs.

We ate on a bench, nodding to a family with rucksacks and chubby knees who came down a cliff path, probably following the GR34 around Brittany's coast.

'I'm glad we saw that,' Adi said as we turned our wheels northwards from Doëlan, replete, for now, with views of western seas.

We were soon cursing. The wind left us alone for half an hour, until it worked out which direction we were going, then pounced. Imminent grumpiness was averted when we arrived at St-Thurien. Twinned with Kilmacow, Irlande! We rode up a barrier-lined street, waved on by officious volunteers, to sniggers from onlookers, minutes ahead of a swoop of multi-coloured lycra.

'Has the Tour de France started?' It had started a week ago, we discovered later, reading about Bradley Wiggins in the yellow jersey. Neither of us had been interested in the Tour before, but from then on we started to read the sports pages of the free newspapers. An Englishman winning, and popular with the French?

On and inland through Moëlan-sur-Mer (which wasn't) past a game of fancy dress football in the communal village grounds. Its Breton name, Molar-ar-Mor, turned into my earworm of the day, chanting round and round in my head. Through tiny Baye to Le Trevoux. We were getting better at spotting the necessities. Apparently moribund villages would have a give-away little door round the corner from the Mairie, housing a toilet and sink and drinking water. Tiny signs you'd miss if you blinked led to tardis-like shops. We found one in Le Trevoux, staffed by a smiley-eyed lady and patrolled by a tiny yowling cat, skinny-legged but healthy with a muscly little body that he rubbed against my legs. We sat by the old communal oven in the square and munched the remains of the lunchtime baguette (fantastic, from the bakery in Guidel-ville), watching the scooter boys speeding around being cool and the old man who'd bought a handful of carrots and a huge bottle of brandy in the shop (with a shot from the shop's bar in the process) totter about the square towards a proper bar.

It was glorious cycling weather: breezy, high clouds, sun, in and out of shadow on the lanes, changing light on the land and full Atlantic skies full of movement and just plain, plump, life. It lasted the rest of the afternoon.

Through St-Thurien and on to Scaër (Skaer, if you prefer the Breton). The cycling was lovely, on minor C-roads and then the D6, a country road, down sweeping descents and up long, gentle ascents, never too strenuous but plenty of them. Fields of wheat and sweetcorn, woods everywhere, mostly of sweet chestnut, with pine by the coast and more oak as we rode inland. Purple heather was just beginning to flower, warming the hedgerows. Houses were varied in styled; some looked just like the sturdy, four-square nineteenth-century Welsh-English standard but with more steeply pitched roofs.

We cycled around Scaër and found three boulangeries, the tourist office and a sign for the campsite. It was quite late and I was hungry but happy, perched on the wall outside the tourist office while Adi went in for the bumph. We didn't really need the bumph; there was a sign for the campsite just beside me, pointing down the hill. I could see the top of a building and a couple of tents showing through the trees. We could do the poring over maps after dinner. God, I was getting hungry.

Adi came out of the tourist office with a bundle of leaflets, all of which he placed in his bar bag except for one sheet.

'Now,' he said, shaking out the map of the village and sitting down on the wall beside me, 'let's see where we are.'

I'm very proud of the fact that I managed not to shriek what was in my head, which was, 'It's THERE, it's THERE, it's down the FECKING hill, I can fecking SEE IT!'

'Shall we go down and get pitched up first and have a look at it over dinner?' I said politely.

He looked down the hill and at the map. He was dying to look at it but he was strong. 'Okay, yep, we can do that.' And he put it away and we rode down the hill and got pitched up and showered just before the rain came.

I loved Brittany's municipal campsites. We'd expected to be paying a bit more for campsites up north but the opposite was true. A pretty girl who looked astonishingly like my youngest sister - fair freckled skin, black hair and blue eyes - booked us in, writing the details in a little book and giving us the carbon copy. The shower block was old and solid, and the washing machine and dryer were free! At a one-star municipal campsite! 'But you have to put in your own laundry liquid,' the girl told me anxiously. We assured her that was entirely acceptable.

Adi managed to cook in the doorway of the tent, killing the stove every time the rain got heavy enough to force us to close the door, letting the food stew in the pan. The picnic table squatted wetly, tauntingly close and useless. Despite the difficulties, dinner was delicious. Adi had perfected the art of cooking camping chips. A cheese, tomato and pepper sauce, a couple of thick slices of pain complet to mop up.

Saturday night. Distant sounds of festivity in the village. There'd been some sort of event in every village we'd passed through today. Adi suggested it was a Breton festival: the annual "Stuff-France Day"..

CHAPTER FIFTY

To Huelgoat

Huelgoat was our destination for the second interior night. More than halfway, we stopped for lunch in Landeleau. It was dry and sunny, which partly made up for the fact that we were sitting at a decrepit picnic table in the car park of a builders' yard.

We'd crossed the Nantes-Brest canal at a depressed-looking Pont-Triffen, getting there partly by cycle track along a disused railway line as far as Gourin (the line goes all the way to Roscoff).

'I am done with cycle tracks!' I announced dramatically as we left the track. Adi just gave me that look.

'Is that right.'

'Yes. Treedy—'

'Treedy.'

'Treedy, gloomy, cut-off from the landscape.'

'Not always, but I see what you're saying.'

It hadn't been completely unpleasant. The surface was good and we rode swiftly along, separated from traffic but also separated from the patchy sunshine. The gloomy track was brightened by two lovely old station houses, one now a café and the other a halt for randonneurs. Even so, it was a relief to get out onto roads again. A weather system was heading our way - from the northwest, naturally - and we wanted to make progress. We'd decided to camp in Huelgoat no matter how far ahead of schedule we arrived.

We carried on, up through sweet chestnut and oak woods and over the Montagnes Noires. The second Black Mountains of the trip. The col wasn't exactly 'Brittany's Col du Tourmalet', as one leaflet had dubbed it, but the views were broad and sweeping. Patchwork fields of crops and grass in yellows and greens. Skylarks soaring on threads of song. Yellowhammers yelling. Scattered cows chewing cud, hip-deep in grass. Rolling country. I fell into a sort of pedalling daze, counting the gentle ascents and descents. Down-up-down-up-down.

Cycling along in Adi's wake, I realised that I'd fallen totally in love with cycling. My body was doing everything I asked of it. I felt strong. I felt chocolatey. I felt a deep, secret satisfaction with myself. I felt like, goddam, I can do something hard and enjoy it! I can cycle through another country and feel proud of myself, not because it makes me better than anyone else, but because it makes me better than myself, than what I used to be.

And, I realised with a shock, I'd become more patient. Less melodramatic. I had grown up a bit, at the age of forty-one. Who knew?

By four o'clock we were in a bar-creperie beside Huelgoat's lake, a breeze-ruffled sheet of mercury in a bowl of lush, khakhi shrubs and trees. We were inside the bar with beer and tea while everyone else was outside, because they were English and rich and we didn't want to talk to people just because we shared the same language.

'I feel like a right miserable sod and I don't care.' Adi sipped his horrifically expensive beer. 'Anyway, they're only southerners.'

'Yep. You are a miserable sod.' Truth is neither of us is the most sociable, and while we really do like talking to others we both find it tiring. Fortunately, our peaks and troughs of introversion don't usually coincide; normally, one of us is in the mood to strike up conversations with strangers.

The campsite had been located, opening hours of shops, tourist office and boulangerie ascertained. After our drink we pitched up early and I lay and read beside the river, enjoying an hour to myself while Adi went to read over a quiet beer at the bar-tabac. All our bedding lay draped on rocks and over branches. The evening passed with our rituals of food and maps and decisions about route and destination. The whole if-we-get-there-by-lunch-that-means-we-can-head-for-there-which-looks-really-pretty calculations. Washing up, sip of wine, a last wander round the campsite checking for the Dutch campervan and the small girl turning cartwheels. Both present. It was safe to turn in.

CHAPTER FIFTY-ONE

To Tréguier

N o headwind. At all. All day!'
We were marvelling in hushed tones, toasting the god of tailwinds in the bar-tabac in Tréguier's cathedral square. No tourists, just a weathered man reading the paper, a quiet barmaid and a resident boxer dog who came over, sniffed us with an air of great politeness, then settled down and licked our toes.

The day had started off in Huelgoat with a regression into shop-dawdling on Adi's part and melodramatic protestations on mine. So much for patience and maturity.

Quickly friends again, we went to explore the Forêt d'Huelgoat behind the bar-tabac, a chaotic, wooded mass of huge, rounded granite boulders, crevasses and chasms and holes amongst them. We descended with the aid of minimalist footholds into the Devil's Cave, then wandered to the trembling rock – La Roche

Tremblante – where a startlingly-dressed person was wandering about. The name recalled a popular medieval trial for witches; the Great Orme's Rocking Stone in North Wales is a famous one, where or accused criminals would be thrown off the cliffs if it wobbled when they were forced to stand on it. Or was it if it didn't wobble? When we got to the Virgin's Place – La Ménage de la Vierge – a young lady in a pink evening dress was draped prettily on a green mossy boulder, smiling yes when I waved my camera across the chasm at her with a question on my face. Rather sweetly, my photo caught her jeans peeking out from under her dress.

The weather threw fresh challenges at us. The headwind had dropped – we avoided speaking this out loud all day – but it was the coldest cycling day so far.

I felt good and sturdy in my legs, despite a wobbly tummy. That didn't stop me eating lunch, which was delicious, an excellent baguette from Huelgoat which we ate stuffed with cheese, apple and tomatoes in Guerlesquin, in a lovely tree-shaded garden in the middle of the village. The village's requisite little brown dog – there was almost always one, never far from the boulangerie – patrolled as we ate with numb fingers and brown, goose-bumped knees. The morning market had just closed down and dreadful music was being piped through loudspeakers, a sort of middle-of-the-road pan-Celtic crap. Another Irish bar.

We didn't stop for long. 'Too fecking cold for this,' as Adi put it.

I wished I'd brought gloves.

The cycling was lovely, on teeny roads. I startled a Shetland pony, almost invisible in his giant-grassed paddock. We cycled for miles across an undulating plateau to Plouaret, which got the award for the most useless - possibly the only useless - tourist office we'd encountered in France. It was staffed by an indifferent woman and an uninformed but eager-to-help young man.

'Do you have any information about campsites in the area?'

He looked to the woman for help.

'Non.' She didn't look up. He looked at us.

'Non.'

And that was that. We asked if there were toilets nearby and, almost beside himself with pleasure at being given the opportunity to be useful, the young man led us to them himself, down a side street off an unpleasant little square, past mobs of teenagers. Adi took one look in and walked straight back to me, refusing even to describe them.

Up more hills to pretty Pluzunet. Goats in a paddock, llamas over a hedge. Yellowhammers.

Skylarks. The easy and slightly busy D33 to La Roche-Derrien, with its lovely timbered-and-rose-bushed square and hilltop church. The last few miles to Tréguier along rush-hour roads. The traffic was as respectful as ever. I love French motorists.

We found the campsite a mile or so from the village, well ready for it after over fifty chilly miles. Dour-looking farmers stared at us as we cycled past. It was just like the more insular bits of Ireland and Wales, the 'Who are these, now?' sort of looks. The farmer on the campsite, in contrast, was friendly and curious about our travels.

Cheap and basic: three showers, two toilets, two washrooms, each a little concrete cubicle opening directly onto the grass, the showers lacking even the barely adequate plyboard partition. But the water was hot, it was quiet, the ground was soft with not a sign of an ant, and it was only a kilometre from the boulangerie.

After the showers, we rode into Tréguier to spy it out. Narrow streets, half-timbered buildings everywhere, a goodly proportion of them apparently occupied by artists. After the tea overlooking the square, we left the bar-tabac with well-licked toes. The boxer watched attentively as we rode off. I love the way an intelligent dog looks at you when you cycle past with pannier-heavy bicycles, working out exactly what you are.

We took a little spin around the streets, down to the tiny harbour. Tréguier is near the head of a tidal inlet, a southern mirror of the ones I know from West Cork. Adi took a photo that I treasure, of me on my bike, in silhouette at the bottom of a narrow wooden street. I look, in the fading light, happy. I am a happy shape.

It wasn't the best campsite in the world but it was blissfully mosquito-free, rain-free and noise-free, until the leaders of the groups of kids camping over the hedge in the next field decided it was time to rouse them all to go to the toilet and brush their teeth. Loud exhortations and grumbles. When they'd all finished, the man started playing a fecking guitar and singing. At that time of night. After a short rendition, apparently encouraging participation but getting none even from the two other leaders, he gave up. Three cheers for tongue-tied teenagers.

CHAPTER FIFTY-TWO

To Loguivy-de-la-Mer

Next day was one of the most difficult. I felt knackered, drained, and Adi was rapidly drained by my brooding presence twenty metres behind him. For variety we had a strong northerly crosswind instead of a headwind, but it was a struggle to keep upright, the panniers catching the air like chunky sails, knocking me sideways. Ahead of me, Adi and his bike made an impossibly acute angle with the ground. The Legs were struggling, empty. I can't remember anything about the countryside we rode through, though I know we went north on minor roads and back south to Lézardrieux. By the time we reached Paimpol I was shattered, achey and unhappy. I took an instant dislike to Paimpol and to the campsite just south of it. Adi, wonderfully, didn't press the point but led me back north.

So began a long search, cycling all over the peninsula north of Paimpol seeking a village called Ploubazlanec and its alleged myriad campsites. By the time we'd found Ploubazlanec and found that none of the campsites were anywhere near it we were both utterly fed up. I remember staring glassy-eyed and aggrieved at the countryside, thinking 'It's not THAT bloody pretty.'

Finally we found a campsite and I collapsed. It was cold. We were bone-weary. It was just one of those bad cycling days, where nothing you do - stretching, eating properly, drinking regularly, pacing yourself - will make the pedalling any easier, or counteract the sensation that the road is actively gripping your tyres like sand.

But it ended well. The tiny municipal campsite we'd found was on a small bay sheltered by Loguivy-de-la-Mer's headland, a mile from the village over a short but nasty little hill. The campsite hid behind a shingle dune backing the beach; we couldn't see the sea from our pitch, but we could hear it. The other campers were a mixed bunch; some elderly, with a smattering of the usual middle-aged early retirees and a few families from Germany and Portugal. Nobody English, but there was the compulsory Dutch tent. Everyone was very quiet. As we walked around, examining pitches, with our eyes on one near the toilet

414 | MARIE MADIGAN

block, a man popped out of his campervan and shook his head. He pointed to a large tent close by.

'They make a lot of noise,' he said. 'You don't want to go there.'

'They' turned out to be a couple of Polish lads working in a fish factory up the road. They were huge, and they came home from work in the early evening, showered noisily, rinsed their rubbery overalls out noisily, talked noisily to each other over their dinner in their tent and abruptly fell asleep. I thought the man had been a bit unfair about them. I did try to engage one of them in conversation as he rinsed his overalls out in the washing up sink next to me, but he couldn't understand me, or maybe couldn't hear me three foot below him. He didn't look interested anyway.

After we'd got the tent up and I'd had a cup of tea I started to perk up. I'd just come over all tired and melodramatic when I really just needed a cup of tea, I told myself. But when Adi came back after talking to the campsite man he said he'd paid for two nights.

'You need it, and I won't complain.'

He was right. It had been - we worked backwards - Nantes since we'd had a rest day. Nine days on the road: our longest continuous stretch. The rush of relief when he said he'd paid The Man for two nights told its own tale. I was profoundly grateful, especially as this was not the sort of place Adi would have chosen for a two-night stop.

'It's time,' he repeated, waving away my thanks. 'You need it. We both do.'

The loveliest evening turned the day on its head. A lovely pizza and pudding in the village. Eavesdropping revealed that word about us had already got around, as I caught quiet references to 'les Gallois' in the conversation at the bar. A scramble on the low-tide shingle and pink-and-grey islets in the harbour. A speedy bike ride around tiny alleys and lanes in the toe-tingling wind. The perfect finish at the tent: a couple of squares of chocolate under a huge, rosy sky.

CHAPTER FIFTY-THREE

Loguivy-de-la-Mer

My turn to get the breakfast croissants. The prospect of a rest day lent my wheels wings. Up that short but vicious hill – 25%! – on cold legs with no tea. I couldn't stop congratulating myself when I got back.

'Yes, yes, you're wonderful!' Adi grunted. But he was smiling, and it was he who dealt with the stove and provided the tea, as usual.

We had no plan. I promised The Legs, and the rest of my body, that I'd do some yoga and stretches, but after that there would be nothing to do but read, write, read, write, sleep, more stretches, sit on the beach and read, come back to the tent and read... All to be accomplished whilst as horizontal as possible.

Adi checked his bike computer after breakfast. We'd averaged over fifty miles a day over the last seven days. We both felt pleased, as it had been moderately hilly and we'd also done plenty of exploring on foot, not just stuck in the saddle all day, every day.

Weather-wise, we decided to pretend we were on a Scottish island. If we were in the Western Isles we'd be delighted with this weather, and we'd be thrilled with all the fresh fruit and vegetables, of which there is a dearth in the shops on the islands. I'm convinced that this is because the islanders all know when the ferry with all the fresh produce arrives - I'm sure it can't be daily - and they're all there at seven in the morning, queueing down the road like it's the sales, and there's nothing left by 9.30 when the cycle tourers show up except for the same venerable orange and soft onion that have been on the shelf getting rejected for weeks.

The wonderful thing about stopping in a place where there's not much to do is that you don't do anything. Adi pottered about with small jobs unhurriedly, cleaning the stove, checking the various sewn-up bits of the tent. I sorted out and washed clothes, then lay outside the tent to read. Salad and a baguette for lunch; reading in the intervals of sun and light wind; throwing the ball to each other on the green. A bike ride into the village and a wander on foot to the GR38 on the other side of the bay. A drink in the bar-tabac, a dark, homey sort of pub. Courteous landlady and a fisherman bid us bonsoir as we left. Adi produced a full-flavoured aubergine curry for dinner, with a nugget of Cantal cheese. Eaten looking towards the sea, which we could almost see over the shelly, shingle dune. Chocolate and wine and a walk east around the bay. A kestrel swooping, hovering, staring at us. Another calling from the sweet chestnut wood. Islets dark and pink-crested against the turquoise sea. A little egret, snowy white. They alway seem to me to be egret-shaped windows into another, blindingly white world. More chocolate.

I was in bed before ten, before the Portuguese and French children I could hear playing, after the loud Polish lads, before the German family and their dogs. In the tent as I scribbled in my diary I could hear Adi's music in his headphones, his breathing; voices, the German children; dogs barking on the beach; blue tits; the wind in the poplars.

The wind that hasn't stopped for three weeks, I thought, but not for long because I was falling deeply, blissfully, restfully asleep.

PART FOURTEEN

Tailwind: Loguivy-de-la-Mer to St-Malo

CHAPTER FIFTY-FOUR

To Lermot

I softened towards Paimpol when we stopped there on the way through the next morning. The tourist office staff were helpful, the ice-creams we bought (illicit morning treat) were creamy and generous, and Adi found the correct replacement batteries for his bike computer. It had started to act up intermittently, apparently protesting at the cold: it worked fine in the sunshine and turned itself off in the cold winds. Much like my legs. A couple of days ago we'd spent a half-hour by the side of the road while Adi fiddled with the computer trying to work out what was wrong with it, while I cycled up and down the lane trying to keep warm. A numb patch developed on the underside of my left thumb, due to the chill.

It never ceases to amaze me, the way that Adi just stops to fix whatever is wrong. No matter what the conditions – busy crossroads, hailstones, shrieking girlfriend – he just whips out the spares and the toolkit and starts pulling and poking. My approach (not recommended) is to pedal as fast as possible to somewhere I can deal with the offending part in comfort, ignoring any ominous sounds and hoping it doesn't drop off before I get there. Probably making the problem worse along the way, I acknowledge.

We were full of a sense of accomplishment as we left Paimpol. We'd eaten our usual breakfast, packed away, done all these extra jobs and were in the saddle again by 10.30! Finally, we were getting the time down. It had only taken eight weeks.

Our goal was to get as far east of St-Brieuc as possible before the rain. Though we had started in sunshine, the skies were purple and heavy, biding their time, and the forecasts on the back pages of the newspapers did not feature little yellow suns.

For most of the way we'd followed the D786, a red-coloured road that would normally have had me baulking, but most of the traffic seemed to take a straighter major road further inland, leaving us in relative peace. Rumpled green headlands fell steeply into a moody sea, and we rode down and up them, following for a while a signed cycle route. Lunch was taken in a tiny shelter, just big enough for two friendly people if they didn't mind total thigh contact, on a tiny road just outside Porlaix. It was the wrong road, as it happened, though in view of the depths of grumpiness we'd sink to later I'm now glad we didn't know that at the time. No idea what the shelter was for. No sign to indicate it was a bus stop, though that might not mean anything. A few houses huddled nearby. A small tortoiseshell cat streaked out of a field of dripping sweetcorn.

We managed an unintended detour which would have been lovely if it hadn't been just after lunch when our muscles were cold and tired and the rain at its heaviest. The detour, naturally enough, took us down a steep hill to a tiny cove and up again, winding through fields and meadows and looking south along the coast to the bay of St-Brieuc. Soaked but stoic, The Legs instructed me to click down the gears and they'd do their bit. They did, even on the steepest hills. 'Just take your time,' they advised. At the top of hills I'd find myself looking back down, then at The Legs in amazement – had they really just pulled me up that? – and giving them a little pat.

It had been a long 35 miles by the time we stopped at a PMU bar in St-Laurent-de-la-Mer. A charming barmaid sat us beside a heater and served me the most delicious hot chocolate I'd had in France – very hot and chocaholic chocolatey. I had discovered in last hour that my waterproof jacket was no longer waterproof. Both cuffs had breached, sending cold, wet tendrils creeping up my arms; my left arm was now soaked to above the elbow. Wet patches across my shoulders, seepage around my neck – a revolting sensation – and a damp patch over my belly button. I needed that hot chocolate.

The rain continued after the break, and we continued to plod along what was a really lovely route: little lanes along the top of steep slopes down to the sea, to little coves surrounded by toothy rocks, through picturesque fishing villages. It reminded me of the Ceredigion coast of south Wales.

Our road approached St-Brieuc from the north, with a long ride in along its river mouth and over a tiny river-traffic bridge. As we started up the hill on the other side, weaving between old port buildings, the rain strengthened, pelting down painfully. I hunched over my handlebars, squinting, following the spray from Adi's rear wheel.

Over the noise of the rain I heard him yell suddenly but couldn't make out the words. An instant later I saw the old tram tracks embedded in the road and felt my front wheel slip on the metal.

It's amazing how time slows down or, to perceive it another way, how the body speeds up. An awful instant of skid and wobble. I wrenched the handlebars uselessly and felt Bike topple beneath me. I leapt clear, vertically up into the air, limbs flung wide in a star jump. It felt as if I was up there for weeks, while Bike lay prostrate on the road below me. Then time and my body sorted themselves out. I plummeted, landing with such force that my feet slipped through my soaked sandals. I ended up on my bare feet on the gritty road, my sandals forced up around my ankles. Still in the pouring rain, in the middle of the road, I wiped as much road grit out of my feet as I could, and picked up my bike.

I'd been worried about buckling the wheel but thankfully there was no obvious damage. I gave the thumbs-up to the rain-blurred figure of Adi, waiting just up the road, and we started again. I'm too small to push my bike up hills when it's laden, it just does my back in, so I got on, slightly wobbly of thigh, and set off carefully. The tyres just about held their grip on the steep, wet tarmac. The Legs did their bit. But the hill hadn't done with us yet. There was another shout, full of hard consonants, from up ahead. One of Adi's gears had slipped and he was wobbling crazily. He managed a sideways vault using the handlebars and then threw the bike down on the road. He was furious.

I cycled past him at a slug's pace – there was no point in stopping – and found an ornately decorated alcove next to a Turkish-style public toilet, perched bizarrely at the top of the hill. Adi reached me a few minutes later, in a furious, jaw-clenched temper. He went for a short walk, came back, shouted at the bike, went away again, came back and fiddled and threatened it with scrappage. I huddled in the alcove, trying not to let the wet bits of my jacket touch my neck, and tried not to hear his shouting while I pulled some more gravel out of my feet.

It was a low point.

Bizarrely, the rest of the ride was lovely, though cold and wet. We were filthy of leg when we found the campsite at Lermot, on a headland looking out over St-Brieuc Bay. Every bit of sprayed-up road grit had glued itself to our exposed skin. The showers were lovely, hot and clean, and there was a small bar. We ensconced ourselves there with our massive bar of chocolate after dinner. (Another successful meal despite Adi having to cook in the doorway again.) The sky was interesting with clouds, which is the only way to look at it sometimes.

Cycling makes you dirty. If it's not sweat, it's rain. I'd lost count of the number of times I'd hesitated to enter cafés, knowing that I smelt very strongly of myself. I invariably decided that the lure of the tea outdid my concerns about my aroma. Fortunately, the French respect for cyclists meant than we were never looked at askance.

The flipside of getting filthy is getting clean. Some of the most blissful moments of the tour were those spent standing under a shower of the perfect temperature, scrubbing at the grime, feeling it release its hold on my skin and slide away. The environmental brownie points gained by two months of sustainable travel was probably negated by the volume of water I consumed in showers, but I had long ago decided I could live with that.

Over a drawn-out beer in the bar we settled on a plan for our last five nights. One more stop on the coast, then we'd go on to Dinan, have two nights there, and then go on to St-Malo for the last two nights. We were winding down. For once I didn't protest. The prospect of being tourists for the last three days was an enticing one.

An invigorating but very short walk from the campsite along a cliff path in the dusk. The rain had stopped and the wind was cool but not freezing. Cool enough to send a soft Irishwoman running for her sleeping bag though, particularly one who'd got drenched three times that day. Rain came again in the evening but passed, just leaving the wind. I fell asleep hearing: tent skins' snapping; someone whistling in the showers; no birds. I missed the swifts, their constant screams.

CHAPTER FIFTY-FIVE

To Pléhérel-plage

Morning greeted us with a chilly, swirling drizzle, irritating but not enough to threaten the camping stove and the stewing of the tea and coffee. Everyone else seemed to have the same idea as us – move on, maybe it will be better somewhere else – and the campsite was full of people flapping tents and awnings in a futile attempt to get some of the rain water off them. We went through our own flapping and packing, then Adi went to hand a plastic mug of coffee to the large Italian man, a solo cycle tourer, who was flapping his little tent alone. We'd met him in the bar last night.

'I am living in Marseille,' he had said, gloomily looking at the forecast and a map and trying to work out how to get back to some sun. 'I am not used to this.'

He and Adi exchanged a few words, then the Italian man went back to his flapping, taking a sip of coffee. The flapping paused. With a smile like sunshine, he raised the mug to Adi.

'Fantastic! FANTASTIC!'

Adi's coffee percolator had come with us on every single cycle tour, but this time he'd contemplated leaving it behind. I'd caught him holding it with a speculative air on packing day.

'Don't even think about it,' I said.

'What?' He looked startled. 'You think I shouldn't bring it?'

'No! Bring it, bring it for Christ's sake! We need our luxuries.'

And I, I said silently, need you to have your coffee in the morning. Actually, having on rare occasions spent mornings in Adi's company when coffee had not been available, it doesn't actually count as a luxury. It's essential, just like tea with me. And it was wonderful that morning to be able to share it in soggy fellowship.

Finally, we had a tailwind, though it did its best to fox us. Whenever we had to turn our noses south for just a minute it seemed to leap upon me. I swear I could hear it going 'Yeeehaaaahhhh!' as I gripped and battled with the weight of the bike, ambushed by gusts on corners.

We swooped down a lovely hill to cross the river that comes out at Morieux and pedalled past an expanse of a reeds, full of moorhen chicks and mallard ducklings. A steady, gentle climb brought us back up to the plateau and the pleasant minor roads north-east towards Erquy. The Legs were expert at hills now. 'You want us to go up there, is it? No problem. Take your time, now.'

I knew we'd be rained on, so I had resolved to treat myself as soon as possible to a tartelet fraise, one of those delicious melt-in-the-mouth-pastry tartlets with custard and a topping of glazed strawberries. I'd drooled over them daily but had only eaten a couple in the entire trip; their fat content was stratospheric enough to dissuade me until I'd earned them by cycling ninety miles, which of course had never happened. (This earning-treats thing is a bit of a curse. A vestige of the old Catholic hair-shirt.) Today, I would not restrain myself until I'd earned it.

It's amazing what the thought of a treat can do. I remember cycling doggedly, getting much pleasure out of the landscape. Again and again the road dropped from the plateau down to little coves, with steep climbs back up, around exciting blind bends. I loved every minute of it. I went into every single boulangerie we passed, and if they didn't have a tartlet, I bought something anyway. The treat count went (look away if you're diabetic): one large chocolate chip cookie, fresh from the oven, the best I'd tasted in years; one pain au chocolat; a pineapple fritter from the market in Le Val-André and finally, a tartlet from an artisan pâtisserie, also in Le Val-André. I ate it on a bench on the promenade in sunshine and wind. Stuffed as an armchair. Of course, the fritter and the tartlet counted as health food, having fruit in the name.

The Rough Guide had raved about Erquy, but when we got there we thought 'Yeah, nice enough, but...' We were not impressed, for the very best of reasons: that in our lucky, lovely lives we have lived in and have visited places lovelier than this. The sun came out as we sipped a decadent glass of afternoon wine in a cool café. A slim, elegant woman with yellow cat presided; reggae music drifted onto the little terrace. The sun spotted us and hid behind a cloud. We spun the drinks out, feeling lazy, talking idly. It was nearly three before we left, with altered plans - I don't know why we bothered making them - and headed further west.

I couldn't make out whether I was enjoying Brittany or not. It wasn't just that the countryside in Scotland, West Cork and some parts of Wales could knock spots off it, in my opinion, but also that, especially on the north coast, there was an increasing number of what I can only call dour Celts. I am one myself, so I feel qualified to judge. But even as the thought crossed my mind, all the exceptions rose up in my memory to chastise me: the nice man today who asked us where we were going and directed us towards Erquy and insisted we go to Dinan. The campsite man last night was friendly, and the girl in the bar, even though, according to Adi, she had no idea how to pull a pint of lager. The nice couple who ran the bar in Tréguier and their toe-licking dog. The man who'd shouted out a huge 'Chapeau!' as we chugged up a hill towards Scaër. Sundry helpful shopkeepers and people who'd pointed the way whenever I momentarily lost Adi. Maybe I was the one who was dour.

Rain found us and cleaved to us after Erquy but The Legs and I were still in sturdy mode and Bike was stoic as always. If it hadn't been raining it would have been delightful. The campsite we pitched up at in Pléhérel-plage was enormous and friendly, spread out over and behind dunes and under trees, with bars and places to buy chips and loads of cheerful campers and campervanners. A break in the rain gave us just enough time to pitch the tent before it came down harder than ever in heavy, vicious drops, lashing us. The tent was dry, but we and all our panniers were wet, which necessitated complicated rolling back and forth of the awning floor so as to get everything in while keeping a patch of dry floor for us to sit on.

I got soaked again in a futile mission, cycling around the headland looking for some where to buy a bottle of wine and a bag of pasta. I flew through the scattered villages and found, spread out over the headland, a boulangerie, a charcuterie and a boucherie, but no wine cheap enough and no pasta. By the time I'd decided that we could afford that expensive wine and went back to the charcuterie where I'd seen it, it had closed. Mission failed, I got lost on the way back in the confusing tangle of lanes.

Adi was lovely when I finally arrived at the tent, sodden and declaring that I was never in my life going to go outside again. He looked at all the positives: the tent on dry ground, the excellent girlfriend for buying him a bottle of beer at the campsite bar (my only successful purchase), a big baguette, a campsite where we could buy chips and, most importantly, the fact that we had already bought the chocolate. 'Otherwise you'd be going to that place ten miles back,' he grinned.

Cheered, I went for my shower. When I got back Adi had found wine on the campsite somewhere; I suspected he'd bartered for it. 'But you've got to get the chips,' he said.

Ten cold minutes waiting for chips in a draughty marquee was worth it: they were great, the wine was great, Adi's accompanying veggie sauce was great.

The rain paused after dinner, long enough for us to get dressed up in our fleeces and trainers (I can't believe I almost hadn't brought my fleece) and follow a path that led to the top of the dunes behind the beach. We looked at the clouds, leaden and turgid, and the sea, blue-grey and white-tipped, like a Scottish island in November. Adi took a photo of the two of us, hair wind-whipped, sea roiling behind as we shouted on the count of three, 'It's FECKING JULY!'

CHAPTER FIFTY-SIX

To Dinan

I can't remember a thing about the ride to Dinan. It must have happened, because we woke up in Pléhérel-plage and we ate our dinner in Dinan, but all I recall is a peleton of elderly cyclists who overtook me slowly as we left the Baye de la Frênaye and headed inland.

'Bon courage, ma petite dame!' shouted a lady, petite enough herself, as she inched past me on her shiny road bike. I liked that. Not just a madame but a petite dame.

But soon we'd be back in the land where people didn't know what to call each other when they met in random situations, those tiny little things that make rubbing along with strangers easier. I suppose that's why we talk about the weather.

Given the wiggle room we had for making our ferry, I was a bit sad that we hadn't seen a little more of Brittany's western shores. Adi and I discussed this as we cycled along. We could, perhaps, have gone a day's ride further west, had another day on the north coast, and then still maybe had a day in hand in St-Malo. But you never know. Our tyres, which had behaved themselves beautifully - not a single puncture! - could have thrown a wobbly. The Knee could have acted up again. My knee could have acted up.

It was cheering to see that London had already had three times its normal July rainfall. Whenever the weather since Orléans had got us down, we'd been heartened by the fact that it was worse at home. Apart from Scotland, which had had a dry, warm summer the like of which it hadn't seen for centuries (true fact), the rest of Britain had been under a rain cloud for two months. It's not a particularly nice characteristic, this strand of schadenfreude, but Adi and I agreed that we couldn't have borne it if Anglesey had been cooking in a heatwave while we were cooking our dinner in the rain again.

At least the tent had been dry when we'd dismantled it that morning, apart from a little condensation. We erected the outer up as soon as we arrived in Dinan, giving it a chance to air in the breeze before the clouds came over again.

The big Italian man was already there and greeted us with a smile. Over a shared baguette he told us that the Bastille Day celebrations for the night had been cancelled on account of the forecast rain.

'It has broken all records, this weather,' he said. 'Lucky for us, non?' And he ate a big bite of baguette.

I couldn't help thinking it was a bit wimpy of them to have cancelled their national holiday celebrations on account of the weather. St Patrick's Day parades are never cancelled, no matter what the weather does. Then again, they are held in the middle of March on a rainy island where sun is not expected. Not quite the same as France in the middle of July although - I looked at the sky - it was hard to tell the difference right then.

For the last couple of weeks campsites had gradually been getting busier. I liked it. It had been lovely to be one of the few campers, sometimes the only campers, but we'd always enjoyed chatting or at least nodding to others, even if they did shock us a little at times (the nice people who wanted to kill the ants; the man who didn't know what a boulangerie was). It had been nice to see school-aged kids appearing. The English schools had another week to go, but Bastille Day seemed to be the point where most of the European school holidays started. Instead of having the showers almost to myself, suddenly I was sharing them with teenage girls brushing their hair and hogging the mirrors. I found it rather sweet.

'It's been nice to see it change,' Adi agreed, from the doorway of the tent again. I was squashed beside him, holding the door flap over when the rain threatened to put the stove out, opening it up again to let it vent when the rain eased off. Cooking in the rain for the third night running. This was a record. Even in Scotland we hadn't had it so bad.

It struck me then; we really were going home soon. Despite everything, I just loved being on the road. Even when we stopped for a day or more, we'd been free. Our days had been full of motion and exploration and curiosity. All we had to think about was where to go, how to get there, where to buy food, which café to favour with our custom. And endless new corners to ride around, new views to see, new rumples and curves of the world to feel under our wheels.

'It's not quite over yet,' Adi said, seeing my expression. 'Give us your plate.'

CHAPTER FIFTY-SEVEN

Dinan

A nd it wasn't, of course. Next day dawned sunny. 'You know, nearly all the days that we have rested have been sunny?' Adi said over breakfast.

We'd passed through Dinan years earlier when we drove from Santander to Cherbourg in our Landrover. This time we'd pitched our tent almost on the same spot where we'd pitched the Vango's big brother eight years before. The great buttresses of the old town wall started beside us and rose up, imposing.

I was quite excited about today, mingled with the niggling distress in my belly that it would all be over. Ready to go home? Yes, in some ways. But in another we felt like we'd just made it, just got fit enough, just got the confidence to know that we could do it.

We spent the day mostly apart. I wandered around on the town walls, in churches, in the cathedral and down by the river, where the picturesque old low bridge and the long front of the low town were crowded with people watching one of the events laid on for the holiday weekend: water jousting! Picture rowing boats, teams of four in each, with a coxswain and a person I can only describe as a jouster, plumped up with a lifejacket and standing on the end of a sloping platform projecting from the stern of the boat and gripping – I am not joking – a lance. Over a loudspeaker the MC for the day was commented cheerfully and incessantly. Two boats rowed away from each other, the plump men in the stern balancing their lances and looking very precarious. When they each reached their start point and turned to face each other the MC shouted, 'Alors. Musique!' And from somewhere came a medieval piped sort of tune, exactly what you'd expect at a joust while two horses charged towards each other. Two boats rowing at each other took a bit longer than two charging horses, so we all got to learn the music intimately as its eight bars came around again and again. The oars dipped, the boats surged and the jousters on the sterns swayed and gripped their lances. The boats gathered speed, then the music stopped and the MC shouted something like 'Ramassez les rams! Ramassez les rams!' The rowers shipped oars, the momentum kept the boats gliding towards each other, the jousters lifted their lances and as the boats passed alongside they lunged. One long bendy lance tipped a fighter into the water, to huge cheers and applause.

This went on all afternoon, with a crowded, cheerful audience on the banks, eating, drinking and cheering, while teams of rowers jousted and fell in to roars of approval. Every three or four jousts, there was a sort of interval entertainment race, which consisted of pairs of men on rafts made out of plywood apparently strapped to the inner tube of a tractor tyre, racing each other madly across the river.

In a quiet park high above all the excitement, I sat in the shade and watched a man and his teenage daughter practising aerial silks, turning gracefully while suspended by the long white fabric, in the shade of the tree.

That night we found a bar that sold stout. Adi was delighted. And I drank too much wine after weeks of moderation, and discovered that it is not wise to cycle down a street, be it ever so deserted, after half a bottle of wine. But on the plus side, I can now testify to the fact that you don't bruise or break if you are totally relaxed when you fall from your saddle.

CHAPTER FIFTY-EIGHT

To St-Malo

Bradley Wiggins was still leading the Tour de France. We'd started paying attention to the sports pages of the free newspapers in cafés, and catching the highlights of the day's stage while we avoided the rain in bars in the evenings.

This will sound ridiculous, but I felt as if I had some insight into the life of a Tour de France cyclist, some tiny glimpse of a chink of a whisper of understanding. Our sixty or seventy kilometres, with leisurely lunch, doesn't at first glance have an awful lot in common with a 190 km stage race, but what we did do was cycle every day. We had to. Obviously, Adi and I had chosen to do this but, having committed ourselves to it, in another sense we had no choice. Without blowing our tiny budget, we had no choice but to get on our bikes and plough through whatever the terrain and the weather flung at us. Like those super athletes, this was just what we did.

On the other hand, this comparison is complete tosh.

We rode through gentle, lovely countryside, following the Rance north as it broadened from river to inlet. I remember a little village, Le Minihic-sur-Rance, where we bought apples and oranges and I wandered around trying to find shade. I was feeling slightly desiccated from the night before. Where are clouds when you need them?

The sun shone, the road was easy, with the mouth of the Rance slowly widening down to our right. The best bit was the cycle path beside the enormous bridge that crosses the Rance estuary on the big D168, south of St-Malo. It was the only crossing of the estuary and we had no idea if there'd be a cycle path or not, but just trusted to experience. Sure enough, a weedy but entirely adequate concrete track appeared a couple of hundred yards before the bridge and took us alongside the traffic racing above and beside us. The track was on the seaward side and we sped along, with the ramparts of St-Malo rising into view across the water.

The final approach was outstanding. St-Malo's old town sits at the end of an east-west spit. Nowadays it's connected by a causeway and bridge to a headland to the south, built upon what was originally shifting sands. To the east is a huge lagoon filled with industrial shipping and pleasure boats. We waited with a crowd of pedestrians and cyclists, while cars and trucks waited further back behind a barrier, because a ship was leaving through the locks that connect the lagoon to the sea. The road bridge over the lock retracted itself like something out of Thunderbirds. People stood where the road ended, while a huge industrial-looking ship passed through the lock about two foot in front of them. I'm sure you'd never get within a hundred yards of it in Britain without fences and notices everywhere. Adi and I tried to imagine someone suing the port authorities if they fell in. The Gallic shrug, the slight puzzlement.

'But there is the water. Did you not see the water? Hmm?'

Then we were cycling over it, up to the huge walls that enclose the old town. We wheeled into the car park beside the tourist office and leant our bikes up against the wall, as we'd done at dozens of tourist offices before.

'My turn?' said Adi.

While he collected the bundle of bumph, it hit me. We'd done it. Two thousand miles, two months. Taking out all our non-cycling days, I thought, that probably makes our average higher than you'd think at first – and then I told myself to stop it. With all our setbacks, we'd cycled two thousand miles through France. We'd explored villages and towns, eaten and drunk and chatted and walked and cycled, cycled, cycled. We were here, at the top. We had done it. I patted Bike. I patted The Legs.

Adi came out with a fistful of leaflets. And we were still together! I patted him too.

The campsite was back over the Thunderbirds bridge in the Cité d'Alet, a large and cheerful park backed by a little green wooded hill topped with a graveyard. Cheerful manager. Large showers full of teenage girls brushing their hair. Small girls turning cartwheels. We wheeled our bikes towards our final pitch through the campervan field, lined with barbecues and deck-chairs. At the doorway of every caravan a terrier stood, looking sternly over his patch. Large cheerful groups, a few lone walkers.

We were fizzy and relaxed, sad and elated. Emotional. I put on my dress bought long ago in Aigues-Mortes and we cycled into the old town. Inside the citadel the streets were full of stout north-European types, accents from everywhere from Dublin to Prague. We ate pizza and ice-cream, dirt cheap and delicious, before taking a walk through the old streets and up onto the ramparts. Terns dived into cobalt-blue water; small boats puttered out in the channel. A bright orange kayaker paddled out towards a group of tiny sailboats. The swifts had gone to bed by the time we left.

CHAPTER FIFTY-NINE

St-Malo and Home

The last day. We split up again, after our breakfast – a two-mug morning. I explored all the lovely back streets of the citadel. St-Malo was almost flattened by the Allied forces in the bombardment that accompanied the D-Day landings in 1944, and had been lovingly restored stone by stone. A discreetly signed historical trail led me around deserted streets, within earshot of the crowds who didn't venture further than a couple of streets of the gates of the old town. I could have been the only person in the town.

Through a gate in the ramparts on the north side to sit on rocks overlooking the beach outside the grey granite walls. The Plage de Bon Secours was busy but not crowded, with people going out and back to the little island of Grand Bé while the tide allowed. I could see the beaches beneath the ramparts westward, the lighthouse on its promontory and beyond, the beaches

446

and headland past the mouth of the Rance. The tide was low but lads were still leaping off a diving platform into a pool cut into the rocks.

I took out my feet and looked at them. Despite the weather I'd managed to get a ridiculous stripey tan. I felt happy.

It was delightful, just leaning back against the rocks, looking at the blue and gentle sea, the islets, the islands, the coast stretching away. The people up on the ramparts behind me, the empty boat-trailers, sunbathers on the soft sand. Voices, voices everywhere, and the calling of gulls. I heard rock pipits, fledgeling gulls plaintive and pleading.

I bought a double museum ticket and climbed 169 steps to the top of the castle, now the Musée d'Histoire de la Ville, for a swift's eye view of the town. Later, on the same ticket, I visited the Cap-Horner museum in St-Servan, a small town on the headland just to the south. I was in a bit of a daze by now. It took me a while to register that Cap-Horners were sailors who'd sailed around Cape Horn.

I floated through the day, an odd mix of wanting to make the most of Saint-Malo, but not feeling like a tourist. Still in that same mood, happy and sad, elated and bereft. I scribbled in my diary, trying to capture what I felt, and failing. In the end I wrote 'Mostly Very Happy!', underlined it, gave up on profundity and went for a cup of tea in a café. To my joy, it was served in a pot. I opened my diary and crossed out the word 'Mostly.'

Adi had wanted our last dinner to be a camp stove dinner. To our delight, the sunny weather held. Our last dinner, not hunched in the door of the tent!

'This is the first time we haven't cooked—'

'We?' Adi interrupted.

'The first time YOU haven't cooked in the rain for…' We counted back.

'Five nights?'

'Tréguier.' It seemed ages ago.

The wind was still with us but it was warm. Weather demons smiling on us at last. An Adi special, a mushroom and aubergine curry, spiced with the last of the mix he had discussed with the stall holder Figeac. Dark hazelnut chocolate.

We had a few euros to use up. Into St-Malo on the bikes for a last, enormous scoop of ice-cream. A pleasant bar, playing Lynnard Skinnard. Another, dark and gothic, playing easeful reggae.

Swifts, still there, the soundtrack to our trip. Adi took pictures of the ramparts, illuminated for the night. I felt sad. Our last night in France.

'Not our last night ever,' said Adi, chinking mugs with me in the tent. 'Next year.'

Why did we do it? Not as long a trip as some, not as epic as some, but it was epic to us. Two thousand and forty miles, nine and a half weeks, sixty-five days.

At the end, we were a unit: the two of us, our bikes and our tent. I'd grown more patient; Adi'd grown more conscious of time. We both took a little more time to listen to each other. I hadn't come on this tour thinking we had something to save, but I did think we might have something to lose if we didn't learn to rub off each other's corners. We didn't lose anything. We gained memories. Cycling with someone else lends authenticity to the experience. We shared roles, we fought and we made up. We waited for each other – well, Adi waited for me, but I would have waited for him. That's the thing.

And then it was morning, the port, a ten-hour crossing to Portsmouth, a B&B, two train journeys, and a ride home from the station via the pub. Beaumaris was buzzing with tourists. After a drink with friends we cycled the last four miles home. We lifted the panniers up the steps and piled them on the study floor, then cycled up the road to our spot, a quiet cliff above an old quarry that looks uninterrupted over the Menai Strait to the mountains of Snowdonia.

'If we'd arrived somewhere like this at any point on our tour, we'd have been delighted,' Adi said, as we rode home in the dusk. 'But we're still going back.'

I agreed. The Legs agreed.

'Ready for a bit more?'

Oh, yes!

Afterthought: Distances

Day 1: Avignon: 14 miles

Day 2: To Maubec: 37 miles

Day 3: To Apt: 23 miles

Day 4: Apt: 7 miles

Day 5: To Forcalquier: 44 miles

Day 6: To Beaumont-de-Pertuis: 34 miles

Day 7: To Cucuron: 27 miles

Day 8: Cucuron: 12 miles

Day 9: To Roussillon: 26 miles

Day 10: To Robion: 24 miles

Day 11: To St-Rémy: 25 miles

Day 12: St-Rémy: 19 miles

Day 13: To Arles: 21 miles

Day 14: Arles: 6 miles

Day 15: To Saintes-Maries-de-la-Mer: 34 miles

Day 16: To Grand Motte: 32 miles

Day 17: To Marseillan-Plage: 54 miles

Day 18: To Le Grau d'Agde: 12 miles

Day 19: Le Grau d'Agde: 20 miles

Day 20: To Capestang: 38 miles
Day 21: To Bois-Bas: 43 miles
Day 22: To Olargues: 33 miles
Day 23: Olargues: 0 miles
Day 24: To Mazamet: 38 miles
Day 25: To Castres: 23 miles
Day 26: To Albi: 36 miles
Day 27: To Figeac: 14 miles
Day 28: Figeac: 0 miles
Day 29: Figeac: 8 miles
Day 30: Figeac: 12 miles
Day 31: To Cabrerets: 37 miles
Day 32: To Rocamadour: 43 miles
Day 33: To Carennac: 20 miles
Day 34: To Meyronne: 22 miles
Day 35: La Roque Gageac: 48 miles
Day 36: Les Eyzies: 21 miles
Day 37: To Orléans: 36 miles
Day 38: To Blois: 52 miles
Day 39: To Ballan-Miré: 59 miles
Day 40: To Neuil-sous-Faye: 43 miles
Day 41& 42: Neuil-sous-Faye: 0 miles
Day 43: To Montsoreau: 35 miles
Day 44: To Gennes: 30 miles
Day 45: St-Florent: 52 miles
Day 46: To Nantes: 43 miles
Day 47: To Nantes: 14 miles
Day 48: To Blain: 41 miles
Day 49: To St-Martin-sur-Oust: 49 miles

Day 50: To Vannes: 40 miles

Day 51: To Carnac: 35 miles

Day 52: To Guidel: 38 miles

Day 53: To Scaër: 44 miles

Day 54: To Huelgoat: 39 miles

Day 55: To Tréguier: 53 miles

Day 56: To Loguivy de la Mer: 46 miles

Day 57: Loguivy de la Mer: 4 miles

Day 58: To Lermot: 47 miles

Day 59: To Pléhérel-Plage: 36 miles

Day 60: To Dinan: 30 miles

Day 61: Dinan: 0 miles

Day 62: To St-Malo: 31 miles

Day 63: St-Malo: 6 miles.

Acknowledgements

Thanks to my family for encouragement: sisters Noreen and Theresa, and the Anderton men, Dave and Harry; my mother and father; and to Trowell for dropping us at the station at silly o'clock.
Extra special thanks to Adi Moore, again and always. I might never have started cycle touring without him, and he *still* waits for me at the tops of hills.

ABOUT THE AUTHOR

Marie Madigan is an Irish writer and nature conservationist living in North Wales, who spends most of her time walking, cycling and writing. It is her ambition to cycle along every road marked in yellow on the Ordnance Survey map of the UK.

Did you enjoy this book? An honest review left wherever you bought it is always welcome, and really important for indie authors! The more reviews an indie book gets, the easier it is to promote and reach new readers. Even a line or two at the store where you bought it, or on Goodreads, would be an enormous help.

Want some more of Marie Madigan's work for free? Subscribers to her mailing list get a free digital copy of Southern France In Low Gear and a free Countdown To Your Cycle Tour Check List in PDF. You'll only be contacted when there is an offer, news or a new book is about to be released. Your email address will never be shared and you can unsubscribe at any time. Find out more:

www.mariemadigan.co.uk

Cycle Touring For Beginners
This concise guide covers everything beginners and more experienced cycle tourers need to know,

including what you *don't* need in order to enjoy cycle touring. Covering what sort of bike you need, how fit do you need to be (not super-fit) and whether or not you should bring luxuries (of course you should), Cycle Touring For Beginners encourages you to try exploring your world by bicycle, whether that's an overnight trip in your own county or a two-month tour in another country, and whether you're staying in guest houses or camping. With encouragement and tips on everything from how to eat to keep yourself healthy to what to bring in your tool kit, this book will have you itching to saddle up and start your own bike touring adventure this weekend.

Southern France In Low Gear

During a cycle tour in France in 2012, Marie's legs started talking to her. A year later, pedalling up the first long hill in Corsica, The Legs piped up again.

'And how long is it for this time? Two months? And we're going where? Oh, just to the Atlantic. Fine. No problem.'

With the same sturdy old bikes, the same stoic Legs and the same measure of stubbornness and stamina, Marie and Adi chug around Corsica, pedal through Provence, skirt the Cévennes and plod through the Pyrenees. With encounters with booted eagles, friendly farmers, cycle tourers of all description and a thrilling glimpse of the Yellow Jersey, the hilly regions of France charm them once again.

A Short Ride Round North Wales

Proving to themselves that a cycle tour needn't be a cross-continental expedition, Marie and Adi pedal out of their front gate and off into the Welsh summer. Six short days spin out into miles of lanes, crisscrossing borderland valleys and majestic uplands where they discover new lanes and vistas in their home of North Wales, rediscover old ones, and remind themselves once again that there's no better way of exploring than on the back of a bike.

Say Hello!

Visit Marie's website at **www. mariemadigan.co.uk**, where you can download a free 'Countdown To Your Cycle Tour Check List' and a free digital copy of 'Southern France In Low Gear.'

You can follow her on Twitter: **@mariethemadigan**

Or email Marie at **marie@mariemadigan.co.uk**

21388568R00270

Printed in Great Britain
by Amazon